福建省文化和旅游厅 组织编写

编著
张美娜

翻译
罗 睿

摄影
陈英杰
成冬冬
张清杰
吴云轩
吴刚强
许兆恺等

福建的世界遗产

World Heritage Sites in Fujian

U0112698

泉州

Quanzhou

海峡出版发行集团
THE STRAITS PUBLISHING & DISTRIBUTING GROUP ｜ 福建人民出版社
FUJIAN PEOPLE'S PUBLISHING HOUSE

图书在版编目（CIP）数据

泉州：汉英对照 / 张美娜编著. —— 福州：福建人民
出版社，2023.6（2024.5重印）
　（福建的世界遗产）
　ISBN 978-7-211-09001-3

　Ⅰ.①泉… Ⅱ.①张… Ⅲ.①文化遗产—介绍—泉州
—汉、英 Ⅳ.①K295.73

中国国家版本馆CIP数据核字(2023)第031812号

泉 州
QUANZHOU

编　　著：张美娜	
翻　　译：罗　睿	
责任编辑：周跃进	
美术编辑：陈培亮	
责任校对：陈　璟	
装帧设计：〔澳〕Harry Wang	
内文排版：雅昌文化（集团）有限公司	

出版发行：福建人民出版社	电　　话：0591-87533169（发行部）	
地　　址：福州市东水路 76 号	邮　　编：350001	
网　　址：http://www.fjpph.com	电子邮箱：fjpph7211@126.com	

经　　销：福建新华发行（集团）有限责任公司
印　　刷：雅昌文化（集团）有限公司
电　　话：0755-86083235
地　　址：深圳市南山区深云路 19 号
开　　本：787 毫米×1092 毫米　　1/16
印　　张：19.25
字　　数：427 千字
版　　次：2023 年 6 月第 1 版
印　　次：2024 年 5 月第 3 次印刷
书　　号：ISBN 978-7-211-09001-3
定　　价：108.00 元

目 录

Contents

01

世遗档案

UNESCO's Introduction to Quanzhou: Emporium of the World in Song-Yuan China

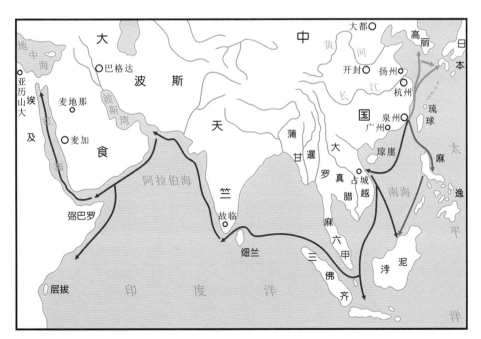

◎ 宋元时期泉州海上交通示意图。（方圆 供图）

Diagram of maritime transportation from Quanzhou during the Song and Yuan Dynasties. (Courtesy of Fang Yuan)

名　　称：泉州：宋元中国的世界海洋商贸中心
列入时间：2021年7月列入《世界遗产名录》
遗产类型：世界文化遗产

遗产价值

　　该遗址群体现了泉州在宋元时期（公元10—14世纪）作为世界海洋商贸中心的活力，及其与中国腹地的紧密联系。泉州在亚洲海运贸易的这个重要时期蓬勃发展。该遗产地包括多座宗教建筑，如始建于公元11世纪的清净寺（中国最早的伊斯兰建筑之一）、伊斯兰教圣墓，以及大量考古遗迹，如行政建筑、具有重要商贸和防御意义的石码头、制瓷和冶铁生产遗址、城市交通网道的构成元素、古桥、宝塔和碑文。在公元10—14世纪的阿拉伯和西方文献中，泉州被称为刺桐。该遗产地还包括一座保留了部分原貌的元代寺庙，以及世界上仅存的摩尼石像。摩尼是摩尼教的创始人，该教约于公元6—7世纪传入中国。

Quanzhou: Emporium of the World in Song-Yuan China

Inscribed in 2021 on the World Heritage List

Cultural Property

The serial site of Quanzhou illustrates the city's vibrancy as a maritime emporium during the Song and Yuan periods (10th—14th centuries AD) and its interconnection with the Chinese hinterland. Quanzhou thrived during a highly significant period for maritime trade in Asia. The site encompasses religious buildings, including the 11th century AD Qingjing Mosque (one of the earliest Islamic edifices in China), Islamic tombs, and a wide range of archaeological remains: administrative buildings, stone docks that were important for commerce and defence, sites of ceramic and iron production, elements of the city's transportation network, ancient bridges, pagodas, and inscriptions. Quanzhou was known as Zayton in Arabic and western texts of the 10th to 14th centuries AD. The heritage site also includes a partially preserved Yuan Dynasty temple and the only remaining Mani stone statue in the world. Mani is the founder of Manichaeism, which was introduced to China around the 6th—7th centuries AD.

◎ 夕阳下的东塔西塔。（何国辉 摄）

The East and West Towers at sunset. (Photo by He Guohui)

入选理由

坐落于中国东南沿海的系列遗产"泉州：宋元中国的世界海洋商贸中心"以特殊方式反映了，产—运—销功能高度整合的区域一体化空间结构以及重要的制度、社会和文化因素，共同促成泉州在10—14世纪逐渐崛起并蓬勃发展，成为东亚和东南亚贸易网络的海上枢纽。宋元泉州商贸系统以位于江口平原的城区为运行中枢，东南面的辽阔海域是对外联系门户，西北面的广袤山区是产业基地，水陆复合的运输网络连通其间。

承载着宋元泉州整体关键价值特征的系列遗产组成部分包括了行政管理机构与设施遗址、多元社群宗教建筑和造像、文化纪念地史迹、陶瓷和冶铁生产基地，以及由桥梁、码头、航标塔组成的水陆交通网络，完整地体现了宋元泉州富有特色的海外贸易体系、多元社会文化和贸易结构。

"泉州：宋元中国的世界海洋商贸中心"系列遗产突出展示了在公元10—14世纪亚洲海上贸易的高度繁荣时期，其整体的地域结构以及主要的制度、运输、生产、销售和社会文化因素，这些促使其成为全球性的商贸中心。作为世界海洋贸易中心港口的杰出范例，该遗产展示了宋元泉州对东亚和东南亚经济文化发展的巨大贡献。

这一系列遗产包含了必要的遗产点和价值特征，阐释了泉州作为10—14世纪世界上首要的海洋商贸中心的史实。系列遗产点及其要素之间保持了功能上以及社会、文化和空间的紧密联系，并共同阐释了宋元时期泉州海洋贸易体系的完整治理体系、关键特征和要素。遗产直接所在的区域、重要景观以及其他支持的区域或价值特征均被包含在缓冲区内。与系列遗产地整体有所关联、容易影响遗产地景观的地区和周边环境，均划定了关联环境区域并已得到有效保护。通过一系列的保护和管理措施，城市发展压力、气候变化的影响、自然灾害的威胁和旅游压力都得到了有效的控制。

该系列遗产作为一个整体，包括其各遗产点和遗产要素，真实可信地反映了宋元时期泉州作为世界级海洋商贸中心的整体区域布局、历史贸易体系功能、社会结构和历史年代信息。各原始位置尚存，历史功能信息能被清晰识别和理解，实物遗存及其历史记录中反映的形式、材料、工艺、传统维护机制与技术体系的历史信息，以及这些古迹和遗址所承载的现存信仰和文化传统，所有这些都证明了各遗产点的高度真实性和可信性。大量的历史文献以及中国与国际的研究成果，可作为其物证。

◎ 明何朝宗塑白瓷观音像。（成冬冬 摄）

The white porcelain statue of the Goddess of Mercy sculpted by He Chaozong in the Ming Dynasty.
(Photo by Cheng Dongdong)

Outstanding Universal Value

Located on the southeast coast of China, the serial property Quanzhou: Emporium of the World in Song–Yuan China reflects in an exceptional manner the spatial structure that combined production, transportation and marketing and the key institutional, social and cultural factors that contributed to the spectacular rise and prosperity of Quanzhou as a maritime hub of the East and South-east Asia trade network during the 10th—14th centuries AD. The Song-Yuan Quanzhou emporium system was centred around and powered by the city located at the junction of river and sea, with oceans to the south-east that connected it with the world, with mountains to the far north-west that provided for production, and with a water-land transportation network that joined them all together.

The component parts and contributing elements of the property include sites of administrative buildings and structures, religious buildings and statues, cultural memorial sites and monuments, production sites of ceramics and iron, as well as a transportation network composed of bridges, docks and pagodas that guided the voyagers. They comprehensively reflect the distinguishing maritime territorial, socio-cultural and trade structures of Song-Yuan Quanzhou.

Quanzhou, Emporium of the World in Song–Yuan China, outstandingly illustrates, through its component parts, the territorial integrated structure and the key institutional, transportation, production, marketing and socio-cultural factors that turned it into a global-level emporium and key commercial hub during a highly prosperous stage of Asia's maritime trade in the 10th—14th centuries AD. The property demonstrates Quanzhou's great contributions to the economic and cultural development of East and South-east Asia.

The serial property includes the necessary components and attributes that reflect Quanzhou as a premier maritime emporium of the world of the 10th—14th centuries AD. The component parts and contributing elements maintain close functional, social, cultural and spatial links with each other, altogether illustrating the integrated territorial system and also key facets and factors of Quanzhou's maritime trade system in the Song and Yuan periods. The immediate setting of the property, important views and other supporting areas or attributes, are all included in the buffer zone; areas sensitive to visual impacts and background environments demonstrating overall association with the serial property are all contained in demarcated wider setting areas and placed under effective protection. Urban development pressures, impacts from climate change, natural threats, and tourism pressures appear under effective control, through a set of protective and management measures.

◎ 安平桥又称五里桥。（陈英杰 摄）
Anping Bridge is also known as Wuli (2.5 kilometers) Bridge. (Photo by Chen Yingjie)

The series as a whole, comprised of its component parts and contributing elements, credibly conveys the overall territorial layout, functions of the historical trade system, social structure, and historical chronological information of Quanzhou as a global maritime emporium in the Song and Yuan periods. Surviving original locations; information of historical functions that can be clearly recognized and understood; historical information of forms, materials, processes and traditional maintenance mechanisms and technical systems reflected in physical remains and their historical records, as well as surviving beliefs and cultural traditions that these monuments and sites carry; all testify to a high degree of authenticity and credibility of the component parts. The physical evidence can be confirmed by a wealth of historical documentation and Chinese and international research results.

unesco

World Heritage Convention

CONVENTION CONCERNING THE PROTECTION OF THE WORLD CULTURAL AND NATURAL HERITAGE

The World Heritage Committee
has inscribed

Quanzhou: Emporium of the World in Song-Yuan China

on the World Heritage List

Inscription on this List confirms the outstanding
universal value of a cultural or
natural property which requires protection for the
benefit of all humanity

DATE OF INSCRIPTION

31 July 2021

Audrey Azoulay

DIRECTOR-GENERAL
OF UNESCO

02

泉州：宋元中国的世界海洋商贸中心

Quanzhou:

Emporium of the World in Song-Yuan China

◎ 开元寺镇国塔。（陈英杰 摄）
Zhenguo Pagoda of Kaiyuan Temple. (Photo by Chen Yingjie)

万国之城——东方第一大港的航海通商史

泉州，位于中国东南沿海，自古就是一个港口城市。

新石器时代，古越族人在这片土地上开始从事渔猎、农耕。古越族人在造船、制陶、石雕、建筑等方面造诣非凡，独领风骚。西晋末年，战乱连年，中原晋人衣冠南渡，入闽来泉，沿江而居。中原文化于此生根发芽。因思念故土，他们将此江命名为"晋江"。晋江自此成了泉州人的母亲河。晋江流域出口，是江海交汇的港口，亦是宋元时期古刺桐港"三湾十二港"的中心。

唐嗣圣初年（684年）首置武荣州，州治在今南安丰州古城。唐久视元年（700年）武荣州治迁至丰州东南十五里，即今泉州鲤城区。唐景云二年（711年）改武荣州为泉州，泉州之名自此开始。此后，泉州别名有清源、温陵、刺桐城、鲤城。

泉州这座城市，以海为起点，因海而荣耀。

唐和五代时期，泉州海交贸易蓬勃发展，海外文化如潮奔涌。古越文化、中原文化、海外文化在泉州相互碰撞，交汇融合。

◎ 晋江两岸。（陈英杰 摄）
Both sides of the Jinjiang River. (Photo by Chen Yingjie)

The City of Nations: the History of Seafaring and Trading in the Largest Port of the East

Quanzhou, located on the southeast coast of China, has been a port city since ancient times.

In the Neolithic Age, the ancient Yue people began to engage in fishing, hunting, and farming on this land. In such aspects as shipbuilding, pottery, stone carving, and architecture, the ancient Yue people have had enormous accomplishments, and have been leading figures in these fields. At the end of the Western Jin Dynasty (265—317), wars continued for years. The Jin people from the Central Plains brought their civilization to the south and entered Fujian and its southeast area Quanzhou, where they lived along the river. Hence, the Central Plains culture took root here. As they missed their homeland, they named this river "Jinjiang (Jinjiang River)". Since then, Jinjiang River has become the mother river of Quanzhou people. The estuary of the Jinjiang River Basin is the port where the river and the sea intersect. It is also the center of the "Three Bays and Twelve Ports" of the ancient Zayton Port during the Song and Yuan Dynasties.

In the year of 684 of the Tang Dynasty, Wurong State was first established, with the state government in the ancient city of Fengzhou, Nan'an. In the year 700 of the Tang Dynasty, the Wurong State Government was moved 7.5 kilometers to the southeast of Fengzhou, which is now Licheng District, Quanzhou. In the year of 711, Wurong State was renamed as Quanzhou—this was when the name of Quanzhou began. Since then, Quanzhou has had aliases such as Qingyuan, Wenling, Zayton City, and Licheng.

Quanzhou is a city of glory that started with the sea and because of the sea.

During the Tang and Five-Dynasties period, Quanzhou's marine trade flourished and overseas cultures rushed in. Ancient Yue culture, Central Plains culture, and overseas culture collided in Quanzhou and intersected and merged.

◎ 泉州湾来往的船只。（陈英杰 摄）

Ships coming and going in Quanzhou Bay. (Photo by Chen Yingjie)

宋元时期，刺桐港成为世界上最重要的港口之一，并对世界产生巨大影响。

作为10—14世纪世界海洋商贸中心，其海洋大通道的独特经历，让刺桐港闻名于世。历史上，无数来自世界各地的船只和商人都曾聚集于此，他们带着凌云的壮志和梦想，于宋元时期，参与了那段风云激荡的岁月，并留下了海上交通和海洋贸易高度发达的史迹。

航标、渡口、石桥、海港……都是那段历史的重要见证者，它们在岁月的演变中，向人们展示历史的回响。

古城泉州，有着绝无仅有的古迹。如今，这些见证中外古老文明交融的历史遗迹依然存在于泉州大地上，等待世人再次用心领略其风采。

你可以怀着一颗安静的心，吹着海风，漫步石桥之上；你也可以眺望远处的石塔，徜徉在古老海丝之城的历史长河里。驻足于曾经宏阔的东方第一大港，海上丝绸之路的历史气息扑面而来。

During the Song and Yuan Dynasties, Zayton Port became one of the most important ports in the world and had a great influence on the world.

Its unique experience as the emporium of the world from the 10th to the 14th centuries and its great maritime route made the port of Zayton famous. Throughout history, countless ships and merchants from all over the world have gathered here, and with dreams of overriding ambition, they participated in those stormy years during the Song and Yuan Dynasties, and left behind abundant historic relics of highly developed maritime transportation and trade in Quanzhou.

Navigational markers, ferries, stone bridges and harbors ... are all important witnesses of that history, and they show us the echoes of history in the evolution of the years.

The ancient city of Quanzhou has an unparalleled number of once-and-one monuments. Today, these historical relics that have witnessed the intersection of ancient Chinese and foreign civilizations still exist on the land of Quanzhou, waiting for the world to once again appreciate their elegance with heart.

You can walk on the stone bridge with a quiet heart while the sea breeze blows on your face; or you can look at the stone pagoda in the distance and wander in the history of the ancient city of the Maritime Silk Road. Stopping at the once largest port of the East, you can feel the historical atmosphere of the Maritime Silk Road.

◎ 古老的六胜塔与现代的石湖港。（吴刚强 摄）
The ancient Liusheng Pagoda and the modern Shihu Port. (Photo by Wu Gangqiang)

九日山石刻：海交祈风盛典的不朽记忆

在科技尚不发达的千百年前，无论是出海还是耕作都靠老天爷赏饭吃，天气未知，收成便是未知的。举行祈风仪式，祈求风调雨顺，是劳动人民最原始的诉求。拥有坚定信仰，便不再心生恐惧。

北宋元祐二年（1087年），泉州设市舶司，昭惠庙祈风仪典成为国家级典祀。此后，每逢船舶往返季节，泉州郡守和市舶司的高级官员就率领相关僚属到南安丰州九日山下延福寺旁的昭惠庙，举行祈风仪式。

昭惠庙的通远王为东南沿海的第一代海神，其灵显长达四百多年。"时舟舶遮江，旗幡蔽日，香烟缭绕，鼓乐喧天""车马之迹盈其庭，水陆之物充其俎"。由上面古人对祈风仪式的描述语中可见其隆重。官方祈风盛典的仪式，步骤大致如下：先设祭坛，再摆祭品，接着奏迎神曲，最后宣读《祈风文》，待到礼成后，石刻以记之，也就是我们现在看到的九日山祈风石刻。整个仪式典雅庄重，先人们对海洋神秘力量的信任就来自这隆重的仪式。借由祈风仪式，人们试图与心中的海神建立某种联系与沟通，并希望得到其庇佑。

"冬遣舶、夏回舶"两次祈风盛典加上神圣的祭海仪式，先民们便坚信海神能保佑出入刺桐港的船队，夏季可御西南风而来，冬季可逐东北风而去，也坚信"涨海声中万国商"的繁荣会一直持续。

◎ 九日山祈风仪典。（张清杰 摄）
The wind-praying ceremony in Jiuri Mountain. (Photo by Zhang Qingjie)

Stone Inscriptions in Jiuri Mountain: the Immortal Memory of the Wind-praying Ceremony for Maritime Trade

Thousands of years ago, when technology was not yet developed, both seafaring and farming depended to a great extent on Nature. As the weather was unknown, the harvest was unpredictable. It was the most primitive demand of the working people to hold the wind-praying ceremony to pray for timely wind and rain. With a strong faith, there would be no more fear.

In the year of 1087 of the Northern Song Dynasty, the Maritime Trade Office was established in Quanzhou, and the ceremony of praying for favorable wind at Zhaohui Temple became a national ritual. Since then, every time

◎ 祀奉通远王的昭惠庙通远殿。（成冬冬 摄）
The Tongyuan Hall of Zhaohui Temple dedicated to King Tongyuan. (Photo by Cheng Dongdong)

when ships were going back and forth, the Governor of Quanzhou and senior officials of the Maritime Trade Office took their relevant bureaucrats to Zhaohui Temple, which was next to Yanfu Temple at the foot of Jiuri Mountain in Fengzhou, Nan'an, to hold a wind-praying ceremony.

King Tongyuan of Zhaohui Temple was the first sea god of the southeast coast, with his spirit manifested in theophany for more than four hundred years. "At that time, boats and ships covered the river, flags and streamers covered the sun, smoke of joss sticks was draped around, and drums and music were loud" "The traces of carriages and horses filled its court, and the tributes from land and water filled its stands". From the above descriptions the grandness of ancient people' wind-praying ceremony can be well reflected. The general procedures of the official ceremony of praying for the favorable wind are roughly as follows: first set up the altar, and then present the offerings, then play the god-welcoming songs, and finally read the Wind-praying Text. After the ceremony, stone inscriptions were made to record the event, which are the Jiuri Mountain Wind-praying Inscriptions as we can see today. The trust of the ancestors in the mysterious power of the sea came from this grand ceremony, which was elegant and solemn. By the ceremony, people tried to establish some kind of contact and communication with the sea god in their hearts, and hoped to get his blessing.

With the two wind-praying ceremonies of "sending ships in winter and returning ships in summer" and the sacred sea ritual, the ancestors firmly believed that the sea gods could bless the fleet of ships safely entering and leaving Zayton Port, making them come with the southwest wind in summer and go with the northeast wind in winter. They also firmly believed that the prosperity of "the Emporium of the World in the sound of the rising sea" would continue.

◎ 高不足百米的九日山，却有三十六奇景胜迹。（陈英杰 摄）
Less than 100 meters high, Jiuri Mountain boasts 36 scenic spots. (Photo by Chen Yingjie)

祈风仪式不再，那些石刻却悄悄留下印记，使得今日之人能一窥当年盛景。从海上丝绸之路吹来的海风徐徐缓缓拂过九日山的每一方石刻，山风大声朗诵着祈祷文，一旦靠近，往日的气息就像潮水般涌来。位于南安丰州镇的九日山，距离泉州城约七千米远。九日山以"山中无石不刻字"闻名于世。自唐以来，文人墨客就喜游览此山，灵感来了，石头就成了天然之纸，用纸固然好，用石却更为恒久，许多珍贵的摩崖石刻因此遗留至今，石头因字亦有了灵魂。

九日山如同一部古老的书，每方石刻都是书中的一页。那些石刻的篇章，也许只有几个字，却可以引人揣摩其背后的万千世界。如今，全山自唐至清的摩崖石刻尚存75方，其中景迹题名15方，登临题诗11方，游览题名29方，修建纪事7方，海交祈风及市舶司事13方。

九日山祈风石刻集历史、文物、诗作、书法为一体，堪称石刻之经典。现存的10方海交祈风石刻中2方在东峰，8方在西峰，分别记载了早至南宋淳熙元年（1174年）晚至咸淳二年（1266年）共11次祈风的详细情况。其中，淳熙十五年（1188年）石刻全文如下："舶司岁两祈风于通远王庙，祀事既毕，登山泛溪，因为一日之欢，淳熙戊申夏四月。会者六人，林枅、赵公迴、胡长卿、韩俊、折知刚、赵善棐。冬十月，会者五人，赵不遏、胡长卿、韩俊、赵善棐、郑颐孙。"此一石刻明确记载了祀事地点，一年有"夏四月"的遣舶和"冬十月"的回舶两次祈风，"登山""泛溪"尽"一日之游"及参加人员等。

九日山祈风石刻力证了泉州作为海上丝绸之路重要港口的历史，也见证了我国与世界各国人民跨越万里进行海交贸易、相互往来结下深厚友谊的宝贵岁月。这些留住时光的石刻，成了人类永恒的礼物。它们比创造它们的人更加永恒。祈风石刻的存在，让人们一踏进九日山除了惊艳还有心动。何其有幸！当初，先人在此对话海神；而今，世人在此对话历史。

◎ 福建陆路提督马负书所题 "九日山"。（成冬冬 摄）

The Chinese characters "九日山(Jiuri Mountain)" inscribed by Ma Fushu,

the commander-in-chief of Fujian. (Photo by Cheng Dongdong)

Although the wind-praying ceremonies are gone, those stone inscriptions have quietly left their marks so that people today can have a glimpse of the scenes back then. The sea breeze blowing from the Maritime Silk Road gently brushes every stone inscription on the Jiuri Mountain, and the mountain breeze recites the prayers loudly. Once you get close, the atmosphere of the past will come like a tidal wave. Located in the town of Fengzhou, Nan'an, Jiuri Mountain is about seven kilometers away from Quanzhou City. The mountain is famous for "no stone in the mountain without inscriptions". Since the Tang Dynasty, the literati liked to visit this mountain. When their inspiration came, the stone became a natural paper. Many precious stone inscriptions were thus left to this day, and the rocks were given a soul by the inscriptions.

Jiuri Mountain is like an ancient book, with each stone inscription being a page of the book. Chapters of those stone inscriptions may only have a few words, but they can lead people to guess the great world behind them. Nowadays, 75 stone inscriptions from Tang to Qing Dynasties still exist on the mountain, including 15 scenic inscriptions, 11 inscriptions of poems, 29 inscriptions of touring, 7 inscriptions of construction chronicles, 13 inscriptions of maritime trade and wind-praying and the affairs of Quanzhou Maritime Trade Office.

Combining history, cultural relics, poetry, calligraphy as a whole, Jiuri Mountain Wind-praying Inscriptions can be called the classic stone inscriptions. Among the 10 existing stone inscriptions of maritime trade and wind-praying, 2 are in the east peak and 8 are in the west peak. They record the details of 11 praying for favorable wind from as early as the year of 1174 and as late as the year of 1266. Among them, the full text of the stone inscription in 1188 of the Southern Song Dynasty reads as follows: "The Maritime Trade Office prays for favorable wind twice at the King Tongyuan Hall in the year. After the sacrifice, we climb the mountain and raft the stream, as a one-day entertainment. It is now lunar April in summer of the year 1188. Six people attend the meeting: Lin Ji, Zhao Gongjiong, Hu Changqing, Han Jun, She Zhigang, and Zhao Shanshen. In the lunar October in winter, there are five participants: Zhao Buti, Hu Changqing, Han Jun, Zhao Shanshen, and Zheng Yisun." This stone inscription clearly records the place of worship, and there are two times of praying for favorable wind in a year, "in the lunar April in summer" and "in the lunar October in winter". In addition, activities of "mountain climbing", "stream rafting", the "one-day trip" and the participants are clearly recorded.

Jiuri Mountain Wind-praying Inscriptions have strongly proved the history of Quanzhou as an important port on the Maritime Silk Road, and have also witnessed the precious years when people from all over the world crossed thousands of miles for maritime trade and made profound friendship with each other. These stone inscriptions cherishing time tightly have become an eternal gift to mankind. They are more eternal than the people who created them. The existence of the wind-praying stone inscriptions touches people's heart once they step into the mountain. What a privilege! At that time, our ancestors talked to the sea gods, and now, we talk to history here.

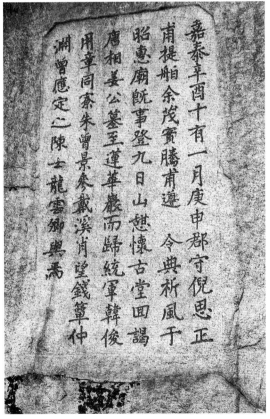

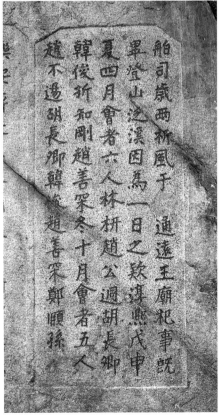

◎ 九日山祈风石刻。（陈起拓、成冬冬 摄）

The wind-praying stone inscriptions in Jiuri Mountain. (Photo by Chen Qituo & Cheng Dongdong)

◎ 九日山延福寺。（成冬冬 摄）
Yanfu Temple in Jiuri Mountain. (Photo by Cheng Dongdong)

　　九日山也见证了早期中外宗教交流的历史。南朝时，梁武帝派张汜送扶南国使返国，印度高僧拘那罗陀随其来华，先后到达南海郡（今广州）、京城建康（今南京）。南朝陈永定二年（558年），拘那罗陀乘船从梁安港（九日山下金鸡古渡）上岸，住在九日山延福寺，并在此翻译《金刚经》。九日山上有块刻着"一眺石"字样的石头，又名"翻经石"，相传拘那罗陀曾在此翻译经书。

　　由于九日山的独特魅力，曾在此山间留下活动遗迹的各界名流达六十多人，山上不仅有唐代秦系、姜公辅、欧阳詹和韩偓四大文人墨客的四贤祠，南宋大儒朱熹也曾在山中建"思古堂"。千年的岁月帮世人留下高士峰、秦君亭、姜相峰、姜公坟、棋盘石等人文胜迹，等待着游人驻足游览。

Jiuri Mountain also witnessed the early history of religious exchanges between China and foreign countries. During the Southern Dynasties (420—589), Emperor Liangwu assigned Zhang Si to send the envoy of the Kingdom of Funan back to their country. An eminent Indian monk, Guṇarata, came to China with Zhang, and visited Nanhai County (now Guangzhou) and Jiankang the capital city (now Nanjing). In the year of 558 of the Southern Dynasties, Gunarata disembarked from Liangan Port (ancient Jinji Ferry at the foot of Jiuri Mountain) by boat and stayed at Yanfu Temple on Jiuri Mountain, where he translated the *Vajra Sutra* into Chinese. There is a stone on Jiuri Mountain with the inscription "Yitiao Stone", also known as the "Stone of Sutra Translation", where it is said that Gunarata translated the sutra.

Due to the unique charm of the mountain, more than 60 celebrities from all walks of life who have visited here left their traces. There are not only the Four Sages' Shrine of Qin Xi, Jiang Gongfu, Ouyang Zhan and Han Wo constrained in the Tang Dynasty, but also "Si Gu Tang" built by Zhu Xi, a great Confucian of the Southern Song Dynasty. Thousands of years have left behind the Gaoshi Peak, Qinjun Pavilion, Jiangxiang Peak, Jianggong's Tomb, Chessboard Stone, and so on, waiting for visitors' visit.

◎ 九日山西峰最高处"石佛亭"内有一尊五代时期雕刻的石佛。（成冬冬 摄）
A stone Buddha carved during the Five Dynasties in the Stone Buddha Pavilion at the pinnacle of the west peak of Jiuri Mountain. (Photo by Cheng Dongdong)

泉州市舶司：管理海洋贸易事务的行政机构

海上贸易是宋王朝重要的经济来源，朝廷空前重视。北宋元祐二年（1087年），宋哲宗正式下令在泉州设立市舶司。泉州正式成为开放的国家对外贸易口岸，拥有绝对的海洋贸易自由。南宋时期，刺桐港发展成为全国最大的对外贸易港。开放的港口，迎来送往，梯航万国，舶商云集，刺桐港迈入海洋贸易经济的新征程。元代，刺桐港成为全世界最重要的贸易大港之一。

南宋时，泉州市舶司设置提举1员，同提举、副提举各2员。元时则设置提举2员，同提举2员，副提举2员。提举一职，官阶略次于太守，专任，或由太守兼任。市舶司的主要职能和现在的海关类似，负责管理进出口船舶、货物、人员，行使"抽解""禁榷""博买"等职责，同时招徕、接待、管理外商，还兼具治理港口、修筑城池、维护地方治安、剿灭盗贼等职能。

泉州市舶司的设立，让泉州在海洋贸易方面有了诸多便利，商船出海可以在泉州当地申办手续，而不用再像以前舍近求远，去广州市舶司办理。如此，既可以省去大量的人力物力，又可以更加合理安排船舶的出海及回港时间，大大提高了经济效益。

◎ 泉州市舶司遗址。（陈英杰 摄）

The site of Quanzhou Maritime Trade Office. (Photo by Chen Yingjie)

Quanzhou Maritime Trade Office (Municipal Customs): Administrative Agency Managing Marine Trade Affairs

Maritime trade was an important economic source for the Song Dynasty, attracting the imperial court's unprecedented attention. In 1087 of the Northern Song Dynasty, Emperor Zhezong officially ordered the establishment of the Maritime Trade Office (Municipal Customs) in Quanzhou. Thus Quanzhou officially became a national foreign trade port with absolute freedom of maritime trade. During the Southern Song Dynasty, the port of Zayton flourished as the largest foreign trade port in the country. Zayton Port started a new journey of marine trade economy with ships ushering in from and destined for the rest of the world and merchants gathered. During the Yuan Dynasty, Zayton Port became one of the most important trading ports in the world.

In the Southern Song Dynasty, Quanzhou Maritime Trade Office set up one Tiju (administrator) and other four officers of lower-ranking—two Tong Tijus and two Vice Tijus. In the Yuan Dynasty, there were two Tijus, two Tong Tijus, and two

◎ 旧时可让船只直达泉州市舶司的河道如今只剩下狭窄的壕沟。（陈英杰 摄）

In the old days, the river used to be wide enough for ships to reach Quanzhou Maritime Trade Office. Now only narrow trenches remain. (Photo by Chen Yingjie)

Vice Tijus. The official ranking of Tiju was slightly second to that of the governor. It was a full-time post, or held by the governor as an adjunct post. The main function of the Maritime Trade Office was similar to the present-day customs, responsible for the management of import and export of goods, ships and personnel, and the implementation of the duties of "taxing in kind", "monopoly" and "buying foreign goods on behalf of the government", as well as recruiting, receiving and managing foreigners. It was also responsible for managing the port, building the city walls and moats, maintaining the local public security, and suppressing the thieves.

The establishment of Quanzhou Maritime Trade Office gave the city a lot of convenience in marine trade. Merchant ships could apply for local procedures in Quanzhou instead of going to Guangzhou Maritime Trade Office as before. In this way, a lot of manpower and material resources could be saved, and ships could be more reasonably arranged to go to sea and return to port, which greatly improved the economic efficiency.

泉州市舶司收入丰厚，对于国库的充盈起到了不可或缺的作用。由于利润可观，南宋朝廷除了不断放权给泉州市舶司，还加强对泉州市舶司的扶持，两种政策相互支撑。据载，建炎二年（1128年），南宋朝廷一次性拨给泉州市舶司20万贯本钱，助力泉州市舶司扩大海外贸易规模。彼时，南宋朝廷每年财政收入大约4,500万贯，而泉州市舶司一年的收入就达到百万贯之多，泉州因此被称为"富州"。

◎ 泉州市舶司遗址挖掘现场。（王俊 摄）
Excavation of the site of Quanzhou Maritime Trade Office. (Photo by Wang Jun)

在泉州市舶司的规范管理下，泉州海外贸易空前繁荣，从刺桐港出发的商船从这里挺进更广阔的海洋世界，由此形成的海洋贸易网络，改变泉州，改变中国，改变世界。

据考证，泉州市舶司的遗址位于泉州市区中山南路水仙宫。这个遗址，也是全国唯一保存下来的古海关遗址，见证了宋元时期"东方第一大港"的海外交通和海外贸易的鼎盛繁华。市舶司的旧建筑已不在，只留下水仙宫和鹊鸟桥。

泉州市舶司历经宋、元、明三朝，于明成化八年（1472年）迁至福州，前后达386年之久。在将近400年的时间里，泉州的市舶司制度，为刺桐港商船的远洋贸易，提供了最大便利，推动泉州成为宋元中国的世界海洋商贸中心。

Quanzhou Maritime Trade Office had a rich income and played an indispensable role in filling up the national treasury. Because of the considerable profits, the imperial court of the Southern Song Dynasty not only continuously empowered Quanzhou Maritime Trade Office, but also strengthened the support for it. The empowerment and support policies propped against each other. It is recorded that in 1128, the imperial court of the Southern Song Dynasty allocated a one-off capital of 200,000 Guan(unit of Chinese cash, which refers to "string of cash coins") to Quanzhou Maritime Trade Office to help it expand its overseas trade. At that time, the annual revenue of the Southern Song imperial court was about 45 million Guan, while the revenue of Quanzhou Maritime Trade Office reached a million Guan a year. Quanzhou was thus called a "rich state".

Under the standardized management of Quanzhou Maritime Trade Office, the city's overseas trade flourished like never before, from which merchant ships departed from the port of Zayton and advanced into the wider ocean world, thus forming a maritime trade network that have changed Quanzhou, China and the world.

According to research, the site of Quanzhou Maritime Trade Office is located in Shuixian Palace, South Zhongshan Road, Quanzhou City. This site, the only preserved ancient customs site in China, bears witness to the prosperity of overseas transport and trade of the "Largest Port of the East" in the Song and Yuan Dynasties. The ancient buildings of Maritime Trade Office are gone, only Shuixian Palace and Magpie Bridge remaining there.

Lasting for three dynasties of Song, Yuan, and Ming, Quanzhou Maritime Trade Office was moved to Fuzhou in 1472, after a period of 386 years. For nearly 400 years, the system of Quanzhou Maritime Trade Office provided the greatest convenience for the ocean-going trade of merchant ships in the port of Zayton and promoted Quanzhou as Emporium of the World in Song-Yuan China.

◎ 泉州市舶司遗址出土陶瓷器。（成冬冬 摄）
Ceramics excavated from the site of Quanzhou Maritime Trade Office. (Photo by Cheng Dongdong)

真武庙：泉州海神信仰的重要遗存

供奉真武大帝的泉州真武庙始建于五代南唐，是真武大帝信俗传入八闽的首站，故而得名"玄天上帝八闽第一行宫"，其分炉遍布全省乃至东南亚地区。泉州真武庙位于东海街道法石社区的石头山上，山之绝顶有数十块大石相叠。现存建筑为明清时期的建筑风格，布局精巧，其朝向坐东朝西，山门、凉亭、大殿等主体建筑依山而建。

历史上，真武庙吸引了众多文人墨客、社会贤达到此留下墨宝。《真武殿祝文》为南宋泉州太守真德秀撰写，至今尚存。山门柱上的对联"仰之弥高大观在上，过此以往联步而升"，意境悠远，由清代著名书法家庄俊元手书。

沿着山门后的石阶而上可见一台地，台地上状如龟蛇的岩石上有一方"吞海"石碑，是明嘉靖十二年（1533年）晋江县令韩岳所立。"吞海"二字，既彰显了真武大帝的气势，也是泉州海洋文化的历史见证，张扬了泉州行船人势可吞海的气概，同时也寄托着靠海为生的沿海人民最原始的诉求——祈求船吞海，万勿海吞船。这一独特的海神信仰，是对大海神秘力量的敬畏，代表了民间朴素的海洋观。

◎ 真武庙山门为重檐歇山顶，檐下施如意斗拱，典型的四柱三间牌楼式建筑。站在山门前，极目远眺，晋江波澜壮阔，气吞山河。（陈英杰 摄）
The mountain gate of Zhenwu Temple is a typical four-column, three-*chien* memorial-arch building with a double-eave gable, a hipped roof and Ruyi-shaped bracket sets under the eaves. Standing in front of the arch gate, you can see the magnificent Jinjiang River in the distance. (Photo by Chen Yingjie)

◎ 真武庙祭海仪典。（吴云轩 摄）
The ceremony of offering sacrifices to the sea in Zhenwu Temple. (Photo by Wu Yunxuan)

　　泉州人民与海洋渊源深厚。有些史学家认为，先秦时，生活在泉州的古越人就已经与生活在中原的周人有了海上交通的先例。隋唐时期，泉州海上交通开始兴盛，宋元发展至鼎盛时期，前后繁荣达四百年之久，海洋文化对泉州人民影响深远，直至今日。

　　对于靠海吃海的泉州人来说，"讨海"是他们赖以生存的重要技能。人们对于海洋的崇拜和敬畏，来源于海洋丰富的资源和海上未知的凶险。"以海制宜、经营海田"的渔民们，需要强有力的海上之神来给予他们庇佑和勇气。智慧又虔诚的泉州人民，找到了掌管北方的水神——真武大帝。真武大帝的形象威武，横眉怒目，左手执剑，右手执戟，足踏龟蛇，被泉州人民视为能镇妖驱邪的海上尊神。

　　祈风和祭海是启航海上丝绸之路最重要的两个仪式，缺一不可。得天独厚的地理位置，加之真武大帝传说在民间广泛流传，因此宋代起每有郡守举行海事活动，必到真武庙祭海，以祈求海神保护商船平安往返。《泉州府志》曾记载道："玄武庙在郡城东南石头山，庙枕山漱海，人烟辏集其下，宋时为郡守望祭海神之所。"祭海一年举行两次，一次是端午前后的"回舶祭海"，另一次则是秋冬的"遣舶祭海"。

Zhenwu Temple: an Important Remnant of Quanzhou's Sea God Beliefs

Zhenwu Temple, dedicated to Zhenwu Celestial Lord, was built in the Southern Tang State (937—975) during the Five Dynasties, and was the first stop for the beliefs of Zhenwu Celestial Lord to be introduced to Fujian. That is why it was named "the first palace of Xuantian God (Zhenwu Celestial Lord) in Fujian", and its subordinate temples can be seen all over the province and even in Southeast Asia. The temple is located on the stone hill, Fashi Community in Donghai Street, with dozens of boulders stacked at the top of the hill. The existing buildings of the temple are of the architectural style of the Ming and Qing Dynasties with exquisite layout. Sitting east and facing west, the main buildings such as the mountain gate, the pavilion, and the main hall were built on the hill.

◎ 真武庙大殿祀奉真武大帝。（陈英杰 摄）
The Main Hall of Zhenwu Temple dedicated to Zhenwu Celestial Lord. (Photo by Chen Yingjie)

Throughout history, Zhenwu Temple has attracted many literati and sages to leave their calligraphy here. *The Blessing of Zhenwu Temple* was written by Zhen Dexiu, the governor of Quanzhou in the Southern Song Dynasty, and still exists today. The couplet on the pillar of the mountain gate, "Look up to the great view on the top, pass this past joint step and ascend", has a far-reaching meaning and was written by the famous calligrapher Zhuang Junyuan in the Qing Dynasty.

Going up the stone steps behind the mountain gate, you can see a platform with a rock like a tortoise and a snake, on which there is a stone tablet called "吞海(Swallowing the Sea)", which was erected by Han Yue, the magistrate of Jinjiang County in 1533 of the Ming Dynasty. The words "Swallowing the Sea" not only highlight the momentum of Zhenwu Celestial Lord, but also are a historical testimony of Quanzhou's maritime culture. They promote the temperament of Quanzhou boaters who can swallow the sea, and also hold the most primitive appeal of the coastal people who lived off the sea for their livelihood—praying for ships to swallow the sea, and never letting the sea swallow the ships. This unique belief in the sea god is the reverence for the mysterious power of the sea, representing the simple folk view of the sea in Quanzhou.

◎ 明刻"吞海"石碑。（陈英杰 摄）
A stone tablet inscribed "吞海 (Swallowing the Sea)" carved in the Ming Dynasty. (Photo by Chen Yingjie)

The people of Quanzhou have a deep connection with the sea. Some historians believe that the ancient Yue people living in Quanzhou already had a precedent maritime exchange with the Zhou people living in the Central Plains during the pre-Qin (221 BC) period. During the Sui and Tang Dynasties, maritime transportation in Quanzhou began to flourish, and developed to its peak during the Song and Yuan Dynasties—a prosperity for four hundred years. The maritime culture has had a profound influence on the people of Quanzhou until today.

For the people of Quanzhou, who live near the sea and live off the sea, "fishing" is an important skill that they rely on for survival. People's worship and reverence for the sea comes from its rich resources and the unknown dangers. The fishermen, who "make use of the sea to manage the sea fields", need a strong sea god to give them shelter and courage. The wise and pious people of Quanzhou found Zhenwu Celestial Lord, the god of water in charge of the North. The image of Zhenwu Celestial Lord is powerful, with crossed eyebrows and angry eyes, a sword in his left hand, a halberd in his right hand, and a turtle and a snake under his feet. Zhenwu Celestial Lord is regarded by the people of Quanzhou as a powerful god of the sea who can suppress demons and drive away evil spirits.

Praying for favorable wind and offering sacrifices to the sea are the two most important and indispensable rituals to set sail on the Maritime Silk Road. Zhenwu Temple occupies the unique geographical location and the legend of Zhenwu Celestial Lord was widely spread in the folklore. Since the Song Dynasty, for every governor who held maritime activities, they would come here to pray to the gods of the sea to protect the safe return of merchant ships by "offering sacrifices to the sea". According to the *Annals of Quanzhou Prefecture*: "Zhenwu Temple is located at the stone hill to southeast of the city. It pillows on the hill and borders on the sea. People converge under it. In the Song Dynasty, it was the place where the governor offered sacrifices to the god of the sea." The "sea sacrifices" were held twice a year, once around the Dragon Boat Festival when ships returned from afar, and the other in autumn or winter when ships departed from Quanzhou.

◎ 天后宫山门。（蒋长云 摄）
The Mountain Gate of Tianhou Temple. (Photo by Jiang Changyun)

天后宫：海内外规格最高、规模最大的妈祖庙之一

在泉州，老百姓供奉的神明众多，而妈祖则是他们供奉的神祇中对海峡两岸信众影响最大的神明之一。向海而生的泉州人，渴望海神的庇佑；发达的刺桐港，需要海神来镇守一方。泉州的海神从昭惠庙的通远王，到真武庙的真武大帝，再到天后宫的天后娘娘，从来不曾缺失。

天后娘娘，又称"妈祖"或"妈祖娘"，俗名林默娘，世居湄洲岛。林默娘出生于北宋建隆元年（960年），民间传说她能驾驭风云，预知天象，常泅水救难，驱瘟除病而受到当地人爱戴。殁后的林默娘依然经常出现在海上，救助受苦受难的渔民和船商，以一己之力保一方海域平安。世人因而尊称她为"海上女神"，并建庙祀奉。

南宋庆元二年（1196年），在泉州城南，天后宫拔地而起。这里是笋江和巽水二流汇合之处，也是蕃舶客航聚集之地。从此，官方最高规格的祭海仪式从真武庙转移到了天后宫，祭海的主祭对象从真武大帝变成了妈祖。

Tianhou Temple: One of the Largest and Top Level Mazu Temples at Home and Abroad

In Quanzhou, people worship many gods and goddesses. Mazu is one of the worshipped godesses that has the greatest influence on the faithfuls on both sides of the Taiwan Straits. The seaward people of Quanzhou long for the blessings of the sea gods; the properous port of Zayton needs to be under guard of the sea gods. The sea gods are never missing in Quanzhou: from King Tongyuan in Zhaohui Temple, to Zhenwu Celestial Lord in Zhenwu Temple, and to Mazu (the Queen of Heaven) in Tianhou Temple.

The Queen of Heaven, also known as Mazu or Mazu Niang and commonly known as Lin Moniang, once lived on Meizhou Island. Born in 960 of the Northern Song Dynasty, she was loved and adored by the locals for her ability to harness the winds and clouds, foresee celestial phenomena, and often swim in water to save lives and drive away plagues and diseases. After her death, Lin Moniang still often appeared on the sea to rescue the suffering fishermen and ship merchants, to ensure the safety of the people and ships with her own strength. She was thus honored as the "Goddess of the Sea" and temples were built to worship her.

◎ 天后宫正殿。（陈英杰 摄）
The Main Hall of Tianhou Temple. (Photo by Chen Yingjie)

In 1196 of the Southern Song Dynasty, Tianhou Temple was built in the south of Quanzhou City, where the two streams of Shunjiang River and Xunshui River converge and where foreign ships and sailors gathered. From then on, the highest official ritual of sea worship was transferred from Zhenwu Temple to Tianhou Temple, and the main object of sea worship was changed from Zhenwu Celestial Lord to Mazu.

宋元时期，刺桐港成为世界上最大的贸易港口之一，海上贸易进入鼎盛时期，海神信仰也愈加浓烈。朝廷顺应民间需求，加封民间神祇。至元十五年（1278年），元世祖忽必烈下诏敕封妈祖为"泉州神女""泉州海神"，号"护国明著灵惠协正善庆显济天妃"，并举行盛大的御祭加封典礼。清康熙二十三年（1684年），妈祖地位再次升级，由"天妃"晋封为"天后"，"天后"之称从此名扬海内外。

泉州天后宫的香火从南宋庆元二年延续到现在。这座八百余年历史的海神庙，是海内外规格最高、规模最大的妈祖庙之一，也是我国台湾地区和东南亚许多妈祖庙的祖庭。她见证了泉州"涨海声中万国商"的繁华，也见证了"寸板不许下海"闭关锁国后的落寞。如今，信众们从我国台湾地区、东南亚甚至更远的地方来到这里祭拜他们心中的神祇，祈求平安和幸福。

◎ "乞龟"是闽台两地流传久远的传统民俗。这一习俗两百多年前由泉州传到澎湖。2007年开始，泉州天后宫和澎湖天后宫携手合制"大米龟"，联合举行"乞龟祈福"民俗活动，为两岸民众祈福。如今，每年的"乞龟"俨然成了泉台两地一项极具传统味道的元宵节民俗活动。（吴云轩 摄）

Qigui is a long-standing traditional folk custom in Fujian and Taiwan. This custom was spread from Quanzhou to Penghu more than 200 years ago. Since 2007, the two Tianhou Temples in Quanzhou and Penghu joined hands to make the "rice turtle" and hold the folklore activity of "praying for the blessing of the turtle", to pray for people on both sides of the Taiwan Straits. Nowadays, the annual *Qigui* has become a traditional folklore activity of the Lantern Festival in Quanzhou and Taiwan. (Photo by Wu Yunxuan)

During the Song and Yuan Dynasties, the port of Zayton became one of the largest trading ports in the world. The maritime trade of Quanzhou entered its heyday, and the belief in sea gods became stronger. The imperial courts responded to the demand of the local people by ennobling folk gods and goddesses. In 1278 of the Yuan Dynasty, Kublai Khan issued an imperial edict to confer on Mazu the titles of "Goddess of Quanzhou" and "Sea Goddess of Quanzhou", and a grand ceremony was held. In 1684, the status of Mazu was upgraded again from "Tianfei (Princess of Heaven)" to "Tianhou (Queen of Heaven)", and the name "Tianhou" became famous at home and abroad from then on.

The worshipping activites of Quanzhou Tianhou Temple has continued from 1196 in the Southern Song Dynasty to the present. This sea goddess temple, which is more than eight hundred years old, is one of the largest of its kind at the highest standard at home and abroad, and is also the ancestral temple of many Mazu temples in Taiwan as well as Southeast Asia. It has witnessed the prosperity of Quanzhou—the "Emporium of the World in the sound of the rising sea"—as well as the desolation of the "sea ban" country. Today, believers from Taiwan, Southeast Asia and even further afield come here to worship the deity in their hearts and pray for peace and happiness.

◎ 2019年，泉州澎湖信众妈祖会香庆典在泉州天后宫举行。（成冬冬 摄）
　The 2019 get-together for Mazu of congregations from Quanzhou and Penghu was held in Quanzhou Tianhou Temple. (Photo by Cheng Dongdong)

泉州天后宫，位于泉州中山南路末段东侧，坐北朝南，面对镇南门，和德济门遗址紧挨着。天后宫占地面积7,200余平方米，大门呈牌楼式，两侧有浮雕麒麟石垛及石雕花窗，整体结构华丽壮观，宁静肃穆。进门抬头可见"海邦砥柱"四个鎏金大字，这是台湾鹿港天后宫赠予泉州天后宫的牌匾。闽台之间神缘深厚、源远流长，由此可见。

天后宫正殿为全宫建筑中心，砖木结构，保存完好。卷棚式檐廊，四角柱头为圆形浮雕仰莲连珠斗，方形斗拱接连四挑，独具一格。前檐一对雕龙廊柱，雕工细致，活灵活现；"鲤鱼化龙""八骏云火""鹤舞云中"等图案雕刻于须弥座，艺术造型典雅优美，和女性神灵的属性相得益彰。

殿中正龛供奉妈祖神像，龛后木板壁有清代绘制的大型湄洲岛壁画一幅，珍贵异常。廊庑位于殿前东西两侧，内祀辅助天后诸神二十四司，东廊仍在。从明代保存至今的寝殿位于正殿之后，木构建筑，古朴厚重。作为主祀女性神灵的宫殿，天后宫还设有梳妆楼。这一系列建筑共同构成了泉州天后宫极为完整的建筑体系，其规模宏伟壮丽，独具女性神灵特色，是海内外天后宫建筑的典范之作。此后国内其他地方的天后宫建筑规制多有仿照泉州天后宫而建。山东烟台天后宫就完全仿造其规制，连建筑材料都在泉州预制好再运往烟台，而台湾仿建的天后宫更达数百座之多。

几百年间，妈祖信仰随着海上贸易商船由海上丝绸之路一路传开，在我国台湾地区和越南、马来西亚等国家，生根发芽，绵延香火，让处在海洋周边的人们有了坚定的信仰。

◎ 代表最高级别官方表彰的御书匾额"神昭海表"，从清雍正元年（1723年）至今仍高悬于正殿中。（成冬冬 摄）

The imperial plaque representing the highest level of official recognition, "神昭海表 (Goddess of the Sea)", still hangs high in the Main Hall since 1723. (Photo by Cheng Dongdong)

Quanzhou Tianhou Temple is located on the east side of the last section of Zhongshan South Road in Quanzhou. Sitting north and facing south, it is next to the site of Deji Gate and faces Zhennan Gate. The temple covers an area of more than 7,200 square meters. The overall structure is magnificent and serene. The Main Gate is in the style of a memorial-arch building, with relief carvings of stone kylin stacks and stone lattice windows on both sides. When you enter the gate, you can see the big gilt characters that read "海邦砥柱(Mainstay of the Sea State)", a plaque given by Lukang Tianhou Temple in Taiwan to Quanzhou Tianhou Temple. The deep and long-standing divine ties between Fujian and Taiwan are thus evident.

The Main Hall is the center of the temple. Its brick and wood structure is well preserved. The colonnade is of the roll-top style, with the four unique corner pillars rounded and carved in relief with lotus flowers and square four-tier bracket sets. The pair of dragon columns in the front eave are meticulously carved and vivid. The patterns of "carp turning into dragon", "eight stallions in the clouds" and "crane dancing in the clouds" are carved on the sumeru pedestals, which are elegant and graceful in artistic shape, and correspond perfectly with the female deity's attributes.

◎ 天后宫寝殿前檐柱保存有一对宋代婆罗门教寺青石雕花石柱，与开元寺大雄宝殿后檐柱为同一类型石柱。（成冬冬 摄）

Among the front eave columns of the bedchamber, there remained a pair of stone carved-flower pillars of a Brahminical temple from the Song Dynasty, which are of the same type as the rear eave columns of the Mahavira Hall of Kaiyuan Temple. (Photo by Cheng Dongdong)

The main niche in the hall is dedicated to the idol of Mazu, and behind the niche there is a large mural of Meizhou Island painted in the Qing Dynasty, which is very precious. The galleries are located on the east and west sides of the front of the hall, which are dedicated to the 24 gods who assist Mazu. The east gallery is still in place. The bedchamber, preserved from the Ming Dynasty, is located behind the Main Hall and is a wooden structure, with classic simplicity and stability. As a temple mainly dedicated to a female deity, there is also a dressing house in Quanzhou Tianhou Temple. This series of buildings together constitute an extremely complete architectural system of Quanzhou Tianhou Temple. With its magnificent scale and unique characteristics of female deities, the temple is an exemplary work of architecture of Tianhou temples at home and abroad. Since its completion, the architectural system of the temple has been imitated by many Tianhou temples in other places in China. For example, Yantai Tianhou Temple in Shandong is a complete imitation of this system—even the building materials were prefabricated in Quanzhou and delivered to Yantai. In Taiwan, there are hundreds of imitative temples of Quanzhou Tianhou Temple.

Over the centuries, the belief in Mazu has spread along the Maritime Silk Road with merchant ships, taking root in Chinese Taiwan, Vietnam, Malaysia and other countries and regions, extending the worship activities of Mazu and giving people around the oceans a firm belief.

◎ 祖籍福建永春的台湾著名诗人余光中老先生有一首诗《洛阳桥》，开头这样写道："刺桐花开了多少个春天，东西塔对望究竟多少年，多少人走过了洛阳桥，多少船驶出了泉州湾……"（郑文桂 摄）

The famous Taiwanese poet Yu Guangzhong, who is originally from Yongchun, Fujian Province, has written a poem *Luoyang Bridge*. The poem begins like this: "How many springs have the Zayton flowers bloomed /, How many years have the East and West Towers looked at each other /, How many people have walked across Luoyang Bridge /, And how many ships have sailed out of Quanzhou Bay ..." (Photo by Zheng Wengui)

洛阳桥：中国最早的跨海石桥

　　两宋时期，随着海外贸易的发展，连接码头与内陆的交通设施显得愈发重要。彼时的泉州掀起一股气势如虹的"造桥热"，在三百多年间，共建造了一百三十九座跨江、跨海大石桥，每两年多就有一座新桥建成。它们让码头与城区、海港与腹地的联系更加顺畅紧密。这期间建造的最重要的桥梁之一就是位于泉州洛阳江入海口的洛阳桥。

　　洛阳桥本名万安桥，当年洛阳江入海口"水阔五里，波涛滚滚"，百姓为祈求平安过渡，把这个渡口称为"万安渡"，桥名"万安桥"。无论名号是洛阳桥还是万安桥，说到此桥，人们都要提及当年主持修造者、时任泉州郡守同时也是宋代大书法家的蔡襄。他的巨大石像在桥的这一头，为他而立的蔡襄祠在桥的那一头，似乎在共同守护着这座跨江接海的大石桥。

　　蔡襄祠内由蔡襄本人亲撰的《万安桥记》碑，全文仅有一百五十三字，却把造桥的几乎一切重要事项都囊括了，其中包括了建桥的开始时间、意义、资金来源、主要负责官员、竣工通行时间等情况。碑文洗练粹美，书法遒丽，刻功生动，被誉为书法、记文、雕刻"三绝"。

Luoyang Bridge: the Earliest Stone Cross-sea Bridge in China

During the Song Dynasty, with the development of overseas trade, the transportation facilities connecting the docks with the inland area became more and more important. During this time, Quanzhou was the scene of "bridge building craze". Over the course of more than three hundred years, one hundred and thirty-nine large stone bridges were built across rivers and seas. There is one new bridge completed biennially. These bridges provided convenient and close relations between the docks and the city, the harbor and the hinterland. One of the most important bridges built during this period is Luoyang Bridge, located at the estuary of Luoyangjiang River in Quanzhou.

Luoyang Bridge was originally named Wan'an (All Safe) Bridge. At the estuary of the Luoyangjiang River, "the water is 2.5 kilometers wide with the waves rolling". For a safe transition, the ferry was called Wan'an Ferry and the bridge was named Wan'an Bridge. Whether the name is Luoyang Bridge or Wan'an Bridge, when it comes to this bridge, people would mention Cai Xiang, the host of the building project , the then governor of Quanzhou, and also a great calligrapher in the Song Dynasty. His huge stone statue at one end of the bridge and Cai Xiang Shrine erected for him at the other end—both of them seem to be guarding together this big stone bridge that spans the river and connects the sea.

In Cai Xiang Shrine there is a monument of Wan'an Bridge's Record written by Cai Xiang. The full text is only one hundred and fifty-three words, but it covers almost all the important matters of bridge building, including the start time of the bridge construction, significance, sources of funding, the main responsible officials, the completion time, time to use, among others. With concise and beautiful inscription, vigorous and pretty calligraphy, and vivid engraving, the monument is known as a great artefact of "three wonders" in calligraphy, writing, and carving.

◎ 洛阳桥屹立于洛阳江上已近千年。（吴云轩 摄）
  Luoyang Bridge has stood on the Luoyang River for nearly a thousand years. (Photo by Wu Yunxuan)

◎ 时至今日，洛阳桥仍在发挥着它的交通功能。（陈海平 摄）
To this day, Luoyang Bridge continues to perform its transport function. (Photo by Chen Haiping)

横穿江与海的洛阳桥建成后，刺桐港与内陆腹地的陆路交通方便了许多，贸易往来也随之更为畅通发展，尤其中外商人的货物北上，不必再经朋山岭远绕长溪桥，缩短了不少路程，由此也带动刺桐港的货物加快流通速度！

除了发挥沟通山海的重要作用外，洛阳桥的造桥工艺以及在中国桥梁史上的地位也值得一提。中国著名桥梁专家茅以升在他的《中国桥梁史话》一书中，向世界隆重介绍的就有泉州的洛阳桥，并如此赞誉："洛阳桥为福建桥梁的状元。"洛阳桥与北京的卢沟桥、河北的赵州桥、广东的广济桥一起被誉为我国古代四大名桥。"南洛阳，北赵州"享誉海内外，被许多游人誉为一生之中不得不去的历史名桥。

作为我国历史上第一座跨海大石桥，洛阳桥名噪一时。北宋皇祐五年（1053年），洛阳桥开始建造。这一工程极为浩大艰巨，不仅耗费大量人力物力，也给施工人员带来很多挑战。当时的洛阳江水深难测，多有暗涌。为解决此一难题，智慧的工匠们建造时创造性地采用"筏形基础"，而国外采用筏式桥基不过是近一百多年的事。泉州先民们的智慧着实令人叹服，在桥上每走一步，都不由得生出敬佩之情。

◎ 洛阳桥建造时采用了"筏形基础"和"种蛎固基"法。（陈英杰 摄）
In constructing Luoyang Bridge, the "raft foundation" and "culturing oysters to consolidate the base" methods were adopted. (Photo by Chen Yingjie)

Upon the completion of Luoyang Bridge, land transportation between Zayton Port and the hinterland became much more convenient. Trade flows are also more smooth, especially when the goods of Chinese and foreign merchants went northward, they didn't have to go to Changxi Bridge through Pengshan Hills, which shortened the distance a lot and sped up the circulation of the goods in Zayton Port!

In addition to playing an important role in connecting the mountains and the sea, the building technology of Luoyang Bridge and its position in the history of Chinese bridges are also worth mentioning. In his book *The History of Chinese Bridges*, Mao Yisheng, a famous Chinese bridge expert, proudly introduced Luoyang Bridge in Quanzhou to the world and praised it as the No. 1 bridge in Fujian. Luoyang Bridge, along with Lugou Bridge in Beijing, Zhaozhou Bridge in Hebei, and Guangji Bridge in Guangdong, is acclaimed as one of China's four famous ancient bridges. The saying "Luoyang Bridge tops in southern China, Zhaozhou Bridge tops in northern China" is famous at home and abroad, and both bridges are regarded by many visitors as historical bridges that they have to visit once in their lifetime.

As the first stone cross-sea bridge in the history of China, Luoyang Bridge enjoys quite a reputation. The construction of Luoyang Bridge began in 1053 of the Northern Song Dynasty. The project was extremely large and arduous. It not only cost a lot of manpower and material resources, but also brought great challenges to the construction workers. At that time, the Luoyangjiang River was deep and unpredictable, with many dark surges. In order to solve this problem, smart craftsmen creatively adopted the raft foundation when constructing, while the use of the same method abroad is only over a hundred years. The wisdom of the ancestors of Quanzhou is really amazing. With each step on the bridge, people could not help but feel a sense of admiration.

洛阳桥处在"外有海潮冲击，上有江流刷洗"的险境位置，当时又无混凝土工艺，工匠们只能大胆创新，"种蛎以固基"，让洛阳桥经受江水与海水千年的冲击而不倒。所谓"种蛎固基"，是利用牡蛎的胶结特性达到巩固桥基的效果。牡蛎两个壳分工合作，一个用来附着在岩礁上或与其他牡蛎联结在一起，另一个用来保护自己柔软的躯体。牡蛎身体里渗出的胶汁无孔不入，一旦跟礁石胶成一片，铁铲也难奈其何。这个生物学的特性，被智慧的工匠们灵活应用到洛阳桥上。他们在桥基上广泛养殖牡蛎，牡蛎的繁殖能力惊人，几年之后，成片的牡蛎就把原来松垮的石条粘得固若金汤，堪比水泥之功。用牡蛎固基是建筑史上的一大发明，把生物学和建筑学融合得如此完美，是此桥的一大特色。

洛阳桥初建的时候，桥的长度为三百六十丈，宽度为一点五丈，两侧共有石雕护栏五百根。人们以江心岛中洲为界，把桥分为南北两段，桥上分布有七个亭子、九座塔、二十八只石狮子，其中一座婆罗门宝箧印经塔上刻有释迦牟尼成佛的故事。四尊石力神分立桥两端，石琢葫芦刻于桥塅四角石柱上，旁边呈洞状，佛像雕刻其中。江心岛中洲有中亭，中亭左侧有"西川甘露"碑亭，历代摩崖石刻及碑刻遍布四周，桥的北端有昭惠庙、真身庵遗址。

近一千年过去了，洛阳桥上"海内第一桥"的牌匾依然高高挂着，其美誉接受着时间的考验。那些经历了千年风霜的桥基，如今仍然于洛阳江中迎接着潮涨潮落。富有生命力的牡蛎和看似没有生命力的石头，共同演绎了一段可歌可泣的造桥神话。

◎ 洛阳桥中亭历代碑刻。（成冬冬 摄）

Inscriptions of different dynasties in the Central Pavilion of Luoyang Bridge. (Photo by Cheng Dongdong)

Luoyang Bridge was in a dangerous location where there are ocean tides dashing outside, and river water washing downstream. Because there was no concrete technology then, craftsmen could only be bold and innovative. They made Luoyang Bridge withstand the impact of the river and sea water for a thousand years and do not fall down by culturing oysters to consolidate the base. This method is based on the use of oysters' adhesive properties to achieve the effect of consolidation of the bridge's base. Based on the division of labor and cooperation between the two shells of oysters, one shell is used to attach to the reef or to connect with other oysters, and the other is used to protect its soft body. The oyster's body oozes glue that is so pervasive that once it is glued to the reef, it can not be removed even by a shovel. The wise craftsmen flexibly applied this biological characteristics to Luoyang Bridge. They widely bred oysters on the base of the bridge. Oysters' reproductive capacity is so amazing that after a few years, the oysters made pieces of the original sagging stone solid and strong, comparable to the work of cement. The oyster base is an extraordinary invention in the history of architecture. The perfect integration of biology and architecture is a major feature of this bridge.

When Luoyang Bridge was first built, it was about 1199 meters long, 5 meters wide, with a total of five hundred stone guardrails on both sides. People used the small sandbank islet at the center of the river as the boundary and divided the bridge into north and south sections. The bridge is distributed with 7 pavilions, 9 pagodas, 28 stone lions, including a Brahmin Ashoka pagoda engraved with the story of Sakyamuni's becoming Buddha. Four stone *mallas* stand at both ends of the bridge. Stone gourds were carved in the four corners of the bridge side on the stone pillars, next to holes in which Buddha statues were carved. The Central Pavilion is located in the sandbank islet, and the left side of the pavilion is "*Xichuan Ganlu* (Seasonal Rain from Xichuan)" monument pavilion. Cliff carvings and stone inscriptions of past dynasties can be seen around the bridge. In the northern end of the bridge there are Zhaohui Temple and site of Zhenshen Convent.

Nearly a thousand years later, the plaque "First Bridge throughout the Country" is still hanging high on Luoyang Bridge. Its reputation has stood the test of time. Those bridge foundations that have experienced hundreds of years of wind and frost are still welcoming the ebb and flow of the tide in the Luoyangjiang River. Vital oysters and seemingly lifeless stones have together performed a singable bridge-building myth.

安平桥：天下无桥长此桥

安平桥因其长度也称五里桥。古时候，人们用"里"作长度计量单位，一里大概相当于现在的450米，而五里就是2,250米左右。在中世纪，此桥的长度绝无仅有，世间再无比此桥更长的石桥。桥中亭石柱上的对联"世间有佛宗斯佛，天下无桥长此桥"也印证了这样的说法。

安平桥的历史，与海上丝绸之路的发展息息相关。唐宋以来，泉州海外贸易有了空前的发展和繁荣，及至宋末元初，刺桐港成为世界上最大的贸易港口之一。为适应海上交通发展的需要，宋元时期，泉州境内的大型石桥纷纷应时而出。

南宋绍兴八年（1138年），僧人祖派开始主持筹建安平桥，大财主黄护与僧人智渊响应号召带头捐钱。因为各种原因，前后历经十三年，直到绍兴二十一年十一月（1151年），才由当时的泉州太守赵令衿重新主持建造工程，用时一年方建成。安平桥建成后，桥边码头成为停泊点，大大方便了安平港的海陆交通，促进了当地中外贸易的发展。安平商人由此出发，足迹遍及东洋、南洋诸国。

◎ 安平桥所在的安平港在围头湾内，曾是宋代泉州海外交通、对外贸易的重要港口。（陈英杰 摄）
Located in Weitou Bay, Anping Port, where Anping Bridge lies, was an important port for overseas transportation and foreign trade in Quanzhou in the Song Dynasty. (Photo by Chen Yingjie)

Anping Bridge: No Bridge in the World Longer Than It

Anping Bridge is also known as the Wuli Bridge because of its length. In ancient times, people used *li* as a unit of measurement, and a *li* is roughly equivalent to 450 meters today, while five *li* is about 2,250 meters. In the Medieval Age, this bridge was the longest one of its kind, and there is no longer stone bridge in the world. The couplet on the stone pillars of the pavilion in the middle of the bridge says, "There are Buddhas worshipping this Buddha, while no bridge in the world is longer than this bridge". It confirms this statement.

◎ 位于泉州城西南安平港内的安平桥就是为了改善刺桐港南下交通而建。（陈英杰 摄）
Anping Bridge in Anping Port, southwest of Quanzhou City, was built to improve the southbound traffic of the port of Zayton. (Photo by Chen Yingjie)

The history of Anping Bridge and the development of the Maritime Silk Road is closely related. Since the Tang and Song Dynasties, Quanzhou overseas trade has had unprecedented development and prosperity, and to the end of the Song Dynasty and the beginning of the Yuan Dynasty, the port of Zayton became one of the world's largest trading ports. In order to meet the needs of the development of maritime transportation, large stone bridges were built in Quanzhou during the Song and Yuan Dynasties.

In 1138 of the Southern Song Dynasty, a monk named Zu Pai began to preside over the preparation for the construction of Anping Bridge. A local rich man Huang Hu and a monk named Zhi Yuan led donations in response to the call. For various reasons, it took 13 years until November 1151 that Zhao Lingjin, the then governor of Quanzhou, re-led the construction project, and it took one year to complete the project. After the completion of Anping Bridge, the pier by the bridge became a mooring point, which greatly facilitated the land and sea traffic in Anping Port, promoting the development of domestic and foreign trade. Starting from here, Anping merchants left their footprints throughout the East and Southeast Asian countries.

安平桥有两大特点：首先，它是跨海湾式石桥；其次，它的桥墩构造独特。全桥362座桥墩，采用卧水为桩，以沙基为底，枕木交叉相叠，世称"枕木卧基"。墩形设计根据潮汐涨落、江河流向的冲击力情况而定。流向冲力不大的，皆为长方形；一方冲击力大的设半船形桥墩；双方都有较大冲击力如港湾深水处，则采用船形桥墩，以缓和潮水涨落时水流之势，减小冲击力。

安平桥的建造技术，称为"干砌"。这种建筑方法采用花岗岩条石纵横交错叠于桥墩之中，其间不灌灰浆，也不衬石榫，却能够达到上下交接、左右牵制的作用。此建筑技术，不仅用于交通设施上，也用于构筑城墙等古代防御设施上。

◎ 安平桥的修建汲取了洛阳桥的成功技术又不照搬其经验，体现了古人的工匠精神和非凡智慧。（郑文桂 摄）
The construction of Anping Bridge draws on the successful techniques of Luoyang Bridge without replicating its experience, reflecting the craftsmanship and exceptional wisdom of the ancient people. (Photo by Zheng Wengui)

Anping Bridge has two major characteristics. First, it is a cross-bay stone bridge. Second, its pier structure is unique. The 362 piers of the bridge take the water as the pile, the sand base as the bottom, with the sleepers crossed and overlapped. The design is known as "Zhenmu Woji (submerged bases of sleepers lying on sand foundation)". The shapes of the piers were determined according to the tidal fluctuation and the impact force of the river direction. Those with small flow direction impulses were all rectangular; one side with large impact force was set up with semi-boat-shaped piers. When both sides of piles received a large impact force, such as in the deep water of the harbor, the boat-shape piers were applied to ease the trend of water flow when the tide rose and fell and reduced the impact force.

The construction technology of Anping Bridge was called "dry masonry". This construction method uses granite stones staggered in the piers, without injecting mortar or embedding stone tenons, but achieving the role of joining the upper and lower parts, and restraining the left and right parts. This construction technique was used not only for transportation facilities, but also for constructing ancient defensive facilities such as city walls.

◎ 安平桥每段桥面用4到8条大石板铺架，石板长5米到11米，宽0.6米到1米，厚0.5米到1米，重四五吨，最大的则重25吨。（郑文桂 摄）

Every deck of Anping Bridge is covered with 4 to 8 large stone slabs. The stone slabs are 5 to 11 meters long, 0.6 to 1 meter wide, 0.5 to 1 meter thick, weighing 4 or 5 tons with the largest one weighing 25 tons. (Photo by Zheng Wengui)

安平桥桥头的瑞光塔（俗称"白塔"），是安平桥建成后乡人以造桥所余钱财"造砖塔于西桥头，曰：瑞光塔"。瑞光塔高22米，为五层六角楼阁式砖石仿木结构，内空心，有旋梯可上。瑞光塔既是安平桥的"桥头堡"，又作为船舶出入的航标，与安平桥一起构成了一幅"白塔凌空，长虹跨海"的壮美画卷。

明崇祯年间，大海商郑芝龙在安平桥修中亭，清顺治十八年（1661年）朝廷"迁界"，把桥上所有建筑物全部焚毁，中亭也在其内。清康熙二十六年（1687年），中亭西侧填海建寺，以亭名寺称水心亭，即为现在的水心禅寺。1938年9月下旬，弘一法师应丰德法师之请，来到安海的水心禅寺，在安平桥边住了一月有余。这期间，他应安海各界善信之请做了几次佛法讲座，广结善缘。法师的房间就在水心禅寺边澄渟院内的一间僧房。房间里每天可听见桥下海水进退、波涛拍击的声音。

如今的安平桥保存完好，政府还在安平桥周边建起了安平桥公园。兼具古老和现代气息的安平桥公园，吸引了来自各方的游客。不同年龄的人，都可以在这座公园里享受到乐趣。下棋的老人兴趣盎然，挑货的阿婆卖力吆喝，留影的年轻女子身姿动人，骑车的少年轻松愉悦……

◎ 位于安平桥头超然亭东北侧的白塔是安海古镇的标志之一。（施清凉 摄）
The White Pagoda to the north-east of Chaoran Pavilion by Anping Bridge is one of the symbols of the ancient Anhai Town. (Photo by Shi Qingliang)

◎ 水心禅寺。（成冬冬 摄）
Water Heart Temple. (Photo by Cheng Dongdong)

Ruiguang Pagoda (commonly known as "White Pagoda") beside the bridgehead was built by the surplus money after the completion of Anping Bridge. It is said that the local people built a brick pagoda called Ruiguang Pagoda. 22 meters high, the five-story pagoda is a hexagonal pavilion-style brick-stone imitation wood structure. The interior of the pagoda is hollow with spiral staircases to go up. Ruiguang Pagoda is not only the bridgehead of Anping Bridge, but also a beacon for ships to depart and arrive. Together with Anping Bridge, it forms a magnificent picture of "the White Pagoda high in the sky, and the long rainbow over the sea".

During the reign of Emperor Chongzhen (1628—1644), the great maritime merchant Zheng Zhilong built a central pavilion on Anping Bridge. In 1661 of the Qing Dynasty, the Qing Government carried out the policy of "moving the boundary (forcing the local residents to move away 25 kilometers from the coastline)" and burned all the buildings on the bridge, including the central pavilion. In 1687, the west side of the central pavilion was reclaimed to build a temple. The famous pavilion was called the Water Heart Pavilion, which is now the name of the temple. In late September 1938, Master Hongyi, a great Buddhist master, came to Water Heart Temple at the invitation of Master Fengde and lived by Anping Bridge for more than a month. During this period, he gave several lectures on Buddhism at the request of the faithful from all walks of life in Anhai, and made good bonds with them. Master Hongyi was accommodated in a monk's room in Chengting House next to Water Heart Temple. Every day in the room, the advancing and retreating of sea water under the bridge and the waves crashing on the bridges can be heard.

Anping Bridge is well preserved today, and the government has also built the Anping Bridge Park around the bridge. The park, which has both ancient and modern appeal, attracts tourists from all walks of life. People of different ages can have fun in this park. The old men playing chess are full of interest, the old women selling snacks yell hard, the young women posing in pictures are attractive, and the boys riding bicycles are relaxed and happy...

顺济桥：海国冲衢、古城地标

随着海上贸易的日益繁荣，泉州城不断向南扩展。晋江这条河流，环绕着古城泉州的南部，水路发达，利于船舶往来，但是内城区和城南以外的陆路交通，却也被阻隔了。

南宋嘉定四年（1211年），泉州知府邹应龙募集资金，筹建一座横跨晋江两岸的桥梁，因位于顺济宫（天后宫）前面，得名顺济桥，又因建造晚于笋江桥，俗称"新桥"。

顺济桥全长五百米，宽四点六米。桥面为梁式石桥，桥墩采用"筏形基础"建造，与洛阳桥建桥方法类似。全河床抛填石块形成结构基础，其上干砌条石形成桥墩，上部为石梁结构。2006年，顺济桥倒塌，现留存船形桥墩及桥墩遗址约三十处。

宋元四百年间，顺济桥是泉州古城与晋江南岸的陆运节点，是伴随海洋贸易发展而建设的出入古城商业区的主要通道，完善了泉州的水陆转运系统。在古人看来，顺济桥是"下通两粤，上达江浙，实海国之冲衢，江城之险要"的交通生命线。顺济桥见证了泉州南城门一带"朝为原宪暮陶朱"的海外交通贸易的繁华景象。

◎ 顺济桥遗址和不远处的顺济新桥。（陈英杰 摄）
The site of Shunji Bridge and New Shunji Bridge nearby. (Photo by Chen Yingjie)

Shunji Bridge: a Thoroughfare and Landmark of an Ancient Seaside City

With the growing prosperity of maritime trade, the city of Quanzhou continued to expand to the south. The Jinjiang River, which surrounds the southern part of the ancient city of Quanzhou, is a well-developed waterway for ship traffic, but at the same time blocks the land traffic between the inner city and the area out of the southern part of the city.

In 1211 of the Southern Song Dynasty, Zou Yinglong, the governor of Quanzhou, raised funds to build a bridge across the Jinjiang River. As the bridge was located in front of Shunji Temple (Tianhou Temple), it was named Shunji Bridge. And as it was built after Sunjiang Bridge, it is also known as New Bridge.

Shunji Bridge is 500 meters long and 4.6 meters wide. The bridge deck is a beam-type stone bridge and its piers were constructed with a raft foundation, similar to the construction method of Luoyang Bridge. The whole riverbed is filled with stones to form the structural foundation, on which masonry stones form the bridge piers, and the upper part is a stone beam structure. In 2006, Shunji Bridge collapsed, leaving about 30 ship-shaped bridge piers and bridge pier sites at the moment.

During the four hundred years of the Song and Yuan Dynasties, Shunji Bridge was the land transportation juncture between the ancient city of Quanzhou and the south area of the Jinjiang River. It was the main thoroughfare to come and leave the commercial area of Quanzhou. It was built with the development of Quanzhou's marine trade and perfected its land and water transport system. In the eyes of the ancients, the bridge played a very important role as the lifeline of transportation that connected Quanzhou with Guangdong and Guangxi southwards, and reached Jiangsu and Zhejiang northwards. Shunji Bridge witnessed the prosperous scene of overseas transportation and trade in the area around Quanzhou's South Gate, which a poor scholar in the morning might turn into a millionaire in the evening.

◎ 顺济桥曾是沟通晋江两岸的重要
　桥梁。（吴云轩 摄）
　Shunji Bridge was once an important
　bridge linking the two sides of the
　Jinjiang River. (Photo by Wu Yunxuan)

◎ 顺济桥在建造时汲取了洛阳桥的建造经验，桥墩也采用"筏形基础"。（郑文桂 摄）

The construction of Shunji Bridge was based on the experience of Luoyang Bridge, with the piers built on raft foundations. (Photo by Zheng Wengui)

　　顺济桥桥北当年设有一段木梁桥，遇到外敌入侵和海盗滋扰时可以吊起。当年的桥头堡，设置戟门，白天敞开，夜晚则关。南端桥堡上有"雄镇天南"四个大字。

　　1230年前后，古城泉州再一次扩张，在顺济桥与天后宫之间建了南城门德济门。德济门内通城区，外接海港，成为古城泉州的繁华地标。

　　顺济桥与德济门两处遗址，是泉州向南发展和演变的历史印迹，是宋代泉州城市建设的历史产物，见证了刺桐城南商圈的兴衰。

There was a section of wooden beam bridge in the north of Shunji Bridge, which could be hoisted in case of outer invasion and pirate nuisance. The bridgehead then was equipped with a halberd gate, which was open during the day and closed at night. On the south end of the bridge, there are four characters "Xiongzhen Tiannan (Defending the South Frontier)".

Around 1230, the ancient city of Quanzhou was expanded again. Deji Gate, Quanzhou's South Gate, was built between Shunji Bridge and Tianhou Temple. Deji Gate connected inner urban area and the seaport, becoming a prosperous landmark of the city then.

The two relics of Shunji Bridge and Deji Gate are the historical imprints of Quanzhou's southward development and evolution. They are the historical products of the urban construction of Quanzhou in the Song Dynasty and have witnessed the rise and fall of the southern commercial district of Quanzhou.

◎ 古桥遗影。（傅捷雄 摄）
The scene of the ancient Shunji Bridge. (Photo by Fu Jiexiong)

石湖码头、江口码头：水陆转运、古港遗风

刺桐港的桥梁、石塔、航标、码头、古沉船经过悠久的岁月成了历史的背影，却仍以其质朴的生命力，拉近世人和海丝起点的距离。在古刺桐港的"三湾十二港"中，有两个码头特别值得一提，一处是石湖码头，另一处是江口码头。当时的刺桐港分为外港和内港，外港的代表是石湖码头，内港的代表是江口码头。

说到石湖码头，就不得不提林銮。早在唐朝，林銮就声名远扬。这位生于晋江东石的航海家，继承先祖开创的海运事业，把海上贸易的版图一再扩大。在巅峰时期，码头上的几十艘大商船都属于林銮，林銮是他所属时代的海上商贸王者。

为了让从事商贸的中外船舶安全入港，林銮在唐开元年间斥巨资花费近20年时间在泉州围头湾畔建造了7座石塔（称"七星塔"）作为引航航标。这7座石塔犹如天上的北斗七星，指引着海上的航船避开险滩暗礁安全抵达刺桐港。与此同时，林銮还建了一个巨大的水陆转运码头，也就是石湖码头，亦称林銮渡。这个以他名字命名的码头，当时是为了开辟通往勃泥（今文莱）的海上航线而建造的。

◎ 石湖码头建于天然岩石间。（陈英杰 摄）
Shihu Dock was built among natural rocks. (Photo by Chen Yingjie)

◎ 渔民们在石湖码头上整理渔网。（苏德辉 摄）

Fishermen are sorting their nets on Shihu Dock. (Photo by Su Dehui)

Shihu Dock and Jiangkou Docks: Water-land Transfer; Legacy of the Ancient Port

The bridges, stone towers, navigation marks, docks, and ancient sunken ships of Zayton Port have witnessed the history for a long time. But they still use their pristine vitality to shorten the distance between the world and the starting point of the Maritime Silk Road. Among the "Three Bays and Twelve Ports" of ancient Zayton Port, there are two docks that are particularly worth mentioning. One is Shihu Dock and the other is Jiangkou Docks. At that time, Zayton Port was divided into outer ports and inner ports. The representative of outer port was Shihu Dock, while the representative of inner ports was Jiangkou Docks.

As per Shihu Dock, Lin Luan has to be mentioned. As early as the Tang Dynasty, Lin Luan became famous. This navigator, born in Dongshi, Jinjiang, inherited the maritime business initiated by his ancestors and expanded the territory of maritime trade. At his peak, dozens of large merchant ships on the wharf belonged to him, who was the king of maritime commerce in his era.

In order to allow Chinese and foreign commercial ships to enter the port safely, Lin Luan spent huge amount of money and nearly 20 years building 7 stone towers (commonly called "Seven Star Towers") on the banks of Weitou Bay in Quanzhou during 713 and 741 of the Tang Dynasty. These 7 stone towers are like the Big Dipper in the sky, guiding the ships on the sea to avoid dangerous shoals and reefs to reach Zayton Port safely. At the same time, Lin Luang also built a huge water-land transfer terminal, Shihu Dock, which is also known as Linluan Ferry. This dock named after him was built to open a sea route to Boni (present-day Brunei) at that time.

因地处要塞，同时也是海防重地，石湖码头巧妙利用巨大的天然礁石，建于两座天然岩石间，构造精巧、结实牢固。石湖码头总长113.50米，以花岗岩条石顺海岸砌筑，呈曲尺状。现存引堤（称"通济桥"）为宋代修建，长70米，宽2.20米，高2.41米。礁盘边缘有用来给泊船系缆绳的石缆桩。当时在渡头还设有巨大的木吊杆用来装卸货品。中华人民共和国成立后，人们还在渡口的淤泥中，发现了郑和船队遗留下的重达758.30千克的铁锚，让我们再一次了解到直至明代这座码头还在发挥着重要的作用。

遥想当年，石湖码头帆影重重、旗帜飞扬、万商云集。今日的石湖码头略显落寞，只有岸边明崇祯十二年（1639年）重立的"通济桥"残碑尚存，仿佛在诉说着这座古渡头千百年间经历的人来人往、潮涨潮落。石湖码头是刺桐港外港码头的珍贵遗存，它见证了宋元时期刺桐港优越的建港条件，圆满地完成了历史赋予它的使命。

◎ 位于石湖码头不远处的石湖港。（苏德辉 摄）
The Shihu Port is located not far from Shihu Dock. (Photo by Su Dehui)

Shihu Dock is located in a strategic pass and is also an important coastal defense area. Cleverly utilizing huge natural reefs, the entire dock was built between two natural rocks, and has an exquisite and strong structure. The dock, 113.50 meters long, was built with granite strips along the coast in a curved ruler shape. The existing dike (called "Tongji Bridge") was built in the Song Dynasty and is 70 meters long, 2.20 meters wide and 2.41 meters high. There are stone bollards on the edge of the reef for mooring ships. At that time, there were also huge wooden steeves for loading and unloading goods at the ferry. After the founding of the People's Republic of China, people found an iron anchor weighing 758.30 kilograms left by famous navigator Zheng He's fleet in the silt at the ferry. This finding proved that this dock still played an important role until the Ming Dynasty.

Back in those days, Shihu Dock was full of ships with their sails and flags flying, and thousands of merchants gathered. Compared with that, today's Shihu Dock seems a bit lonely. Only the remnant stele Tongji Bridge reerected in 1639 of the Ming Dynasty on the shore still exists, as if telling the ups and downs of this ancient ferry for hundreds of years. Shihu Dock is a precious relic of the outer harbor ferry of Zayton Port. It has witnessed the superior conditions for the construction of Zayton Port during the Song and Yuan Dynasties, and successfully completed the mission entrusted to it by history.

◎ 依托泉州完整的石材产业链，石湖港在石湖码头不远处崛起，成为全国最大的进口荒料石集散地。这或许是石湖港参与新的千年海交史的开端。（苏德辉 摄）

Relying on Quanzhou's integrate stone industrial chain, Shihu Port has risen not far from Shihu Dock and become the country's largest distribution center for imported stone blocks. This may be the beginning of Shihu Port's participation in the maritime trade in the new millennium. (Photo by Su Dehui)

建于宋代的江口码头，处在江海交汇处的咽喉地带，是古代泉州重要内港和商贸码头，因其显要位置，内可进泉州城区，外可通达外海，历宋、元、明、清四朝，一直沿用，屡有修缮。

位于泉州丰泽区法石社区的江口码头由文兴码头、美山码头组成。南北走向的文兴码头，功能属性为驳岸码头，呈石构斜坡阶梯状，以错缝形式为主砌筑，现存部分长34米，宽3.50米。岸边有宋代宝箧印经塔一座，塔身为花岗岩，现存两段，系分别雕凿后再行接合。其中上段四面均存有一尊半浮雕的半身佛像，而下段四面则分别阴刻一字，由右至左顺读为"佛""法""僧""宝"。

于临江之处建造的美山码头呈石构墩台，筑基方式是"一丁一顺"的交替叠砌，现存部分长约30米，宽约20米，墩台东西两侧各附有一条南北走向的石构斜坡式道路，向南延伸至江中。为了给大船提供深水停泊的便利，墩台的台基呈梯形，由下而上逐渐向内收，而外侧壁面则呈斜坡状。

20世纪50年代和80年代分别在江口码头发现了12—15世纪的造船遗址、古船残骸、石碇等历史遗存。令人惊喜的是，继泉州湾后渚港沉船出土之后的又一古沉船——法石港宋船（未发掘）也在此发现。

宋元时期，古刺桐港出海口和晋江两岸为适应海上贸易运输的需要，设置了一系列大小码头，石湖码头与江口码头以及诸多内港码头一起，构成了古刺桐港完整的码头设施，共同向世人呈现了宋元时期刺桐港的水陆转运体系，是泉州海上交通的重要遗存和历史见证。它们汇集了来自世界各地的船只，货物从这里来往于世界各地。它们与当时世界上其他繁华的港口遥相呼应，共同促进海洋商贸合作。

◎ 文兴码头呈阶梯状延伸入江。（吴刚强 摄）
Wenxing Dock extends into the river in a stepped pattern. (Photo by Wu Gangqiang)

Jiangkou Docks, built in the Song Dynasty, is located in the key area at the junction of the river and the sea. They were important inner ports and commercial docks in ancient Quanzhou. Because of their prominent location, ships can enter the inner city of Quanzhou and reach the sea outside from there. They were in use all through the four dynasties of Song, Yuan, Ming, and Qing, and were repaired frequently.

Jiangkou Docks are composed of Wenxing Dock and Meishan Dock and are located in Fashi Community, Fengze District, Quanzhou. The north-south directional Wenxing Dock has a functional attribute of a revetment wharf, which is in the shape of a stepped stone slope and is mainly masonry in the form of staggered joints. The existing part of the dock is 34 meters long and 3.50 meters wide. There is a Song Dynasty Ashoka pagoda which is made of granite on the bank. There are two existing sections, which are carved separately and then joined. Among them, there is a half-relief bust of Buddha on all four sides of the upper section, while the four sides of the lower section are respectively inscribed with the word "Buddha", "Dharma", "Monk" and "Treasure" from right to left.

Meishan Dock built near the river is a stone pier. The foundation-building method is alternate stacking of "out-and-in bond". The existing part is about 30 meters long and 20 meters wide. There is a north-south directional pier on the east and west sides of the pier. The rock-shaped slope-like road that runs towards the south extends to the middle of the river. In order to make it easy for large ships mooring in deep end, the base of the pier is trapezoidal, gradually retracting from bottom to top, while the outer wall surface is slope-shaped.

In the 1950s and 1980s respectively, historical relics such as shipbuilding sites from the 12th to 15th centuries, wrecks of ancient ships, and stone inlays were discovered in Jiangkou Docks. Surprisingly, another ancient shipwreck after the shipwreck unearthed in Houzhu Port of Quanzhou Bay—the Song-Dynasty Ship (not excavated) of Fashi Port was also found here.

During the Song and Yuan Dynasties, a series of large and small docks were set up at the estuary of ancient Zayton Port and on both sides of the Jinjiang River to meet the needs of maritime trade and transportation. Shihu Dock, Jiangkou Docks and many inner port docks together constituted the integral terminal facilities of ancient Zayton Port. The facilities which showed the world the water and land transshipment system of Zayton Port during the Song and Yuan Dynasties, are important relics and historical testimony of Quanzhou's maritime transportation. They brought together ships from all over the world, and goods were imported and exported between Quanzhou and other cities all over the world. They chimed in with other prosperous ports in the world at that time, and jointly promoted the world's maritime trade.

© 美山码头。（成冬冬 摄）
Meishan Dock (Photo by Cheng Dongdong)

六胜塔、万寿塔：石塔为标，守望归航

当年刺桐港的"三湾十二港"中，石湖港是第一个港口，而位于石湖港边的六胜塔是东方第一大港的第一座灯塔，被誉为"海上丝绸之路的第一座灯塔"。

以石塔作为航标，是世界航海史上的一大创举。智慧的泉州先人们在石狮市蚶江镇石湖村东北的金钗山建造六胜塔，便于引导往来船只。历史的辉煌，需要建筑来见证。六胜塔是继开元寺之仁寿、镇国二塔而建造，风格、造型与二塔颇为相似。它雕工精细、造型宏伟，岿然不动地雄视古刺桐港。

时光荏苒，白云苍狗！北宋政和元年（1111年）建造的六胜塔已废弃，如今我们所见的是元至元二年（1336年）重建的建筑。六胜塔下的蚶江、石湖在古代为泉州重要外港。当年这里有18个渡口，停泊着各国番舶，海路交通盛极一时。清初，这里又成为祖国大陆与台湾对渡的中心码头。这座见证了东方第一大港繁华过往的古塔，其诞生和存留也见证着泉州航海设施建设和航海技术的发展。

◎ 六胜塔通高36.06米，底层周长47.5米，占地425平方米。（陈英杰 摄）

The height of Liusheng Pagoda is 36.06m, the circumference of the ground floor is 47.5m, and it covers an area of 425m². (Photo by Chen Yingjie)

Liusheng Pagoda and Wanshou Pagoda: Stone Pagodas as Navigation Marks Watching Homeward Bound

Shihu Port was the first port among the "three bays and twelve ports" in ancient Zayton Port. Liusheng Pagoda located near Shihu Port was the first lighthouse of the largest port in the East and was known as "the first lighthouse on the Maritime Silk Road".

Using stone pagodas as navigation marks is a great innovation in the history of world navigation. The wise Quanzhou ancestors built Liusheng Pagoda on Jinchai Hill in the northeast of Shihu Village, Hanjiang Town, Shishi City, which was convenient for guiding ships. The splendor of history needs to be reflected by architecture. Liusheng Pagoda was built after Renshou Pagoda and Zhenguo Pagoda of Kaiyuan Temple, and its style and shape were quite similar to the two pagodas. It has exquisite carvings and magnificent shapes, steadfastly gazing at the ancient Zayton Port.

Time flies! Liusheng Pagoda built in 1111 has been ruined, and what we see now is the construction rebuilt in 1336 of the Yuan Dynasty. Hanjiang Port and Shihu Port under Liusheng Pagoda were important outer ports of Quanzhou in ancient times. At that time, there were 18 ferry crossings, which were anchored by ships from various countries, and maritime transportation was flourishing. At the beginning of the Qing Dynasty, this place became the central pier for the crossover between the mainland and Taiwan. This ancient pagoda has witnessed the prosperous past of the largest port in the East, the construction of navigation facilities and the development of navigation technology in Quanzhou.

◎ 六胜塔与不远处的石湖港。（陈英杰 摄）
Liusheng Pagoda and nearby Shihu Dock. (Photo by Chen Yingjie)

六胜塔从外形上看颇有开元寺的东西二塔之风，仿木构的楼阁实则为花岗岩石建造，坐北朝南，八角五层。六胜塔的每一层有四个门并配有四龛，龛的两旁有浮雕金刚、菩萨立像，整座塔的浮雕金刚和力士像共计80尊。各层腰檐以上出勾栏，塔身八隅转角处各竖一大圆柱，上置莲花栌斗，两旁浮雕雀替，均有双跳五铺作斗拱40套。

航海的人，平安为重。家人的祈盼，都凝聚在石塔上的每一尊佛、每一尊金刚、每一尊力士像里。

Liusheng Pagoda looks like the two pagodas of Kaiyuan Temple in appearance. But the wood-like pagoda is actually made of granite stone. It faces south and is five-storey high in octagonal shape. On each floor of the pagoda there are four doors and four niches. On both sides of the niches are embossed Vajra and Bodhisattva statues. The entire pagoda boasts 80 relief statues of Vajras and mallas. There are crossing railings above the waist eaves of each layer, and the eight corners of the pagoda body are each erected with a large column, with a lotus cap block on the top, and two embossed sparrow braces on both sides. There are 40 double-tier five-intermediate-layer bracket sets as bucket arches.

Safety is the most important thing for sailors. The prayers of their families are condensed in the statues of every Buddha, every Vajra, and every malla in this stone pagoda.

在石狮，还有另一座石塔和祈盼平安的传说有关。这座塔叫万寿塔，也称姑嫂塔，相传是宝盖山下居住的乡亲们为了纪念望夫望兄的姑嫂二人所建的石塔。

明代方志史学家何乔远所著《闽书》中写道："昔有姑嫂为商人妇，商贩海，久不至。姑嫂塔而望之，若望夫石然。"美丽的传说历久不衰，传说不一定是真的，但它代表了当时老百姓的精神诉求——希望从事航海的人，都能平安返航。

从外看，八角楼阁式的万寿塔有五层，主楼材质为花岗岩。紧挨着塔门之前建有一座方形石亭，与寺庙拜亭相似，为祭塔之用，也用来祈祷平安。

万寿塔第一层的西北面有一个拱形石门，二至四层则分别有两个门洞，"万寿宝塔"四字赫然刻于第二层的门额上。万寿塔从下往上渐次缩小，叠涩出檐的砖石结构令人叹为观止。回廊围栏环护每层塔的四周，空心塔内有石阶可登至塔顶。顶层外壁建有方形石龛，龛内刻着姑嫂二人形象，印证了古老的传说。

望眼欲穿盼亲还，人间最深沉的祈盼，犹如石塔之重，千年不变。除了情感的寄托，万寿塔本身绝佳的地理位置，也让其见证了泉州海外交通贸易的历史进程。万寿塔所在的宝盖山矗立于泉州湾与深沪湾之间的平原丘陵，是泉州湾一带的最高峰。这里控扼泉州湾与外海交界处，古人风水思想认为这里是泉州的"水口"，在此建塔可以锁住水口以保平安。

◎ 俯瞰万寿塔。（陈英杰 摄）
A bird's eye view of Wanshou Pagoda. (Photo by Chen Yingjie)

In Shishi, there is another stone pagoda related to the legend of praying for safety. This pagoda is called Wanshou Pagoda, or Pagoda of Sisters-in-law. According to legend, it was a stone pagoda built by the villagers living at the foot of Baogai Hill to commemorate the two sisters-in-law who expected the return of their brother and husband.

The Book of Min written by He Qiaoyuan, a historian of local chronicles in the Ming Dynasty, reads: "In the past, there were sisters-in-law who were merchant's wife and sister. The merchant did maritime trade and did not return for long. The sisters-in-law set up stone piles to watch out for the husband's return. And after long they became stone statues." Not necessarily true, the beautiful legend lasts forever and it represents the spiritual aspirations of the people at that time—hoping that those engaged in sailing can return safely.

Seen from the outside, the octagonal pavilion-style Wanshou Pagoda is made up of five floors. The main building is made of granite. Right in front of the pagoda gate there is a square stone pavilion, similar to the worship pavilion of a temple, for worshipping the pagoda, and also for praying for peace and safety.

There is an arched stone door on the northwest side of the first floor of Wanshou Pagoda, and there are two door openings on the second to fourth floors separately. The characters "Wanshou Pagoda" were engraved on the forehead of the second floor. Wanshou Pagoda shrinks gradually from bottom to top, and the masonry structure with its eaves is breathtaking. The corridor fence surrounds each floor, and there are stone ladders to reach the top of the pagoda. There is a square stone niche on the outer wall of the top floor, and the image of the two sisters-in-law were engraved in the niche, which confirms the ancient legend.

The deepest prayer for the safe return of family members is like the weight of a stone pagoda, which will not change for thousands of years. In addition to the emotional sustenance, the excellent location of Wanshou Pagoda itself also allows it to witness the historical process of Quanzhou's overseas transportation and trade. Baogai Hill, where Wanshou Pagoda is located, stands on the hilly plain between Quanzhou Bay and Shenhu Bay, and is the highest peak of Quanzhou Bay. This area controls the junction of Quanzhou Bay and the open sea. The ancients believed that this is the "water mouth" of Quanzhou, and the pagoda built here could lock the water mouth to ensure safety.

◎ 位于宝盖山顶的万寿塔，于南宋绍兴元年（1131年）开始建造，至1162年完成，至今巍然屹立。（成冬冬 摄）

Wanshou Pagoda, located on the top of Baogai Hill, began construction in 1131 of the Southern Song Dynasty, was completed in 1162 and stands tall today. (Photo by Cheng Dongdong)

◎ 后渚古沉船挖掘现场。（成冬冬 摄）
The ancient shipwreck excavation site in Houzhu Port. (Photo by Cheng Dongdong)

宋代海船：丝路繁荣、航海发达的见证

　　古刺桐城的绚烂文明曾经产生无数令世人惊艳的宝物，那些宝物的风采，展现了古城泉州独特而迷人的文化魅力。郭沫若先生曾用"地下看西安，地上看泉州"来形容西安和泉州两地历史文化遗存质量之高、数量之多。泉州的文化遗产散落于古城各处。同时，有一些特殊的遗产却因历史原因深藏于海底，直到有一天重见光明，为世人瞩目。它们就是海上丝绸之路上的古沉船。

　　在所有的古沉船中，泉州后渚港古沉船和广东"南海Ⅰ号"最能够佐证海上丝绸之路之辉煌。它们向世人充分展示了宋元时期海上丝绸之路的海船风采，它们用物华天宝极致地渲染了古代海上丝绸之路的繁荣。

　　位于泉州湾西北角的后渚港，是古刺桐港最具代表性的港口，用以佐证其地位的古渡头，从宋元时期遗存至今。五个用于主祭海神的风水塔，也一并保存了下来。塔石上"至元癸未仲夏廿年（1283年），后山杨应祥刻"的字样依稀可见。

Marine Ships in the Song Dynasty: Witnesses of the Maritime Silk Road's Prosperity and the Developed Maritime Industry

The splendid civilization of the ancient Zayton City once produced countless amazing treasures to the world, the elegance of which showed the unique cultural charm of the ancient city of Quanzhou. Mr. Guo Moruo, a famous historian, once used "Looking at Xi'an from under the ground, and Quanzhou from the ground" to describe the high quality and large quantity of historical and cultural relics in Xi'an and Quanzhou. The cultural heritages of Quanzhou are scattered throughout the ancient city. At the same time, there are some special heritages hidden deep in the seabed for historical reasons, until one day they see the light again and attract the attention of the world. They are ancient sunken ships on the Maritime Silk Road.

Among all the ancient shipwrecks, the ancient shipwreck of Houzhu Port in Quanzhou and *Nanhai I* in Guangdong are the best proof of the glory of the Maritime Silk Road. They fully demonstrated to the world the elegance of marine ships on the Maritime Silk Road during the Song and Yuan Dynasties. They used materials and natural treasures to show the prosperity of the ancient Maritime Silk Road.

Houzhu Port, located in the northwest corner of Quanzhou Bay, is the most representative port of the ancient Zayton Port. The ancient ferry which is used to prove its status has survived from the Song and Yuan Dynasties to the present. The five *feng shui* pagodas used to worship the sea god are also preserved. On the pagodas, the words "Midsummer of the year 1283 during the reign of Kublai Khan in the Yuan Dynasty, engraved by Yang Yingxiang in Houshan", are faintly visible.

◎ 后渚古沉船出土地点如今建起交错的立交桥。（苏德辉 摄）
At the ancient shipwreck excavation site in Houzhu now there are interlaced overpasses. (Photo by Su Dehui)

1974年，宋代古沉船在沉寂了700多年后于后渚港被发掘。古沉船上出土有香料、药物、货物木牌、木签、铜钱、陶瓷器、铜器、木器、编织物、皮革制品、文化用品、装饰品、果核壳、贝壳、珊瑚、动物骨骼等，直观再现了宋代泉州海交盛况。

　　这艘古沉船在残长24.2米、宽9.15米的基础上复原，修复后的长度达到30米，宽10.5米，载重量达200吨。尖底造型的船体结构，拥有13个隔舱，以"V"字呈现于世人面前。

　　以福船为代表的船只是福建沿海一带特有的交通工具，同时也是航行于"海上丝绸之路"最优质的木质帆船。泉州后渚港古沉船反映了13世纪泉州造船工艺处于世界领先水平。今时之人以这艘古沉船为载体，回望700多年前那个"以舟为车，以楫为马"的时代，那个古刺桐港风华绝代的生动岁月。

◎ 古沉船经修复处理后被送至开元寺内的古船陈列馆进行陈列。（刘宝生 摄）
The ancient shipwreck was restored and sent to the Ancient Ship Exhibition Hall in Kaiyuan Temple for display. (Photo by Liu Baosheng)

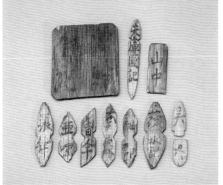

◎ 后渚古沉船上丰富的出土物。（成冬冬 摄）
Rich excavations from the ancient shipwreck in Houzhu Port. (Photo by Cheng Dongdong)

In 1974, the ancient shipwreck of the Song Dynasty was excavated in Houzhu Port after more than 700 years of dead silence. Unearthed from the ancient shipwreck are spices, medicines, wooden cargo signs, pegwood, copper coins, ceramics, bronzes, woodware, weavings, leather products, stationery, decorations, nut shells, seashells and corals, animal bones, etc. They visually reproduce the grand occasion of Quanzhou's maritime transport in the Song Dynasty.

This ancient shipwreck was restored on the basis of its residual length of 24.2 meters and width of 9.15 meters. After being repaired, its length reached 30 meters, its width reached 10.5 meters, and the deadweight of ship was 200 tons. The hull structure of the ship is in a pointed bottom shape with 13 compartments and is presented in front of the visitors with a "V" shape.

Vessels represented by Fu Junks are a unique means of transportation along the coast of Fujian, and they are also the highest quality wooden sailboats sailing on the Maritime Silk Road. The ancient shipwreck in Houzhu Port of Quanzhou reflects that the shipbuilding craftsmanship of Quanzhou in the 13th century was at the world's leading level. Using this ancient shipwreck as a medium, people today can look back at the era of boats as the most important vehicles more than 700 years ago, and the years of unparalleled magnificence of the ancient Zayton Port.

被称为"世界考古珍闻"的后渚港古沉船，是海上丝绸之路国宝级文物。而同样具有代表性的"南海Ⅰ号"是迄今为止国内发现的海上沉船中年代最早、船体最大、保存最完整的远洋贸易商船，被誉为"海上敦煌"。

"南海Ⅰ号"船体约30米长，10米宽，4米高。这艘木质古沉船被波涛汹涌的海水浸泡了800多年，直到1987年8月被广州打捞局无意中发现才为世人所知。2007年，"南海Ⅰ号"被用尽各种奇幻手段打捞上岸，并入驻位于阳江市的广东海上丝绸之路博物馆。

"南海Ⅰ号"古沉船上80,000多件文物造就了考古史上的一项壮举，一个瑰丽的世界被打开了。海上丝绸之路上，茶叶、丝绸和瓷器是三大最主要的出口商品。"南海Ⅰ号"船上装载了许多纸张和丝绸，但船上货品还是以瓷器为主。"南海Ⅰ号"上最令人震撼的，就是目前已发现的20,000余件（套）瓷器。而在大量的瓷器中，经判断，有多半产自德化窑和磁灶窑，其中还发现传世稀少的德化窑大盘，其口径达30厘米至40厘米。宋福建磁灶窑绿釉印花碟，绿得晶莹剔透，夺人眼球；宋福建德化窑白釉四系罐，温润不可言喻，盛放出臻于完美的色彩；宋福建德化窑青白釉印牡丹纹六棱带盖执壶，精致到无以复加；宋福建德化窑印花扁壶，造型别致……

◎ "南海Ⅰ号"古沉船考古现场及出水瓷器。（汇图网 供图）
The archaeological site of the ancient shipwreck of *Nanhai I* and the porcelains from the ship. (Courtesy of *www.huitu.com*)

The ancient shipwreck in Houzhu Port, known as the world's archaeological treasure, is a cultural relic of national-level treasure on the Maritime Silk Road. The equally representative shipwreck, *Nanhai I* is the earliest, largest and most well-preserved ocean-going trader ship among the sunken ships found in China so far, and is known as "Dunhuang on the Sea".

The hull of *Nanhai I* is about 30 meters long, 10 meters wide, and 4 meters high. This ancient wooden sunken ship has been soaked in rough seas for more than 800 years and it was unknown to the world until it was accidentally discovered by Guangzhou Waterway Resue and Salvage Bureau in August 1987. In 2007, *Nanhai I* was salvaged ashore by all kinds of magical means and entered Guangdong Maritime Silk Road Museum in Yangjiang City, Guangdong Province.

◎ "南海 I 号"古沉船出水之德化窑瓷器。（汇图 网 供图）

Dehua kiln porcelains from the ancient shipwreck of *Nanhai I*. (Courtesy of *www.huitu.com*)

More than 80,000 cultural relics on the *Nanhai I* ancient sunken ship created a miracle in archaeological history and opened up a magnificent world. On the Maritime Silk Road, tea, silk and porcelain are the three most important export commodities. The *Nanhai I* ship is loaded with a lot of paper and silk, but the goods on board are still mainly porcelain. The most stunning thing on *Nanhai I* is that more than 20,000 pieces (sets) of porcelain have been discovered so far. Among a large number of porcelains, it has been judged that many of them were produced in Dehua kilns and Cizao kilns. Among them, rare Dehua kiln plates with a diameter of 30 cm to 40 cm were found. The porcelain from Cizao and Dehua was charming and of high quality in various shapes and colors.

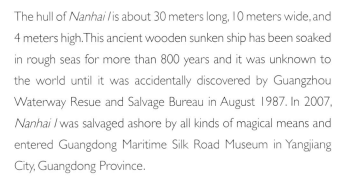

"南海Ⅰ号"船体本身具有极高的文物价值，从船上可以看到宋代的造船技术已经应用了当时可以称得上最尖端科技的水密隔舱技术。这艘福船代表了当时世界造船技术的最高峰。

　　在新科技手段的不断介入下，又一个重要的新发现为世人所知，那就是"南海Ⅰ号"的甲板下船舱内部发现非黄种人遗骸。这些异域特征的发现无疑验证了其他物品存在的合理性。比如船上发现的一方长约20厘米、宽约10厘米，墨池近似高脚杯形状，底部呈现"鸡冠花"纹饰，具有阿拉伯红海地区特征的砚台，以及一条波斯风格的鎏金腰带。

　　让我们想象一下当时的画面："南海Ⅰ号"从泉州驶出，船上载有来自世界各地不同种族、不同肤色的人，他们用精美的瓷器喝着美酒，畅快地聊着中世纪最流行的一切，比如贸易新秩序，比如文化新理念……

◎ "南海Ⅰ号"古沉船出水金器。（汇图网 供图）
Gold from the ancient shipwreck of *Nanhai I*. (Courtesy of *www.huitu.com*)

The hull of *Nanhai I* itself has extremely high cultural relic value. It can be seen from the ship that in the Song Dynasty people has applied the watertight compartment technology in shipbuilding that could be called the most cutting-edge technology at that time. This ship represented the highest peak of the world's shipbuilding technology at that time.

In the continuous intervention of new technology, another important new discovery is known to the world, that is, the remains of a non-yellow guy found inside the under-deck cabin of *Nanhai I*. The discovery of these exotic features undoubtedly verifies the rationality of the existence of other items. For example, the inkstone found on the boat is about 20cm long and 10cm wide, the pond of which was approximately in the shape of a goblet, the bottom was decorated with cockscomb pattern, and with the characteristic of the Arabian Red Sea region. In addition, a Persian-style gilt belt was also found.

Let us imagine the scene at the time: sailing out of Quanzhou, *Nanhai I* ship carried people of different races and skin colors from all over the world. They drank wine in exquisite porcelain, and chatted freely about everything that was most popular in the Medieval Age, such as the new trade order, or the new cultural concepts...

◎　"南海Ⅰ号"古沉船出水之磁灶窑瓷片。（汇图网 供图）
Cizao kiln ceramic chips from the ancient shipwreck of *Nanhai I*. (Courtesy of *www.huitu.com*)

◎ 泉州城夜景。（陈英杰 摄）
Night view of Quanzhou City. (Photo by Chen Yingjie)

光明之城——世界海洋商贸中心的繁华

　　发达的海上交通使得泉州的商贸迅速发展，从这里运往世界各地的商品有瓷器、丝绸、茶叶、铁器……

　　彼时的泉州港，吸引了来自世界各地的商贾。不同民族、不同肤色的人聚集于此，定居，经商，旅游，传教……

　　这座蕴含无穷能量的城市，在商贸交流和文化融合之中，向世人展示出一个海洋贸易中心诞生的故事。

　　1271年，一个名叫雅各的意大利犹太商人有感于泉州的繁荣景象，把泉州称为"光明之城"。那个时期的泉州，夜如白昼，灯火通明。中世纪时期，泉州这个因海洋而兴起的城市，吸引了全世界的目光。

The City of Light: the Prosperity of the World's Maritime Trade Center

The developed maritime transportation enabled Quanzhou's commerce to develop rapidly, and the commodities shipped from here to all over the world included porcelain, silk, tea, and ironware, etc.

In those days, the port of Quanzhou attracted merchants from all over the world. People of different nationalities and colors gathered here, settled, did business, traveled, and preached...

This city of infinite energy showed the world the story of the birth of a maritime trading center through trade exchanges and cultural integration.

Inspired by the prosperity of Quanzhou, Jacob d'Ancona, an Italian Jewish merchant, named it "the City of Light". In that period, with lights on all the time, the nights were as bright as days. During the Middle Ages, Quanzhou, the city that emerged from the sea, attracted the attention of the world.

◎ 渔船驶出泉州湾。（陈英杰 摄）
Fishing boats leaving the Quanzhou Bay. (Photo by Chen Yingjie)

南外宗正司遗址：宋代赵氏皇族管理机构

北宋徽宗时期，宗室人数剧增。为减轻赡养负担，朝廷将部分宗室成员迁往西京河南府（今河南洛阳）和南京应天府（今河南商丘）。迁往南京应天府的宗室，被称为"南外宗"，朝廷设立专门的机构——南外宗正司来管理应天府的宗室成员。

南宋初年，因战争原因南外宗正司不得不一路南迁，最后落地泉州。据考证，泉州鲤城区古榕巷60号院内，是当年南外宗正司的遗址。这一处掌管宋代外居宗室事务的官署和南宋皇族居住遗址，由芙蓉堂、睦宗院、惩劝所、自新斋、天宝池、忠厚坊等构成，面积约45,080平方米。

当时的南外宗正司掌管泉州和漳州两地的宗室。官署中的最高级别官员称为南外宗正司知宗正司事，简称"宗正"或"知宗"。"宗正"最初由宗室武臣充任。自绍兴三十二年（1162年）起，改由宗室文臣充任。南外宗正司还有不同等级官员若干名，用以管理宗室日常事务。

南外宗是宋代皇室的一脉，其官署机构在泉州持续蓬勃发展，机制日益完善。入驻泉州的南外宗给泉州带来了中原的先进工具、技术和文化，促进了地区之间的人文交往和民族融合。自公元1130年以来，迁居泉州的宋代皇族群体，在南外宗正司的管理下，进一步强化了国家政权对泉州海洋贸易的推动，体现了强有力的官方管理保障。彼时，几位宗室成员在泉州担任要职，实施惠政，既提高了泉州的地位，也促进当时海洋经济文化的繁荣。

在当时的大环境下，宗人群体和其他商贾一样，热衷于从事海外经商活动。他们带动了珠宝、香料、丝绸等高档货品的稳定消费，在一定程度上刺激了刺桐港的海外贸易，对海外贸易的兴盛起到促进作用。

◎ 位于泉州鲤城区古榕巷60号院内的南外宗正司遗址。（傅捷雄 摄）

The site of Southern Clan Office is located in the courtyard of No. 60 Gurong Lane, Licheng District, Quanzhou City. (Photo by Fu Jiexiong)

The Site of Southern Clan Office: the Management Institution of the Zhao's Royal Family in the Song Dynasty

During the reign of Emperor Huizong (1082—1135) of the Northern Song Dynasty, the number of imperial clan families increased dramatically. In order to reduce the burden, the imperial court moved some members of the clan to Henan, the west capital (now Luoyang, Henan) and Yingtian, the south capital (now Shangqiu, Henan). The clan moving to Yingtian was called "Nanwaizong(southern clan)", the royal clan members in the south. The imperial court set up a special institution—Southern Clan Office to manage the clan members of Yingtian.

Due to wars, Southern Clan Office had to move all the way south and finally landed in Quanzhou in the early Southern Song Dynasty. According to textual research, the courtyard at No. 60, Gurong Lane, Licheng District, Quanzhou, was the site of Southern Clan Office. The place housed the office in charge of the affairs of the external clan in the Song Dynasty and the imperial families' residence site of the Southern Song Dynasty. It consists of Furong Hall, Muzong House, Correctional Institution, Zixin House, Tianbao Pond, and Zhonghou Lane, and covers an area of about 45,080 square meters.

At that time, Southern Clan Office was in charge of the clan members in Quanzhou and Zhangzhou. The highest official in the office was known as the Officer of Southern Clan Office, Zongzheng or Zhizong for short. Initially, the position was filled by military officials of the clan. From the year of 1162, the position was held by civilian officials of the clan. There were also several officials of different ranks in the office to manage the daily affairs of the clan.

Southern Clan was a lineage of the royal family, and Southern Clan Office continued to flourish in Quanzhou with its official offices and mechanisms increasingly sophisticated. The Southern Clan that settled in Quanzhou brought advanced tools, technology and culture from the Central Plains to the city, promoting human interaction and ethnic integration among the regions. Since 1130, under the management of the office, the Song royal clan that moved to Quanzhou had further strengthened the state power's promotion of Quanzhou's maritime trade and embodied strong official management guarantees. At that time, several members of the clan held important positions in Quanzhou and implemented beneficial policies, which both enhanced the status of the city and promoted the prosperity of maritime economy and culture.

The imperial clansmen, like other merchants, were keen to engage in overseas business activities then. They drove the steady consumption of high-grade goods such as jewelry, spices, and silk, which to a certain extent stimulated the overseas trade in the port of Zayton and contributed to the prosperity of overseas trade.

宗人群体不仅参与海外贸易，也活跃于九日山祈风活动。在九日山上的祈风摩崖石刻中，记录有赵宋宗室成员的文字就有八段：淳熙元年（1174年），赵德李、赵致孚祈风于延福寺；淳熙十年（1183年），有同典宗赵子涛遣舶祈风；淳熙十五年（1188年），赵公迥、赵不遏、赵善桙舶司岁两祈风；淳祐三年（1243年），赵幕崇、赵师恕祷回舶南风；淳祐七年（1247年），赵师耕以郡兼舶祈风遂游；宝祐五年（1257年），宗正赵师淯、别驾赵梦龙等祈风；宝祐六年（1258年），赵梦龙、赵时潘等祈风；咸淳二年（1266年），知宗兼郡事赵希侂、赵东崇等祈风。祈风摩崖石刻记录下了泉州发展海外贸易的轨迹，也是记录宋代南外宗正司对刺桐港海外贸易产生积极影响的珍贵史料。

除了积极参与海外贸易、九日山祈风活动，宗人群体也参与泉州府文庙、安平桥等地方设施的修建活动，推动了泉州地域文化的发展。此外，南外宗正司对于泉州少林的拳术也产生了深远影响。自宋以来，拳术开始盛行。宋时南外宗正司睦宗院设有文臣和武臣主管各一名。武臣负责教授南外宗子们练习武术，而拳术必练。泉州的少林"五祖拳"又名"太祖拳"，因宋太祖擅长三十二式长拳、六步拳、猴拳、花拳等而得名。现在流行的"五祖拳"，极有可能是南外宗室带入泉州，而后在民间传开。

南外宗正司落地泉州，让这个曾经远离中原政治权力中心的刺桐城得以与朝廷有十分密切的往来，并在经济基础方面为延续南宋朝廷的政治生命做出特殊的贡献。遗憾的是，元朝军队一路南下，蒲寿庚投元献城，尽屠刺桐城中赵宋宗室3,000余人，南外宗正司就此走入历史烟尘中，唯留下遗址供后人凭吊。

◎ 南外宗正司遗址挖掘现场及出土文物。（成冬冬 摄）
The excavation site and excavated artifacts in the site of Southern Clan Office. (Photo by Cheng Dongdong)

Apart from participating in overseas trade, the clansmen group was also active in the wind-praying activities on Jiuri Mountain. Among the cliff carvings about wind-praying on Jiuri Mountain, there are eight paragraphs recording members of the imperial clan of the Song Dynasty: In the first year of the reign of Emperor Xiaozong (1174), Zhao Deli and Zhao Zhifu prayed for favorable wind at Yanfu Temple. In the 10th year of the reign of Emperor Xiaozong (1183), Zhao Zitao, a member of the same clan, prayed for favorable wind for departure ships. In the 15th year of the reign of Emperor Xiaozong (1188), Zhao Gongjiong, Zhao Buti, and Zhao Shanshen were sent to pray for favorable wind twice a year. In the third year of the reign of Emperor Lizong (1243), Zhao Muchong and Zhao Shishu prayed for the south wind for returning ships. In the 7th year of the reign of Emperor Lizong (1247), Zhao Shigeng, the governor of Quanzhou and head of the Maritime Trade office, prayed for favorable wind and visited the mountain. In the 5th year of the reign of Emperor Lizong (1257), Zhao Shiyu, officer of Southern Clan Office, and his assistant officer Zhao Menglong prayed for the wind. In the 6th year of the reign of Emperor Lizong (1258), Zhao Menglong and Zhao Shipan prayed for favorable wind. In the 2nd year of the reign of Emperor Gongzong (1266), Zhao Xicha and Zhao Dongchong prayed for the wind. The wind-praying stone inscriptions record the trajectory of the development of overseas trade in Quanzhou, and are also precious historical materials that record the positive influence of Southern Clan Office on overseas trade in Zayton Port in the Song Dynasty.

In addition to actively participating in overseas trade and praying for favorable wind on Jiuri Mountain, the imperial clan community was also involved in the construction of local facilities such as the Confucius Temple of Quanzhou and Anping Bridge, which promoted the development of Quanzhou's regional culture. Besides, Southern Clan Office had a profound influence on Quanzhou's Shaolin boxing. Since the Song Dynasty, Chinese boxing began to flourish. During the Song Dynasty, there was a civil official and a military official in charge of Muzong House of Southern Clan Office. The military official was responsible for teaching the sons of the clan to practice martial arts, and boxing was mandatory. The Shaolin Wuzuquan in Quanzhou, also known as Tai Cho Kun, was named after Zhao Kuangyin, the founder of the Song Dynasty, who expertised in the 32 styles of Changquan (long punch), six-step boxing, monkey boxing, and flowery boxing. Wuzuquan that is now popular was most likely brought to Quanzhou by the imperial clan community, and then spread among the local people.

The landing of Southern Clan Office in Quanzhou enabled the city of Zayton, once far from the center of political power in the Central Plains, to have very close contacts with the imperial court, and made a special contribution to the continuation of the political life of the Southern Song Dynasty in terms of economic base. Unfortunately, the Yuan army went all the way to the south, and Pu Shougeng surrendered to the Yuan army and slaughtered more than 3,000 members of the imperial clan in Zayton City. As a result, the Southern Clan Office went into the dust of history, leaving only the ruins for posterity.

德济门：古刺桐港贸易、文化汇聚地

如今，在北京的韩国人喜欢住在望京，日本人则习惯住在以长富宫饭店、北京发展大厦为中心的两个地区，而德国人喜欢住在以燕莎友谊商城、凯宾斯基饭店为中心的地区。这几个"外国人集中居住区域"，要是用闽南话来说就叫"蕃区"，古时称为"蕃坊"。蕃坊出现于唐代，是唐宋元时期来华贸易的外国商人、侨民聚居的场所，又称番坊、蕃人巷。而早在700年前，泉州就有了"蕃坊"。南宋地理志《方舆胜览》中写道："诸蕃有黑白二种，皆居泉州，号蕃人巷。"至晚自两宋之交起，刺桐城南城门——德济门附近便逐渐形成蕃商聚居街区。

德济门地处蕃商来泉上岸之处。700年前，此处紧邻晋江，利于出海，是进出泉州的要道，外来商贾就近聚居形成了"泉南蕃坊"。位于德济门外的聚宝街和万寿路的富美码头，承担着宋元时期进出口货物集散的重要使命。宋元时期，德济门周边的青龙巷和聚宝街，富商巨贾云集，成为现在人们所说的"富人区"。泉州有句古话"金青龙、银聚宝"形容的就是这两个地方。如今街上遗留的建筑和遗存的风物，依稀可见当年的繁荣与华美。"蕃舶客航聚集之地"，国际观瞻所在，周边配套完善，就连德济门对面的泉州天后宫，都是礼制规格最高的。

宋以前，德济门遗址周边被定位为"海港城"，后来晋江及其入海口一带海岸线退缩、陆地面积不断扩大，具备建城门的条件。彼时的古城泉州拥有七座城门，其他六座均已不复存在，只有德济门遗址被挖掘保留，见证了宋元泉州城市向南拓展的历史。

◎ 德济门遗址与天后宫仅相隔一条马路。（陈英杰 摄）

The site of Deji Gate is just across the road from Tianhou Temple. (Photo by Chen Yingjie)

Deji Gate: The Gathering Place for Trade and Culture in Ancient Zayton Port

Nowadays, Koreans in Beijing like to live in Wangjing area, Japanese are used to living in two areas centered by Hotel New Otani Chang Fu Gong and Beijing Fortune Building, while Germans like to live in areas centered on Beijing Lufthansa Center and Kempinski Hotel. In Minnan dialect, these foreigners' living areas are called *fanqu*, and *fanfang* in ancient times. *Fanfang*, also known as *fanren* lane, appeared in the Tang Dynasty and was the residential place for foreign merchants and expatriates who came to China to trade during the Tang, Song, and Yuan Dynasties. As early as 700 years ago, there are *fanfangs* in Quanzhou. *Fangyu Shenglan*, Southern Song Dynasty's annals of geography, says "There are two kinds of foreigners, black and white, and they all live in *fanren* lanes of Quanzhou." No later than the turn of the Northern and Southern Song Dynasties, Deji Gate, the southern city gate of Zayton City, has been gradually formed as a community for the settlement of the foreign merchants.

Deji Gate is located in the landing point of the foreign merchants who came to Quanzhou. Adjacent to Jinjiang River and conducive to going to sea, Deji Gate was the main road to and from Quanzhou 700 years ago. Foreign merchants gathered nearby to form the "South Quanzhou *Fanfang*". Jubao Street outside Deji Gate and Fumei Dock on Wanshou Road were important for the distribution of imported and exported goods during the Song and Yuan Dynasties. A large amount of wealthy businessmen resided in Qinglong Lane and Jubao Street around Deji Gate, forming an affluent neighborhood as known now. There is an old saying in Quanzhou, "Golden Qinglong, Silver Jubao", which describes these two places. The buildings and relics that remain on the streets today vaguely reflect the prosperity and splendor of those days. As a "place where merchant ships gathered", the surrounding facilities are complete. Even Quanzhou Tianhou Temple opposite Deji Gate boasts the highest standard of etiquette.

Before the Song Dynasty, the area around Deji Gate was positioned as the "seaport town", but later Jinjiang River and its inlet area had a retreating coastline and an expanding land area, which made it possible to build a city gate. At that time, for the ancient city of Quanzhou there were seven gates. Now the other six no longer exist, and only the site of Deji Gate has been excavated and preserved, witnessing the history of the southward expansion of the city of Quanzhou in Song and Yuan Dynasties.

◎ 德济门遗址是我国现存使用时间最长、面积最大的石构古城门遗址之一。（吴云轩 摄）

The site of Deji Gate is one of the longest surviving stone gates in China, with the largest area. (Photo by Wu Yunxuan)

由城门、城墙、门道、墩台、内外壕沟、拱桥以及瓮城和瓮城门等组成的德济门遗址占地面积约2,000平方米，出土的瓷器跨越宋元明清几个朝代，力证了当时人民生活的富庶。埋藏在地下3米左右的德济门遗址呈垒石结构，遗存有14—19世纪的铁炮等。佛教、基督教、伊斯兰教、印度教、犹太教等多个宗教的石刻也于此出土面世。其中有一块宗教石刻与众不同，在此之前从未发现过同类石刻。该石刻一面是古基督教的莲花十字架，另一面则是伊斯兰教的云月图。还有一块石鼓也十分特殊，其基底刻着六角星，中间填刻花卉图案。据专家推测，此石鼓极有可能为宋元时期泉州犹太教堂或者是信奉犹太教大商人住宅的石刻遗物。

宋元时期泉州物质文化交流的昌盛，在德济门的多件石刻文物中得到了印证。德济门遗址完整保存了宋代以来古刺桐城和泉南地区拓建、发展、演变的历史印迹。泉州对外往来由此开始、海上丝绸之路由此发展、多元宗教文化在此融合……

多重叠合的历史印记，在一砖一石中跃然而出，留给世人无尽感叹。那曾是多么壮美的一段人间记忆啊！德济门遗址无言却有力地告诉现在以及未来的人们，那些年关于辉煌、包容和开放的泉州传奇……

◎ 德济门遗址挖掘出土的多种石刻。（成冬冬 摄）
Various stone carvings excavated from the site of Deji Gate. (Photo by Cheng Dongdong)

The site of Deji Gate consists of city gate, city walls, doorways, piers, internal and external trenches, arch bridges, barbican and barbican gate. It covers an area of about 2,000 square meters. The unearthed ceramics were from the Song, Yuan, Ming and Qing Dynasties, which strongly proved the rich lives of the people at that time. The site of Deji Gate, buried about 3 meters underground, has a stone structure with iron cannons from the 14th to 19th centuries. Stone carvings of Buddhism, Christianity, Islam, Hinduism, Judaism, and many other religions were also unearthed here. Among them, one of the religious stone carvings is unique, with no similar stone carving having ever been found before. One side of the stone carving is an ancient Christian lotus cross, and the other side is an Islamic cloud and moon picture. There is also a special stone drum, with a six-pointed star engraved on its base and a flower pattern in the middle. According to experts' speculations, this stone drum is most likely a stone relic of a synagogue in Quanzhou during the Song and Yuan Dynasties or the residence of a great Jewish merchant believing in Judaism.

The prosperity of Quanzhou's material and cultural exchanges during the Song and Yuan Dynasties was confirmed by many stone inscriptions in the site of Deji Gate. The site of Deji Gate has completely preserved the historical traces of the expansion, development and evolution of the ancient Zayton City and southern region of Quanzhou since the Song Dynasty. From here, Quanzhou's foreign exchanges began, the Maritime Silk Road developed, and diverse religious cultures merged …

The multiple overlapping historical imprints leaped out of bricks and stones, leaving the world with endless sighs. What a magnificent memory it was! The site silently but powerfully tells people now and in the future about the glory, tolerance and openness of Quanzhou of those years …

◎ 六角星石鼓。
（成冬冬 摄）
The stone drum with a six-pointed star engraved on its side. (Photo by Cheng Dongdong)

◎ 中山路之所以叫"南北大街"，是因为它全长大约2,500米，贯穿了泉州古城的南北。（吴云轩 摄）

The reason why Zhongshan Road was called South and North Street is that it is about 2,500 meters long and runs through the north and south of the ancient city of Quanzhou. (Photo by Wu Yunxuan)

中山路：闽南建筑艺术博物馆

在中国，将近200个城市有"中山路"。几乎每条中山路都是所在城市商贸繁荣所在、城市繁华的地标。

泉州中山路历史悠久。唐久视元年（700年），泉州成为武荣州的州治，并设置了州治衙署。在衙署前，有一南大街（现在中山路的一部分）被设为市。中山路的繁华由此而开始。泉州中山路原称"南北大街"，"南北大街"改名为"中山路"，是顺应20世纪二三十年代以"中山路"纪念孙中山先生的改名大潮。

宋元时期，泉州是当时世界的贸易中心之一，其地位大抵相当于如今的纽约、巴黎、东京等国际大都市。如果时光倒退几百年，当下那些海外代购们，都得聚集在泉州的各个市场上。你可以想象来自世界各地的采购者从这里买走瓷器、丝绸、香料等备受欢迎的物品。

那时的泉州被马可·波罗称为"东方第一大港"；中山路上车水马龙，呈现出大城市街市的派头，史载"可容十四匹马齐驱"。发展到近现代，但凡泉州名气大、上规模的百货业、图书文具业、照相业、甘味业、药业、金融业、电影业等大多集中在这条街上。

Zhongshan Road: Southern Fujian Architecture Art Museum

In China, there are nearly 200 cities with Zhongshan Road. Almost every Zhongshan Road is a landmark in the city where the commerce and trade are prosperous.

Zhongshan Road in Quanzhou has a long history. In 700 of the Tang Dynasty, Quanzhou became the capital of Wurong State, and the State Government Office was set up here. In front of the government office, a South Street (now part of Zhongshan Road) was designated as a market. The prosperity of Zhongshan Road began from this period. Quanzhou Zhongshan Road was originally called South and North Street. South and North Street was renamed Zhongshan Road in response to the tide of commemorating Mr. Sun Yat-sen with Zhongshan Road in the 1920s and 1930s.

During the Song and Yuan Dynasties, Quanzhou was one of the world's trading centers and its status was roughly equivalent to that of today's international metropolises such as New York, Paris, and Tokyo. If time goes back hundreds of years, the current overseas purchasing agents will gather in various markets in Quanzhou. You can imagine buyers from all over the world buying porcelain, silk, spices and other popular items from these markets.

At that time, Quanzhou was called "the largest port in the East" by Marco Polo. Zhongshan Road was crowded with people and vehicles, showing the prosperity of a street market in a big city. According to historical records, the road "can accommodate 14 carriages". In modern times, most of Quanzhou's famous and large-scale department stores, book and stationery stores, photo studios, sweetshops, pharmacies, financial companies, and cinemas are converged on this street.

◎ 位于中山路与东街、西街交叉口的钟楼是泉州的地标之一。（陈英杰 摄）

The Clock Tower at the intersection of Zhongshan Road, East Street and West Street is one of the landmarks of Quanzhou. (Photo by Chen Yingjie)

唐宋以来各个时期的珍贵建筑、地名故事集中于此，风情万种的多元建筑风格在中山路上被完整保留下来，堪称闽南地区建筑艺术博物馆。罗马式钟楼、大上海理发店、原为施琅后花园所在地的基督教泉南堂、花桥慈济宫、古代秀才读书的泮宫……在中山路均可得见。中山路完整展现了泉州城市的历史风貌，街道至今仍保持着百年前的社会功能和经济文化活力。2001年，泉州"中山路整治与保护"项目获得联合国教科文组织颁发的"亚太地区遗产保护优秀奖"。2009年，中山路入选第二届中国历史文化名街。

漫步中山路，抬头可见许多店铺的老式招牌，让人仿似在历史的烟尘中穿行，好像这里依然是旧日时光。泉州中山路南侧，天后宫、聚宝街、李贽故居、来远驿、富美渡、青龙巷等许多和海上丝绸之路有关的遗址和人物故事，更是体现了泉州古城"市井十洲人"曾有过的辉煌。

"南国多雨天，骑楼可避风"。骑楼，雨天遮雨，晴天遮阳，现代文明的智慧在建筑形式上闪闪发光。如今在马来西亚、新加坡还保留有这种建筑风格的街道。沿着中山路走过一栋栋廊柱式的骑楼建筑，仿佛置身于南洋诸国。泉州中山路是我国少有、保存完整的连排式骑楼建筑商业街，弥足珍贵。

历经朝代更迭，古老的建筑如同凝固的音符，弹奏出对岁月的眷念，让人们对历史不仅止步于想象。2,500米长的街道上，不同地域的人文气息交织在一起。从形成之时到现在，中山路一直都是泉州最繁华的商住两用街，也是"老字号"最集中的一条街，它当得起董必武那句"东西双古塔，南北一长街"的美誉。

◎ 位于中山路上的泮宫是泉州府文庙的主要附属建筑之一。（成冬冬 摄）
The Pan Palace on Zhongshan Road is one of the main outbuildings of the Confucius Temple in Quanzhou. (Photo by Cheng Dongdong)

The precious buildings and stories about the origins of famous places' names of various periods since the Tang and Song Dynasties are concentrated here. The diverse and various architectural styles have been completely preserved on this road. Thus it can be called a museum of architectural art in Southern Fujian area. The Romanesque Clock Tower, the Shanghai Barbershop, the Christian Church where Shi Lang's rear garden was originally located,

the Huaqiao Ciji Temple, the Pan Palace where ancient scholars read books... can all be seen on this road. Zhongshan Road fully displays the historical features of Quanzhou City, and maintains the social functions and economic and cultural vitality of a hundred years ago. In 2001, Quanzhou Zhongshan Road Improvement and Protection Project won the UNESCO Asia-Pacific Awards for Cultural Heritage Conservation. In 2009, Zhongshan Road was selected one of the second group of Chinese Historical and Cultural Streets.

◎ 一千多年后，中山路依然是泉州最繁华的街区之一。（张清杰 摄）
More than a thousand years later, Zhongshan Road remains one of Quanzhou's most prosperous neighborhoods. (Photo by Zhang Qingjie)

Walking along Zhongshan Road, you can see the old-fashioned signboards of many shops, which makes you feel you are walking through the smoke and dust of history, as if this place is still in the old days. To the south of Zhongshan Road, Tianhou Temple, Jubao Street, Li Zhi's Former Residence, Laiyuan Courier Station, Fumei Ferry Pier, Qinglong Alley and many other relics and stories related to the Maritime Silk Road, reflect the glory the ancient city of Quanzhou with "foreign people from various continents" have ever had.

"South China is often rainy; the arcade can be a shelter from the wind." The arcades, sheltering from rain on rainy days and offering shade on sunny days, reflect the wisdom of modern civilization gleams in the architectural form. Today there are still streets in this architectural style in Malaysia and Singapore. Walking along the arcade-style buildings on Zhongshan Road make you feel you are in the Southeast Asian countries. Zhongshan Road is a rare and well-preserved commercial street with rows of arcade structure in China, which is very precious.

Through dynasties, the ancient buildings are like solidified notes, playing nostalgia for the past, making people more than just imagine the history. On the 2,500-meter-long street, the cultural atmosphere of different regions is intertwined. From its formation to the present, Zhongshan Road has always been the most prosperous commercial and residential street in Quanzhou, and it is also the most concentrated street of time-honored brands. It deserves the reputation of Mr. Dong Biwu's poetic praise, "Two ancient pagodas in the east and west, and a long street in the north and south".

◎ 据史料记载，西街成街始于唐开元年间（713—741年），东起双门前（即今钟楼下），西至唐故城西门——素景门（今孝感巷口）。（陈英杰 摄）

According to historical records, West Street became a street during 713 and 741 of the Tang Dynasty, starting from the front of Shuangmen (now the Clock Tower) in the east, and to the west gate of the ancient city of the Tang Dynasty—Sujing Gate (now the entrance to Xiaogan Alley) in the west. (Photo by Chen Yingjie)

西街：充满人间烟火气的千年古街

西街，泉州最早的街道。这条具有1,300年历史的老街，和中国其他城市的著名街道一样，见证着城市的古今繁荣与历史文化。

早在宋朝，西街就是刺桐城繁华的象征，至今仍然保留着完整的古街区。大量具有历史风貌的建筑散落在西街每一条小巷里，诗情画意地占据着来泉州的每一位游人的心。游人们即使要走了，仍会一步三回头地醉心于西街上的小吃、古迹以及别处再也寻不到的万种风情。

西街片区有各级文物保护单位20多处，分属古建筑、古遗址、石刻等多种类别，还有未列入级别但保护较好的古建筑、古民居12处，拥有开元寺、东西塔、肃清门等景点。

West Street: a Thousand-year-old Street Full of Vibrant Urban Street Life

West Street is the earliest street in Quanzhou. With a history of 1,300 years and like the famous streets in Chinese cities, West Street bears witness to Quanzhou's prosperity in ancient and modern times, its history and culture.

As early as the Song Dynasty, West Street was a symbol of the prosperity of Zayton City, and the complete ancient block is still preserved. A large number of historic buildings are scattered in every alley of West Street, and they occupy the heart of every visitor who comes to Quanzhou with their impressing view. Even if the tourists are going to leave, they will still be fascinated by the snacks, historical sites on West Street and thousands of customs and practices that can't be found anywhere else.

There are more than 20 cultural relics protection units at various levels in the area of West Street, belonging to various categories such as ancient buildings, ancient ruins, and stone carvings. There are also 12 ancient buildings and ancient dwellings that are not listed but are well protected. There are Kaiyuan Temple, East Pagoda, West Pagoda, Suqing Gate, and other attractions in the area.

◎ 繁华热闹的西街是国内外游客了解泉州古城的第一站。（陈英杰 摄）
The bustling West Street is the first stop for domestic and international tourists to learn about the ancient city of Quanzhou. (Photo by Chen Yingjie)

未走进西街，先会被红砖墙和火焰窗吸引住目光。一旦走进深处，或深或浅的古巷总像要流淌出故事来留住你，你便愿意驻足，乃至流连忘返。随意拐进一处巷子、一家店面，你可能会惊呼最是此间故事多。

走进西街，你无法避开开元寺，远远地就能看见寺内镇国、仁寿双塔。开元寺虽坐落在充满人间烟火味的西街，却只用一墙紫云屏来把桑莲法界和世俗人间隔开，僧俗各得其所，融洽自在。紫云屏里梵音不绝，清凉自在；紫云屏外商民络绎不绝，人潮如织！于是，西街就和开元寺一起，见证了千年里古城人们的兴衰成败、悲欢离合。

开元寺斜对角的旧馆驿巷是西街众多古巷的一个代表。老泉州人俗称它为"牛仔页巷"或"牛仔驿"。此巷本来是泉州古代驿站（驿站即古代驿吏或来往官员歇宿、换骑之地）所在地。宋代，原泉州官方驿站为晋安驿，设县治西（今中山北路驿内巷）；到了元代，晋安驿迁至旧馆驿巷内，改名清源驿，巷内设有一座专供过往官员或信使住宿和更换马匹的馆舍，称为馆驿；明代天启年间（1621—1627年），迁驿站于城外，原驿站废弃，此处便成为地名和巷名。因为经历过骏马来往的岁月，比起大多数的泉州古巷，旧馆驿巷明显要宽阔些，文化史迹也更丰富。

◎ 西街上玩耍的儿童。（陈英杰 摄）

Children playing on West Street. (Photo by Chen Yingjie)

Before entering West Street, you would be attracted by the red brick walls and flame-shape windows. Once you walk into the street, the long or short ancient alleys there are always like vivid stories to attract you. You will stop, and even linger. Turning into an alley or a store at will, you may exclaim that there are so many stories here.

Walking into West Street, you can't avoid Kaiyuan Temple. You can see Zhenguo Pagoda and Renshou Pagoda in the temple from a distance. Although the temple is located in the West Street full of vibrant urban street life, it only uses the Purple Cloud Screen Wall to separate the mulberry lotus dharma realm from the secular people. The monks and laymen live as they like and are in harmony. There are endless sounds of reciting and chanting Buddhist scriptures within, and it is cool and comfortable; out of the wall was an endless stream of vendors and local people! Thus, West Street and Kaiyuan Temple witnessed the success and failure, the joys and sorrows of the people in the ancient city for over a thousand years.

The Jiuguanyi Alley, diagonally opposite to Kaiyuan Temple, is a representative of the many ancient alleys in West Street. Old Quanzhou people commonly referred to it as Niuzaiye Alley or Niuzaiyi. This alley was originally the location of the ancient stagecoach station in Quanzhou (the stagecoach station was the place where the ancient post office staff or travelling officials came to rest or sleep and change rides). In the Song Dynasty, the former official station in Quanzhou was Jin'an Station, which lied in the west of the county government office (now Yinei Lane of North Zhongshan Road). In the Yuan Dynasty, Jin'an Station moved to Jiuguanyi Alley and was renamed Qingyuan Station. A special station called Guanyi was there for travelling officials or messengers to stay and replace horses. During 1621 and 1627 in the Ming Dynasty, the station was moved outside the city and the original site was abandoned. But the names of the place and the lane remained. Because the horses once ran in and out of the alley, compared with most ancient alleys in Quanzhou, Jiuguanyi Alley is obviously wider and richer in cultural and historical sites.

◎ 每逢农历二十六开元寺勤佛日，西街就变成一个热闹的大集市。（许师伟 摄）
Whenever there is a Buddha Day in Kaiyuan Temple on lunar 26th, West Street becomes a large bustling marketplace. (Photo by Xu Shiwei)

西街的巷弄里还有天室池、明代染织房遗址、定心塔等。达官显赫之家则遍布巷中，其中有明嘉靖年间御史汪旦、户部侍郎庄国桢故居，清道光年间翰林龚维琳胞弟举人龚维琨、清代刑部主事王海文故居，清嘉庆年间进士杨滨海故居，清末状元吴鲁读书处"亦香吟馆"，以及董杨大宗祠、汪氏宗祠等。从某种意义上来说，古厝比它们的主人更会讲故事。这些建筑，或肃穆庄重，或豪迈幽深，但它们都以无言的文明，代替它们的主人，扎根于时间的裂缝中。比如，井亭巷里有闻名遐迩的明代庄国祯侍郎第。这座距今400余年的古大厝，是泉州现存为数不多的较为完整的明代古建筑，年代久远，风采犹存。

《人民日报》副刊曾刊登一篇题为《泉州西街的"美好生活"》的文章。"美好生活"是一个富有温度和人文气息的词，而西街就很符合这样的气质。西街有别于城市高楼的光鲜亮丽，以其古朴的姿态，无须过多繁复的宣扬，便汇集了许许多多想要过美好生活的人。

泉州这座城市的美好样子，深藏于西街每一座或大或小的古厝和每一条或深或浅的巷子里。西街的人间烟火味和超脱世俗的清凉自在同时流淌在纵横交错的安谧古巷中，走过它，就走过了古城的百转千回。

◎ 位于井亭巷的定心塔是一座五层楼阁式建筑，曾被作为泉州城的中心标志。（王柏峰 摄）
Dingxin (Centering) Pagoda in Jingting Alley is a five-story pavilion-style building that was once used as the central landmark of Quanzhou City. (Photo by Wang Baifeng)

◎ 这堵位于西街小西埕的"网红墙"是西街的打卡点之一。（张清杰 摄）
This Instagram-worthy wall in Xiaoxicheng is one of the photogenic spots on West Street. (Photo by Zhang Qingjie)

In the alleys of West Street, there are Tianshi Pond, site of Ming-Dynasty dyeing and weaving house, and Dingxin Pagoda. The homes of prominent officials and celebrities are all over the alleys. Among them are the former residences of Wang Dan, imperial censor in the Jiajing period of the Ming Dynasty, Zhuang Guozhen, deputy minister of the Ministry of Revenue, Gong Weikun, the younger brother of scholar-official Gong Weilin in the Daoguang period of the Qing Dynasty, Wang Haiwen, the director of the Ministry of Punishments of the Qing Dynasty, Yang Binhai, an imperial scholar of the Qing Dynasty, and Yixiang Yinguan, the schoolroom of Wu Lu, the No. 1 scholar in the late Qing Dynasty, as well as Dong's and Yang's Ancestral Hall, Wang's Ancestral Hall, etc. In a sense, ancient houses tell stories better than their owners do. These buildings may be solemn and dignified, or heroic and profound, but they take the place of their owners to root in the cracks of time with speechless civilization. For example, in Jingting Alley, there is the famous mansion of Zhuang Guozhen's. This more-than-400-year-old building is one of the few and relatively complete ancient buildings of the Ming Dynasty in Quanzhou, with longevity and elegance.

The supplement of *People's Daily* once published an article titled "'The Good Life' on West Street in Quanzhou". The phrase "good life" is full of warmth and humanity, and West Street fits this temperament very well. West Street is different from the glamour of the high-rise buildings in the city. With its elegance of classic simplicity, there is no need for too much complicated publicity to bring together many people who want to live a better life.

The beauty of the city of Quanzhou is hidden deep in every old house, large or small, in every long or short alley on West Street. The worldly street life and the detached coolness of West Street flow in the criss-cross, quiet and ancient alleys at the same time. Walking through the street is like experiencing the ancient city's turns and twists.

磁灶窑址：宋元时期福建最重要的外销瓷窑址之一

在闽南语里，"磁"和"瓷"无论在读音或意思上都几乎一致。磁灶以"陶瓷"得名，做陶时间早，走出国门的时间也早。西晋武帝泰始元年（265年），磁灶便开始制陶，至南朝、隋唐以后，手艺更加精湛。此后，磁灶的制瓷业从宋、元、明一直延续到现在。乾隆版《晋江县志》载："瓷器出晋江磁灶乡，取地土开窑，烧大小钵子、缸、瓮之属。甚饶足，并过洋。"千百年前，磁灶金交椅山窑址的土地上，勤劳智慧的工匠们就是在此为普罗大众烧陶、制瓷——小到碗、罐、瓶、碟、盒，大到瓮、缸……这些生活用品，带着磁灶窑的标签，漂洋过海，出现在已知或未知的某户人家里，时光流逝之中，它们或传了下来，或埋于深土。

根据考古发现，磁灶金交椅山窑场创烧于五代，废烧于元末，为宋元时期福建最重要的外销瓷窑址之一，也是磁灶现存12处宋元时期窑址中保存最完好的一处。在4万平方米的西坡上有四条龙形古窑址，其中一条古窑址长达70米、宽有2.5米，可辨认出窑口、火膛、窑壁、窑门等，并有明显的烧制痕迹和大量的器皿、瓷片遗存。

◎ 俯瞰磁灶窑金交椅山窑址。（吴云轩 摄）
A bird's eye view of the sites of Cizao kilns at Jinjiaoyi Hill. (Photo by Wu Yunxuan)

Sites of Cizao Kilns: One of the Most Important Export Porcelain Kiln Sites in Fujian during the Song and Yuan Dynasties

◎ 金交椅山龙形古窑址。（吴云轩 摄）
Dragon-shaped ancient kiln sites at Jinjiaoyi Hill. (Photo by Wu Yunxuan)

In Minnan dialect, "porcelain(磁)" and "china (瓷)" are almost identical in pronunciation or meaning. Cizao Town was named after ceramics. People here made pottery early, and the ceramics went exported early too. In 265 of the Western Jin Dynasty, People in Cizao began to make pottery, and after the Southern Dynasties, Sui and Tang Dynasties, the craftsmanship became more exquisite. After that, the situation remained the same from the Song Dynasty till now. The Qianlong edition of *Jinjiang County Chronicles* contained: "Porcelain came out of Cizao Town, Jinjiang County. Earth was taken to open kilns. Small and big pots, jars, and urns were burned. Large amount of such things were produced and exported to foreign countries." Hundreds of years ago, hard-working and intelligent craftsmen made pottery and porcelain for the general public on the land of the kiln sites at Jinjiaoyi Hill in Cizao Town—from bowls, jars, bottles, plates, boxes, to large urns and crocks...These daily necessities, bearing the label of Cizao Kiln, traveled across the ocean and appeared in known or unknown households. As time passed, they were passed down or buried in deep soil.

According to archaeological discoveries, kiln sites at Jinjiaoyi Hill in Cizao were set up in the Five Dynasties and were abandoned at the end of the Yuan Dynasty. They are one of the most important export porcelain kiln sites in Fujian during the Song and Yuan Dynasties, and the best preserved of the twelve existing Song-Yuan period kiln sites in Cizao. There are four dragon-shaped ancient kiln sites on the west slope of Jinjiaoyi Hill that cover 40,000 square meters. One of the ancient kiln sites is 70 meters long and 2.5 meters wide. The kiln mouth, fire chamber, kiln wall, kiln door, etc. can be identified. We can find obvious burning traces and a large number of utensils and porcelain pieces there.

金交椅山的窑炉采用龙形条构、器物叠烧的工艺技术。这种炉，一次可烧制成千上万件瓷器，当地烧制陶器的规模之大和发展之盛由此可见。有交易才有市场，有需求才会大批量生产。磁灶窑是古代泉州乃至福建外销陶瓷的主要产地之一，其产品种类繁多，器型、釉色多样，装饰手法和纹饰主题丰富，能够满足海内外市场的不同需求。出土或遗存的磁灶窑瓷器中，从生活用品到装饰艺术品，跨度之大令人惊叹，体现了工匠们旺盛的创造力。

近年来，在日本、东南亚以及其他海上丝绸之路沿线国家，不断有宋元时期的中国陶瓷出土或出水，其中相当一部分与福建晋江磁灶窑的器物相同或相似，包括黄釉铁绘大盘、军持、龙瓮等专门为迎合国外消费者需求而组织生产的外销产品。这些陶瓷器的发现，为宋元时期泉州地区外销陶瓷的研究提供了实物资料，同时也让海外发现的部分中国陶瓷找到了原产地，为磁灶窑生产外销瓷的历史提供了确凿佐证。

◎ 晋江市博物馆收藏宋元磁灶窑素胎军持。（林清哲 供图）
Plain Kundika from Song and Yuan Cizao kilns collected in Jinjiang City Museum. (Courtesy of Lin Qingzhe)

The kilns at Jinjiaoyi Hill adopt a dragon-shaped strip structure and a crafting technique of stacking utensils. This kind of furnace can fire thousands of pieces of porcelain at a time, which shows the large-scale and flourishing development of local pottery. Only transactions can generate markets, and only demands generate mass production. Cizao kilns are one of the main producing areas of exported chinaware in ancient Quanzhou and even Fujian. Cizao kilns have a wide variety of products, with various shapes and glaze colors, rich decorative techniques and themes, which can meet the different needs of domestic and foreign markets. Among the unearthed or preserved porcelain, the span from daily necessities to decorative works of art is astonishing, reflecting the strong creativity of the Cizao kiln workers.

In recent years, in Japan, Southeast Asia, and other countries along the Maritime Silk Road, Chinese ceramics from the Song and Yuan Dynasties have been unearthed or salvaged from underwater. Quite a few of them are the same or similar to those of Jinjiang Cizao kilns in Fujian, including yellow-glazed iron-painted large plates, Kundikas, dragon urns, etc, which were specially produced for export to cater to the needs of foreign consumers. The discovery of these ceramics provided physical material for the study of export ceramics in Quanzhou during the Song and Yuan Dynasties. At the same time, it also allowed some Chinese ceramics discovered overseas to find the origin, providing conclusive evidence for the history of exporting porcelain produced by Cizao kilns.

◎ 菲律宾出土宋元磁灶窑黄绿釉军持。（栗建安 供图）
Song-Yuan yellow-greenish glazed Kundikas from Cizao kilns excavated in the Philippines. (Courtesy of Li Jian'an)

德化窑址：千年"中国白"

China，是"中国"的英文译名，同时也是"陶瓷"的译名。追溯历史，陶瓷最初的英文称呼是"chinaware"，直译就是"中国陶瓷器"。唐宋时期，我国的陶瓷制作技艺已经达到很高的水平，各种各样的瓷器销往日本、印度、波斯和埃及等多个国家，因此博得了"瓷国"的美称。

我国有三大瓷都，分别是福建德化、湖南醴陵和江西景德镇。德化县始建于唐开元四年（716年）。这座千年古县用泥土和火锻造成就了特色鲜明的地域文化，也培养了无数的制瓷大师。"白如凝霜冻雪，质如羊脂美玉，精薄如蛋膜，与象牙媲美，釉面晶莹剔透"，这是德化白瓷的真实写照。

千年瓷窑火不熄，未有德化先有瓷。2007年10月6日，泉州市博物馆的考古人员到德化县与永春县交界的寮田尖山野外窑址进行考察，在山包上发现了多处印纹软陶、硬陶和原始青釉瓷器混合叠压的堆积层。与此同时，在寮田尖山南面柑橘园的坡面上发现了一座窑炉的残断面。经过现场勘验，考古专家确认这是一处夏商时期的窑址，德化窑始烧年代定格在了夏商时期。

唐代诗人颜仁郁的侄儿颜化彩编著了一部《陶业法》，总结德化先辈们制作陶瓷的经验和技术。这是世界上第一部完整的陶瓷专著，此书比欧洲同类的陶瓷工艺专著早了800多年。同时，他还绘制了世界上第一幅成体制的陶瓷工厂规划设计图《梅岭图》，里面介绍了德化泗滨梅岭制瓷工场和工艺技术，对后世陶瓷业的发展起了较大的影响。晚唐五代时期，德化的制瓷业已初具规模。1951年1月发现的美湖乡洋田村墓林窑出土了一批青釉瓷器。器型有盘口壶、双耳罐、碗、碟等。

◎ 德化窑屈斗宫窑址。（成冬冬 摄）

Qudougong kiln site of Dehua kilns. (Photo by Cheng Dongdong)

Sites of Dehua Kilns: "Blanc De Chine" for a Millennium

China is the English translation of "中国", as well as the translation of "ceramics". Tracing back to history, the original English name of ceramics was "chinaware", and the literal translation was "Chinese ceramics". During the Tang and Song Dynasties, China's ceramic production skills reached a very high level. All kinds of Chinese porcelain have been sold to Japan, India, Persia, Egypt, and other countries. Thus China got the name "Country of Ceramics".

◎ 明德化窑坐姿白瓷观音塑像。（成冬冬 摄）
The white porcelain statue of seated Guanyin from Dehua kilns of the Ming Dynasty. (Photo by Cheng Dongdong)

There are three major porcelain capitals in China, Dehua in Fujian, Liling in Hunan, and Jingdezhen in Jiangxi. Dehua County was established in the year of 716 of the Tang Dynasty. This thousand-year-old county used earth and fire to forge a distinctive regional culture, and also cultivated countless ceramic masters. "As white as frozen frost and snow, as smooth as suet jade, as thin as egg membrane, comparable to ivory, crystal clear glaze" are the true portrayal of Dehua white porcelain.

The fire of the thousand-year-old porcelain kilns did not go out, and porcelain appeared before Dehua County was established. On October 6, 2007, archaeologists from Quanzhou Museum visited the field kiln site in Liaotianjian Hill, on the border of Dehua County and Yongchun County, and found mixed stacks of geometric soft pottery, hard pottery and primitive celadon glazed porcelain on the hill. At the same time, a broken section of a kiln was found on the slope of the citrus orchard to the south of Liaotianjian Hill. After an on-site inspection, archaeological experts confirmed that this is a kiln site in the Xia and Shang Dynasties, and the beginning of Dehua kilns was fixed in that period.

Yan Huacai, the nephew of the poet Yan Renyu in the Tang Dynasty, wrote a book named *Pottery Industry Techniques*. In the book he summarized the experience and techniques of ceramics of the ancestors in Dehua. This is the first complete monograph on ceramics in the world, which is more than 800 years earlier than similar monographs on ceramic craftsmanship in Europe. At the same time, he also drew the world's first well-established ceramic factory planning and design picture Meiling Map, which introduced Meiling porcelain factory and craftsmanship in Sibing Village, Dehua County. The drawing greatly improved the development of the ceramic industry in later generations. In the late Tang and Five Dynasties, Dehua's porcelain industry had begun to take shape. A batch of celadon glazed porcelain was unearthed from Mulin Kiln in Yangtian Village, Meihu Township in January 1951. Types of vessels included pots with dish-shaped mouths, double-ear pots, bowls, and dishes, etc.

宋元时期，德化制瓷技术取得了长足的进步，规模上也得到了迅猛的发展。泉州市舶司的设立，更是极大地刺激了德化瓷业的发展。德化生产的青白瓷、白瓷大量销往100多个国家和地区，成为"海上丝绸之路"的重要出口商品。德化屈斗宫窑址是德化古窑址的代表。这个宋元时期的古窑址，共有17间窑室，出土了800多件生产工具和6,790多件或完整或残缺的瓷器标本。出土器物胎质白细，釉汁纯净而莹润，已具备明朝象牙白的雏形。屈斗宫瓷窑类型，既不同于龙窑，也不同于阶级窑，而是介于龙窑发展到阶级窑之间的一种独特窑炉类型，人们称之为"鸡笼窑"。

元代德化佛像瓷雕已经盛行，并有瓷塑佛像进贡朝廷得到帝王的赏识，据《安平志》记载："白瓷出德化，元时上供。"马可·波罗在他的游记中也曾写道："刺桐城附近有一别城，名称迪云州（今德化），制造碗及陶器，既多且美。"马可·波罗把德化瓷器带回了意大利，至今意大利博物馆中还保存着他带回的部分德化瓷器。也因此，意大利等欧洲国家学者将德化青白瓷称为"马可·波罗瓷"。

随着刺桐港成为东方第一大港，德化白瓷在国际上声誉远播，广受世界各国的青睐。菲律宾人称它为"奶油白"，日本人称它为"瓷器中的白眉"，而法国人称它为"中国白"。法国人的这个称呼最为贴切，它赋予了德化白瓷更为深层的含义。在世界陶瓷历史上，"中国白"是无可比拟的存在。

◎ 德化窑出土的陶瓷器。（成冬冬 摄）
Ceramics from Dehua kilns. (Photo by Cheng Dongdong)

◎ 德化瓷窑。（陈英杰 摄）
A Dehua porcelain kiln. (Photo by Chen Yingjie)

During the Song and Yuan Dynasties, porcelain making technology in Dehua made considerable progress, and the porcelain industry also developed rapidly. The establishment of Quanzhou Maritime Trade Office also greatly stimulated the development of Dehua porcelain industry. The misty blue porcelain and white porcelain produced by Dehua were sold to more than 100 countries and regions, becoming important export commodities of the Maritime Silk Road. The site of Dehua Qudougong Kiln is the representative of Dehua ancient kiln sites. This ancient kiln site of the Song and Yuan Dynasties had 17 kiln rooms. More than 800 tools of production, and over 6,790 porcelain specimens, intact or incomplete, have been unearthed. The unearthed artifacts are white and thin, and the glaze is pure and lustrous. They adopt the embryonic form of ivory white porcelain in the Ming Dynasty. The type of Qudouggong Kiln is different from the dragon kiln and the ascending kiln. It is a unique type of kiln that is between dragon kiln and ascending kiln. People call it "the chicken coop kiln".

In the Yuan Dynasty, Dehua porcelain carving of Buddha statues became popular. Some porcelain statues of Buddha were submitted as tributes to the imperial court and were appreciated by the emperors. According to the *Local Chronicles of Anping*, "White porcelain was made in Dehua and offered as tributes in the Yuan Dynasty." Marco Polo once wrote in his travel notes: "There is a town named Diyun State (now Dehua) near Zayton City that makes many beautiful bowls and pottery". Marco Polo also brought Dehua ceramics back to Italy, and some of them are still kept in Italian museums. Because of that, scholars from Italy and other European countries call Dehua misty blue porcelain "Marco Polo porcelain".

As Zayton Port became the largest port in the East, Dehua white porcelain's reputation spread far and wide and was favored by countries all over the world. The Philippines called it "creamy white", the Japanese called it "white eyebrows in porcelain", and the French called it "Blanc De Chine". Among these nicknames, the French term is the most appropriate. It gives Dehua white porcelain a deeper meaning. In the history of world ceramics, "Blanc De Chine" is an incomparable existence.

明代，德化窑陶瓷进入了巅峰时期。无论是瓷器的工艺水平、烧制方式，还是审美趣味、装饰艺术都远远超过了宋元时期。彼时，德化涌现出大量技艺高超的匠人。以何朝宗为代表的大师将德化瓷塑艺术推到了前无古人的境界，使之成为"天下共宝之"的珍品。特别是道释人物瓷雕，造型逼真、格调高雅，具有独特的艺术魅力，被世界各大博物馆和私人收藏家争相收藏。

进入清代，德化瓷业更加繁盛，窑场遍布县境，生产青花瓷的窑址多达177处。嘉庆三年（1798年）县邑解元郑兼才《窑工》诗："骈肩集市门，堆积群峰起，一朝海舶来，顺流价倍蓰。"诗中的繁华景象在2000年打捞出的"泰兴号"沉船上得到了印证，船中打捞出的德化青花瓷有35万件之多。

如今，德化陶瓷业依然傲视全球！全县占比80%以上的陶瓷出口海外，行销全球190多个国家和地区。2015年，德化被世界手工艺理事会授予全球首个"世界陶瓷之都"称号。德化的土，经高温燃烧炼就了瓷器中的极品美人——德化瓷。德化瓷在众多瓷器中的地位卓绝，如执掌凤印的皇后，其雍容华美，无可取代。

The Dehua ceramics reached their peak in the Ming Dynasty. Their craftsmanship, firing methods, as well as aesthetic tastes and decorative arts of porcelain all far surpassed those in the Song and Yuan Dynasties. At that time, a large number of skilled craftsmen emerged in Dehua. The masters represented by He Chaozong pushed Dehua's porcelain art into an unprecedented height. Their works became "the world's treasures". In particular, the porcelain sculptures of Taoist and Buddhist figures were lifelike, elegant in style, and had unique artistic charm. They were collected by major museums and private collectors all over the world.

In the Qing Dynasty, the porcelain industry in Dehua became more prosperous. Kilns could be seen all over the county, 177 of which produced blue and white porcelain. Zheng Jiancai, Dehua County's Jieyuan (the scholar who won the first place in provincial imperial examinations), wrote in one of his poem in 1798: "It is very crowded in the market. Ceramics were piled up like mountains. Once cargo ships arrived, the price is doubled". The prosperous scene in the poem was confirmed by the shipwreck of the Taixing salvaged in 2000, with 350,000 pieces of Dehua blue and white porcelain salvaged.

Nowadays, Dehua ceramics industry still arrogantly dominate the world! More than 80% of the county's ceramics are exported, and they are sold in more than 190 countries and regions around the world. In 2015, Dehua was awarded the world's first Ceramic Capital of the World by the World Crafts Council. Dehua's earth, in the high temperature combustion, refines the best beauty in porcelain—Dehua porcelain. Dehua porcelain has an outstanding status among many porcelains. Like the queen in charge of the phoenix seal, its grace and beauty are irreplaceable.

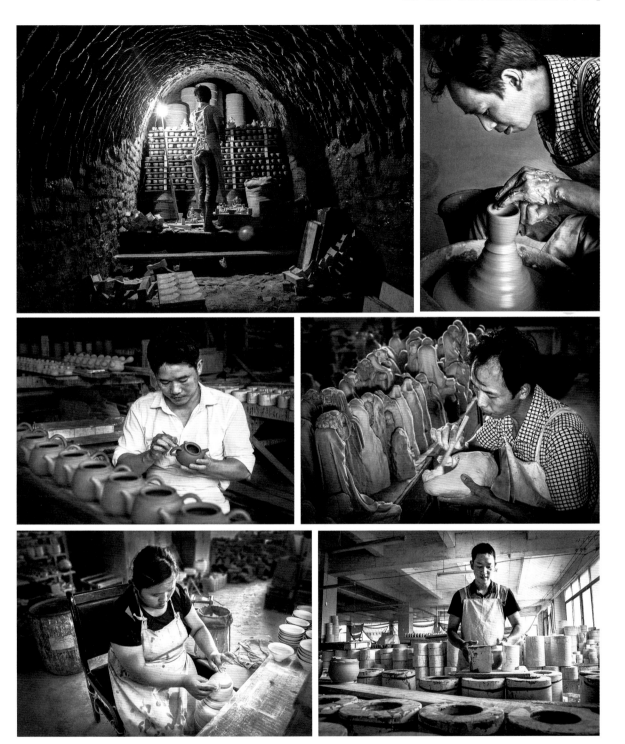

◎ 匠人们制作陶瓷。（陈文 摄）
Craftsmen are making ceramics. (Photo by Chen Wen)

安溪青阳下草埔冶铁遗址：宋代官方炼铁场

青阳卜草埔冶铁遗址位于安溪县尚卿乡青洋村南部的山坡上，为宋元时期留存下来的古铁矿冶炼遗址，是泉州乃至福建重要的冶铁场地。

青阳下草埔遗址面积有一万多平方米，考古发现有炉底、炉壁、冶铁炉渣等冶铁遗迹、遗物。部分探方已揭露至炉渣、木炭屑、黏土、石头形成的锈蚀板结层。目前还发现十余处古矿洞遗迹及两处烧炭遗迹。

该遗址呈现出自下而上、依靠山坡修筑冶炉的冶炼方式，是国内首个考古发掘的块炼铁冶炼遗址。其板结层属于有规划的行为，具体表现为，当冶铁垃圾堆积到一定高度的时候，上端便以"板结层"方式处理，如此操作既可压实、固定冶炼垃圾，又可作为接下来冶炼的新平台。这种处理方法在国际上尚属首次发现。

公元951年，小溪场改为安溪县。首任县令詹敦仁施行"民乐耕耘，冶有银铁"的政策，此举让安溪成为宋元时期泉州内陆腹地最重要的冶铁产地有了坚实的基础。

宋代，泉州矿冶业处于发展和飞跃时期。当时的泉州已经有专门管理冶铁业的官方部门。宋人李焘曾写道："庆历五年（1045年），青阳铁冶大发，即置铁务于泉州。"

◎ 青阳下草埔冶铁遗址挖掘现场。（刘伯怡 摄）

The excavation of Xiacaopu Iron Production Site of Qingyang Village. (Photo by Liu Boyi)

Xiacaopu Iron Production Site of Qingyang Village in Anxi: the Official Iron-smelting Plant in the Song Dynasty

Qingyang Xiacaopu Iron Production Site is located on the hillside south of Qingyang Village, Shangqing Township, Anxi County. Since the Song and Yuan Dynasties, it has been an important ancient iron-smelting site in Quanzhou and even Fujian.

The site covers an area of over 10,000 square meters. Archaeological discoveries include iron smelting remains and relics such as furnace bottom, furnace wall, and iron smelting slag. Some trial trenches have revealed the rusty hardened layer formed by slag, charcoal chips, clay, and stones. At present, more than 10 remains

◎ 安溪青阳下草埔冶铁遗址展示馆。（刘伯怡 摄）

The Exhibition Hall of Xiacaopu Iron Production Site of Qingyang Village. (Photo by Liu Boyi)

of ancient mines and 2 remains of charcoal burning have been discovered.

The site presents a bottom-up smelting method that relies on hillside to construct smelters. It is the first archeologically excavated iron smelting site in China. The compaction layer is a planned behavior. When the garbage is piled up to a certain height, the upper end is treated in a "hardened layer" method. This operation can not only compact and fix the smelting garbage, but also serve as a new platform for subsequent smelting. This treatment method was discovered for the first time in the world.

In 951, Xiaoxichang was changed to Anxi County. At that time, Anxi's first County Magistrate Zhan Dunren applied the policy of benevolence, making the local people enjoy cultivation, silver and iron production. This policy made Anxi the most important iron smelting area in the hinterland of Quanzhou during the Song and Yuan Dynasties with a solid foundation.

In the Song Dynasty, Quanzhou's mining and metallurgical industry was in a period of development and leapfrogging. At that time, Quanzhou had already set up an official department dedicated to managing the iron smelting industry. Li Tao from the Song Dynasty once wrote: "In 1045, Qingyang's iron smelting industry achieved great progress. An iron management office was set up in Quanzhou."

宋代泉州设置坑冶场务201处，公开征铁银税收。安溪青阳下草埔是宋代官方设立的专职铁场之一，其冶铁业蓬勃发展。那时候的匠人们以木炭作为主要燃料，利用喇叭炉配手拉风箱进行块炼铁冶炼。火红滚烫的海绵铁经过初次锻烧，形成基础的铁块、铁片，方便进行加工或再加工。这些半成品，有的在当地被制成锅、鼎、针等制品，运往不产铁的江浙地区，有的则运输至其他地区进行锻造再成型，制成铁器。

洛阳桥建造的时候，已经有了采石和雕石的铁钎等工具；后渚港出土的宋代古沉船中，发现了铁搭钩、斧头、铁锭等用途各异的铁制品；东西塔上有塔刹尖葫芦及大铁链……这些都足以说明宋代泉州锻造及淬炼技术成熟，且广泛使用。

安溪青阳下草埔冶铁遗址是宋元时期泉州冶铁手工业的珍贵见证，与泉州的陶瓷生产基地共同显示出泉州强大的产业能力和贸易输出能力。青阳下草埔冶铁业的发展历程是泉州冶铁历史发展历程的缩影，反映出宋元时期泉州经济的繁荣景象。

在千百年的不断演进中，安溪冶铁的工艺转化成如今的藤铁工艺。安溪藤铁工艺成熟度之高，令人叹为观止。2019年，安溪县被世界手工艺理事会及亚太地区理事会评为全球唯一的"世界藤铁工艺之都"！原国家农业部也将"中国藤铁工艺之乡"的美称授予安溪县。这标志着安溪成为中国最大的藤铁工艺品出口生产基地，实现了历史性的跨越。

冶铁技艺在安溪扎根已久！这种独特的民间技艺，在绵延不断的传承之中保留了下来，不断焕发出勃勃生机与活力。

◎ 2019年，安溪获评"世界藤铁工艺之都"。（刘伯怡 摄）
Anxi received the award of World Craft City for Rattan Iron Crafts in 2019. (Photo by Liu Boyi)

◎学生们正在学习制作藤铁工艺品。（刘伯怡 摄）
Students are learning to make rattan-iron works.
(Photo by Liu Boyi)

In the Song Dynasty, Quanzhou set up 201 pits and smelters and publicly levied iron and silver taxes. Qingyang Xiacaopu in Anxi was one of the professional iron plants officially established by the government in the Song Dynasty, and its iron smelting business flourished. At that time, the workmen used charcoal as their main fuel, and used horn furnaces with hand-drawn bellows to smelt block iron. The flaming hot sponge iron was calcined for the first time to form a basic iron block or sheet, which is convenient for processing or reprocessing. Some of these semi-finished products were made into pots, tripods, needles and other products locally and transported to Zhejiang and Jiangsu where no iron products were made. Some were transported to other regions for forging and re-forming to make ironware.

When Luoyang Bridge was built, tools such as quarrying and stone carving irons were already available. In the ancient shipwreck of the Song Dynasty unearthed in Houzhu Port, iron products for various purposes, such as iron hooks, axes, iron ingots, etc. were found. In the East and West Pagodas, there are sharp gourds on sōrin and large iron chains... These are good sample cases sufficient to show that the forging and quenching technology of Quanzhou in the Song Dynasty was mature and widely used.

Xiacaopu Iron Production Site of Qingyang Village in Anxi is a precious testimony of the iron production industry in Quanzhou during the Song and Yuan Dynasties. Together with the ceramic production bases in Quanzhou, it demonstrates Quanzhou's strong industrial capacity and export capacity. The developing process of the site is a microcosm of the historical development of Quanzhou's iron smelting industry. It reflects the prosperity of Quanzhou's economy during the Song and Yuan Dynasties.

After hundreds of years of continuous evolution, iron smelting crafts in Anxi have been transformed into today's rattan iron crafts. The high maturity of Anxi rattan iron craftsmanship is truly breathtaking. In 2019, Anxi County was selected by the World Crafts Council and the Asia Pacific Regional Council as the only World Craft City for Rattan Iron Crafts! China's former Ministry of Agriculture also awarded Anxi County the title of Hometown of Rattan and Iron Crafts in China, which marks a historic leap forward for Anxi as China's largest production base for exporting rattan and iron handicrafts.

Iron smelting skills have been rooted in Anxi for a long time! This unique folk craft has been preserved in the continuous inheritance, and it is constantly radiating vigor and vitality.

永春：中国香都

在武侠小说里，香是神秘且具不同功用的。香在武侠剧里是江湖人士所用的暗器，可夺人性命；在宫廷剧里是嫔妃所用的秘器，可迷惑君王并借此邀宠，亦可祸害其他嫔妃。当然，香在各大祭祀仪式上是不可或缺的。那些袅袅升起的烟，让普通人相信无论是对先祖的祝祷，还是祈盼神灵庇佑的诉求，都会飘到人类无法抵达的境地——上至九霄，下至九幽。而沉香、檀香、麝香、龙涎香……这些高端香料的名字，因其有助养生保健之功效，也逐渐被世人所熟知。

在泉州的西北方就有这样一座制香的小城，它与河北古城、广东清远、厦门翔安并称"中国四大制香基地"。而说起永春的地位，有些人、有些事，便不得不提。

公元前200年，即汉武帝时期，朝廷开辟对外贸易通道——陆上丝绸之路。彼时，陆上丝绸之路是丝绸、香料等的重要贸易通道。及至唐末，安史之乱使得北方的陆上丝绸之路遭受重创，加之造船和航海技术的进步，因此唐五代后南方的海上丝绸之路逐渐兴盛起来。

泉州是海上丝绸之路的重要起点。宋元时期，在泉州从事贸易的外国商人大多是阿拉伯人。宋时，来中国的阿拉伯商人中，以蒲姓为代表。根据岳珂所著两宋时代朝野见闻的史料随笔《桯史》记载，蒲姓彼时为广东第一富豪，统理外国贸易事务。后蒲氏因"家资益落"，蒲寿庚之父蒲开宗举家自广州徙居泉州，定居临近泉州后渚港的法石乡云麓村，继续从事以贩运大宗香料为主的海外贸易。虽然蒲寿庚长期任职泉州市舶司，然而世事多变，履险蹈危的蒲家后裔移居永春达埔镇汉口村，并将制香技术带到永春。定居永春的蒲氏后裔遂以传统的制香手艺谋生，世代相袭。

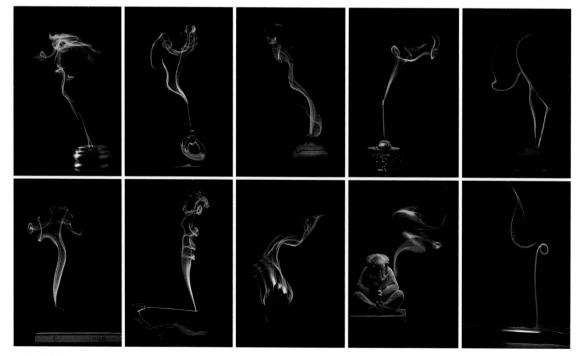

◎ 永春香道。（刘宝生 摄）
Yongchun's incense ceremony. (Photo by Liu Baosheng)

Yongchun: the Incense City of China

In *kung fu* novels, incense is mysterious and has different functions. In the martial arts dramas, the incense is a hidden weapon used by the gangsters, which can kill people; in the costume dramas, it is the secret weapon used by the imperial concubines to confuse the king for his favors or to harm other concubines. Of course, incense is indispensable in major rituals. The smoke that rises up makes ordinary people believe that no matter it is the prayers to the ancestors or the appeals for the blessing of the gods, they will drift to a realm that humans cannot reach—up to the highest heavens, and down to bottom of hell. Agarwood, sandalwood, musk, ambergris…the names of these high-end incenses are gradually being known to the world because of their health-care benefits.

There is a small city named Yongchun in the northwest of Quanzhou, which is famous for making incenses. Yongchun is known as one of "China's four major incense manufacturing bases", along with Gucheng in Hebei, Qingyuan in Guangdong, and Xiang'an in Xiamen. Speaking of Yongchun's status of incense city, there are some people and things that must be mentioned.

In 200 BC, during the reign of the Emperor Wu of the Han Dynasty, the imperial court opened up a foreign trade route, which is the Silk Road on the land. At that time, the Silk Road was an important trade route for silk and spices, etc. After the An-Shi Rebellion in the last years of the Tang Dynasty, the Silk Road in the north was hit hard by wars. In addition to the advancement of shipbuilding and navigation technology, the Maritime Silk Road in the south gradually thrived after the Tang and Five Dynasties.

Quanzhou is an important starting point for the Maritime Silk Road. During the Song and Yuan Dynasties, most foreign merchants engaged in trade in Quanzhou were Arabs. Among the Arab businessmen who came to China, the surname Pu was the representative in the Song Dynasty. According to Yue Ke's historical essay *Ting Shi* written in the Song Dynasty, the Pu family was the richest in Guangdong at that time and was in charge of foreign trade affairs. As "Pu family's fortunes declined", Pu Kaizong, Pu Shougeng's father, moved his family from Guangzhou to Quanzhou, settled in Yunlu Village, Fashi Township, near Houzhu Port, Quanzhou, and continued to engage in overseas trade mainly focusing on the transportation and trafficking of bulk spices. Although Pu Shougeng served in the Maritime Trade Office for a long time, the world was changing. The descendants of the Pu family, who experienced various dangers, moved to Hankou Village, Dapu Town, Yongchun, bringing the technique of making incense to Yongchun as well. The descendants of the Pu family who settled in Yongchun used traditional incense-making techniques to make a living, and they have inherited the techniques from generation to generation.

◎ 工人在制香。（刘宝生 摄）
A worker is making incense. (Photo by Liu Baosheng)

可以说，没有蒲寿庚就没有永春的制香史。蒲家在宋元时期就垄断海上香料贸易，当时香料贸易利润巨大，官方不允许私人贩卖。蒲家把大量香料从阿拉伯、印度诸国引入国门，权贵们享受香料的味道，迷恋香料带来的乐趣。蒲家在泉州一时风头无双，后虽家道中落，但制香手艺却源远流长，未曾受到家道衰败影响。

如今在永春的蒲家后裔，不仅有用香料名给孩子取名的传统，而且所有的孩子5岁便要开始正式闻香、识香，10岁前就要完成一百多种香料的识别，学会闻香识香后，再由上一辈传授纯手工的制香手艺——浸水、打底、搓黏粉、展香、抢香、切香、掷香花，反复操练，力求一气呵成。

经过不断发展完善、发扬光大，永春县目前已成为中国最大的制香基地之一。永春达埔是国内首个荣获国家级制香基地称号的地方。香产业在永春呈现出多样化发展，可作为宗教礼拜、文化礼品、日常调养、医疗保健用品。永春的制香业已经有400余年的历史，目前有制香企业近300家，从业人员超过3万人，销售网络遍布全国，产品出口到欧洲、东南亚等地区。

◎ 在永春，每当天气晴好，各家制香厂都会把半成品的篾香铺开来晒，"香花"朵朵盛开，香气袭来，美不胜收。（刘宝生 摄）

In Yongchun, when the weather is fine, each incense-making factory will dry the semi-finished bamboo incense by spreading them outdoors. The "incense flowers" are in full bloom and the fragrance spreads far and wide. (Photo by Liu Baosheng)

◎ 品香。（王少华 摄）
A smell and appreciation of incense. (Photo by Wang Shaohua)

It can be said that without Pu Shougeng, there would be no history of Yongchun's incense making. The Pu family monopolized the maritime spice trade during the Song and Yuan Dynasties. At that time, the spice trade was so profitable that private sales were not allowed by the government. Pu's family introduced a large number of spices from Arab and Indian countries to the country. The rich and powerful enjoyed the flavor of spices and were obsessed with the enjoyment brought by them. The Pu family was in the limelight in Quanzhou for some time. Luckily, the decline of the Pu family later did not affect the long-term development of the incense-making crafts in Yongchun.

Nowadays, the descendants of the Pu family in Yongchun not only keep the tradition of naming their children with names of spices, but all children start to smell and recognize incense at the age of 5. Before 10, they must complete the identification of more than one hundred spices. After instructing how to smell and recognize fragrance, the previous generation will teach the children the hand-made crafts of incense-making—soaking, primer, rubbing powder, showing incense, scenting incense, cutting incense, throwing incense flowers. The children must repeat practicing and strive to achieve it in one go.

After continuous development and improvement, Yongchun County has become one of the largest incense production bases in China. Dapu Town is the first place in China that has won the title of national incense-making base. The incense-making industry is showing diversified development in Yongchun, which can be used as religious worship incense, cultural gifts, daily nursing, medical and health care products. Yongchun's incense manufacturing industry has a history of more than 400 years. At present, there are nearly 300 incense manufacturing enterprises with more than 30,000 employees. The sales network covers all over China, Europe, Southeast Asia and other regions.

融合之城——刺桐城的多元宗教文化

有人说，泉州的气质里，有着魔幻现实主义色彩。在这里，你可以看到传统的民俗在各个节日里隆重演绎，让人目不暇接；在这里，你也可以看到极具国际化色彩的建筑，使人赞叹不已。无论是魔幻还是现实，它们都真实地存在于泉州这片土地上，犹如千百年前多元文化交融之时的鼎盛。

泉州被誉为"世界宗教博物馆"。其宗教多元且兼容。各种文化在这里相遇，在这里传承，在这里碰撞。走入泉州任何一座庙宇，都会让人心生敬畏之情。庙宇里，或香火鼎盛，或人头攒动，或礼赞静思，它们既见证了信仰的归属，也见证了多元文化的交融。

◎ 开元寺里参与勤佛的信众。（陈英杰 摄）

The Qinfo (Walking Circumambulation) Ceremony in Kaiyuan Temple. (Photo by Chen Yingjie)

The City of Integration: the Multi-religious Culture of Zayton City

Some people say that Quanzhou has a magical realism in its temperament. Here, you can see the traditional folklore activities performed grandly in various festivals, which is a little dizzying. Here, you can also see the highly international architecture, which is awe-inspiring. Whether it is magical or real, they all exist in Quanzhou, as if they were at the height of the integration of diverse cultures hundreds of years ago.

Quanzhou is known as the Museum of World Religions. Its religions are diverse and compatible. Various cultures meet here, pass on here, and collide here. Walking into any temple in Quanzhou will make people feel awe-inspiring. In the temples, the incense is flourishing, the crowd of people gather praising for the gods or meditating. All these witness the affiliation of their faith and the integration of diverse cultures.

◎ 泉州元妙观始建于西晋年间，是道教传入泉州后所建的第一座道观。（黄善哲 摄）
Yuanmiao Taoist Temple in Quanzhou was built during the Western Jin Dynasty, and was the first Taoist temple built after the introduction of Taoism to the city. (Photo by Huang Shanzhe)

泉州府文庙：凝聚古城文脉的儒学殿堂

泉州的历史文化由中原文化、古越文化以及海洋文化融合而成。中原文化，是泉州文化的灵魂。没有中原文化为依托，泉州文化中的海洋文化和古越文化，便缺失独特的醇厚。三种文化的盛衰起承浓缩了泉州历史的风起云涌。

中原文化的南移最先开始于周秦。自汉武帝以来，全国上下大兴儒学，孔子被奉为至圣先师。自中原文化南来后，儒学思想在泉州逐渐取得支配性的地位。

西晋末年，大批晋人衣冠南渡，入闽来泉，沿着晋江流域聚居。由晋人带来的中原文化和土著的越族文化互相吸收，形成了独具特色的地方文化。

到了唐代，中原文化在泉州已经起主导作用。唐和五代时，刺桐港成了重要的对外贸易港口，海外文化随之涌入，如今泉州的诸多史迹，印证了当年的风光。宋元时期，这三种文化的碰撞达到了高潮，形成了泉州特有的"海丝文化"。

泉州府学始建于唐代中叶，各县先后建起文庙，宣扬崇孔、尊孔。泉州府文庙始建于唐开元末年，当时的宰相张九龄题匾"鲁司寇庙"。北宋太平兴国初年（公元976年）迁建于今址。其后府文庙几经修缮，左学右庙，规制逐步完整，规模不断扩大，形成了以儒学为中心的中华传统文化基地。

◎ 泉州府文庙是我国东南地区面积最大的文庙建筑。（陈英杰 摄）
The Confucius Temple and School in Quanzhou is the largest of its kind in southeast China. (Photo by Chen Yingjie)

The Confucius Temple and School in Quanzhou: the Confucianism Palace Condensing the Context of the Ancient City

◎ 泉州府文庙大殿内景。（樊鑫 摄）

The inside view of the Grand Hall of the Confucius Temple and School in Quanzhou. (Photo by Fan Xin)

The history and culture of Quanzhou is an integration of Central Plains culture, ancient Yue culture and marine culture. Central Plains culture is the soul of Quanzhou culture. Without the support of the Central Plains culture, the marine culture and the ancient Yue culture in Quanzhou culture will lack its unique mellowness. The rise and fall of the three cultures condense the ups and downs of Quanzhou's history.

The southward spread of the Central Plains culture began in the Zhou and Qin Dynasties. Since the reign of the Emperor Wu of the Han Dynasty, Confucianism has flourished throughout the country, and Confucius has been regarded as the most sacred teacher. After the Central Plains culture came to the south, Confucianism gradually gained a dominant position in Quanzhou.

At the end of the Western Jin Dynasty, a large number of Jin people entered Fujian and came to Quanzhou, and lived along the Jinjiang River. The Central Plains culture brought by the Jin people and the indigenous Yue culture absorbed each other, forming a unique local culture.

By the Tang Dynasty, the Central Plains culture had played a leading role in Quanzhou. During the Tang and Five Dynasties, Zayton Port became an important foreign trade port, and overseas cultures poured in. Now, many historical sites in Quanzhou confirm the highlight of those years. During the Song and Yuan Dynasties, these three cultures reached a climax of collision and formed the unique Maritime Silk Road Culture of Quanzhou.

Quanzhou prefectural school was built in the middle of the Tang Dynasty. The Confucius temples were built successively in various counties to promote worship of and respect for Confucius. Quanzhou Confucius Temple and School was built at the end of the reign of Emperor Xuanzong of the Tang Dynasty, for which the then prime minister Zhang Jiuling inscribed a plaque *Lu Si Kou Temple*. In the year 976 of the Northern Song Dynasty, it was moved to the present site. Afterwards, the temple was repaired several times. With a school on the left (east) side and the temple on the right (west) side, all kinds of regulations were complete and the scale continued to expand, forming a traditional Chinese cultural base centered on Confucianism.

泉州府文庙地处泉州鲤城区涂门街，占地近百亩，规模为东南七省文庙之最，体现了"海滨邹鲁"的深厚积淀。府文庙的建筑色彩艳丽，雕梁画栋，泥塑、瓷雕、彩绘装饰的飞禽走兽、草木花卉以及农耕狩猎场景，独具闽南特色，其屋脊装饰丰富，在其他文庙难寻。

　　文庙建筑群的中心大成殿是典型的宋代重檐庑殿式建筑，代表了当时最高建筑规格。整个泉州地区，只有府文庙还存有此种建筑结构。大成殿正中供奉孔子像，梁上悬挂有康熙皇帝御书"万世师表"。孔子祀像接受历代泉州人的顶礼膜拜，也凝望着这片土地孕育出一代代儒学人才。大成殿是祭孔的正殿，面阔七间，进深五间。孔庙祭祀之礼，自汉高祖刘邦开始就有，唐高祖时下诏立庙，设乐祭祀开始于宋仁宗景祐年间，所用乐器必须按制备齐使用。目前陈列在大成殿中的祭祀乐器，是清代乾隆年间经过反复考定如式修造的，珍贵异常。

　　位于大成殿东侧的明伦堂是府文庙现存的主要附属建筑，堂前露庭、泮池和石桥均保存完好。泮池筑有元代石桥，桥面铺72块长方形条石，代表孔子的72个得意门生。明正德十五年（1520年），明伦堂开始树立历代各科泉籍进士题名碑，为研究泉州人物及科举史提供重要的实物证据，碑石尚存在开元寺仁寿塔北侧甬道旁。

　　"庙学合一，左学右庙"，泉州府文庙不仅是集闽南古建筑精华为一体的文化珍品，其对培育人才也起到了重要的作用。历代从府文庙走出的进士，唐有16人，五代有11人，宋有872人，元有3人，明有664人，清有248人，充分显示了泉州"人文之胜，甲于闽省"。

◎ 大成殿是泉州府文庙的主体建筑。（陈英杰 摄）

Dacheng Hall is the main building of the Confucius Temple and School in Quanzhou. (Photo by Chen Yingjie)

Quanzhou Confucius Temple and School is located in Tumen Street, Licheng District, Quanzhou, covering an area of nearly 100 acres. Its scale is the largest among the seven southeastern provinces, reflecting the profound accumulation of the land of rich culture. The buildings are colorful, with carved beams and painted rafters, clay sculptures, porcelain carvings, painted birds and animals, plants and flowers, and farming and hunting scenes. It is of unique Southern Fujian style. Its roof ridge is richly decorated, which is hard to find in other Confucius temples.

Dacheng Hall, the center of the building complex, is a typical Song Dynasty double-eave hip roof building, representing the highest architectural specifications at that time. In the entire Quanzhou area, only Quanzhou Confucius Temple and School adopts this kind of architectural structure. In the middle of Dacheng Hall, a statue of Confucius is enshrined, and on the beam is the plaque *A Model of Virtue of All Ages* written by Emperor Kangxi of the Qing Dynasty. The statue of Confucius has been worshipped by generations of Quanzhou people, and it also looks at the generations of Confucian talents that have been nurtured in this land. Seven *chien* wide and five *chien* deep, Dacheng Hall is the main hall for worshipping Confucius. The ritual of sacrificial in the Confucius temples has been in existence since the beginning of the Han Dynasty. Li Yuan, the first emperor of the Tang Dynasty, ordered the temple to be erected. The ritual of playing music when worshipping began during 1034 and 1038 in the Song Dynasty. The musical instruments must be used in accordance with the requirements. The sacrificial musical instruments currently displayed in Dacheng Hall were made during the reign of Emperor Qianlong in the Qing Dynasty. These instruments are precious for they were made after researching over and over and following suit.

Minglun Hall, located on the east side of Dacheng Hall, is the main existing auxiliary building of Quanzhou Confucius Temple and School. The open courtyard, Pan Pond, and stone bridge in front of the hall are all well-preserved. Pan Pond is built with a stone bridge of the Yuan Dynasty. The bridge surface is paved with 72 rectangular stones, representing Confucius' 72 favorite students. In the year of 1520 of the Ming Dynasty, steles inscribed by the successful candidates in the highest imperial examinations from Quanzhou in the past were erected in Minglun Hall, providing important physical evidence for the study of eminent figures in Quanzhou and the history of imperial examinations. The steles still stand beside the corridor on the north side of Renshou Pagoda of Kaiyuan Temple.

"It is an integration of temple and school, with school on the left and temple on the right." Quanzhou Confucius Temple and School is not only a cultural treasure that integrates the essence of ancient architecture in Southern Fujian, but also plays an important role in cultivating local talents. For the successful candidates in the highest imperial examinations from here, there are 16 in the Tang Dynasty, 11 in the Five Dynasties, 872 in the Song Dynasty, 3 in the Yuan Dynasty, 664 in the Ming Dynasty, and 248 in the Qing Dynasty. This fully demonstrates Quanzhou's reputation of "No. 1 in culture and education in Fujian Province".

开元寺：集多元宗教文化大成的唐朝古刹

同是多元宗教信仰的城市，耶路撒冷神圣却悲壮，泉州显得温暖写意，轻松许多。比如著名的开元寺就坐落在鲤城区西街。没有名山大川的依傍，开元寺紧临着人间烟火，和市井生活的近距离接触并没有削弱它的庄严。反之，开元寺在古城民众的心里一直有着特殊的地位。

开元寺始创于唐垂拱二年（686年），最初名叫"莲花道场"，由当地富户黄守恭捐出自家的桑园而建。为感谢黄守恭的乐善好施，寺庙僧人建造了专门供奉黄守恭的檀樾祠。唐开元二十六年（738年），唐玄宗下旨诏令天下各州都要建一座以年号"开元"命名的寺院，以彰显大唐的开元盛世，"莲花道场"遂更名为"开元寺"，并沿用至今。

开元寺现存主要建筑为明清两代修建，南北长260米，东西宽300米，占地面积约7.8万平方米，是福建省规模最大的佛教寺院。中轴线自南而北依次为紫云屏、山门（天王殿）、拜亭、大雄宝殿、甘露戒坛、藏经阁。东翼有檀樾祠、泉州佛教博物馆（弘一法师纪念馆）、准提禅院，西翼有安养院、功德堂、水陆寺等。

开元寺除了历史悠久之外，还有一个特别之处，那就是一座佛教的寺庙里有着诸多其他宗教的元素。中外尤其是中印的宗教文化元素在这里和谐融合，保存至今。开元寺内，可以看到须弥座的人面狮身石刻浮雕像，还可以看到印度教中的神话故事出现在石柱上；寺内的飞天群受腾云驾雾的印度女神、背负双翼的希腊天使以及我国敦煌壁画的"飞天"形象的共同影响。

◎ 开元寺以其独特的文化融合，将优美的艺术形象和雄伟的结构造型和谐地结合在一起。
因其融合闽越、中原、海外多种文化的独特魅力，令世人为之神往。（陈起拓 摄）
Kaiyuan Temple, with its unique cultural integration, harmoniously combines the beautiful artistic images with the majestic structure. Because of its unique charm of integrating various cultures of Minyue, Central Plains, and overseas, it is fascinating to the world. (Photo by Chen Qituo)

Kaiyuan Temple: an Ancient Temple of the Tang Dynasty with a Collection of Multi-religious Cultures

Also cities with multiple religious beliefs, Jerusalem is sacred but tragic, while Quanzhou seems warm and much more relaxing. For example, the famous Kaiyuan Temple is located on the West Street of Licheng District, Quanzhou City. It is not surrounded by famous mountains or rivers. The temple is close to the hustle and bustle of the city life. The close contact with city life has not weakened its solemnity. On the contrary, in the hearts of the people in the ancient city, the temple always has a special status.

Kaiyuan Temple was founded in the year of 686 in the early Tang Dynasty. It was originally named Lotus Place for Buddhist Rites. The local wealthy Huang Shougong donated his own mulberry garden to build the temple. To thank Huang Shougong for his kindness, monks in the temple built Tanyue Hall dedicated to him. In 738 of the Tang Dynasty, Emperor Xuanzong ordered each state in the country to build a monastery named after "Kaiyuan" to show the prosperity of the Kaiyuan era of the Tang Dynasty. Thus the Lotus Place for Buddhist Rites was renamed Kaiyuan Temple and it is still in use today.

◎ 开元寺大雄宝殿斗拱上的飞天乐伎。（陈英杰 摄）
The Flying Apsaras on the arch of the Mahavira Hall of Kaiyuan Temple. (Photo by Chen Yingjie)

The main existing buildings of Kaiyuan Temple were built during the Ming and Qing Dynasties. It is 260 meters long from north to south and 300 meters wide from east to west. It covers an area of about 78,000 square meters. It is the largest Buddhist temple in Fujian Province. From south to north, the buildings on the central axis are the Purple Cloud Screen, the Mountain Gate (the Devaraja Hall), the Worship Pavilion, the Mahavira Hall, the Ganlu Altar of Precepts, the Scripture Repository. On the east wing, there are Tanyue Hall, Quanzhou Buddhist Museum (Master Hongyi Memorial Hall), and Zhunti Buddha Hall; In the west wing, there are Nursing Home, Memorial Hall, Water and Land Temple, etc.

In addition to its long history, Kaiyuan Temple has another special feature, that is, there are many other religious elements in this Buddhist temple. The religious and cultural elements of China and foreign countries, especially China and India, have been harmoniously integrated here and preserved to this day. In Kaiyuan Temple, you can see the carved stone Hindu Kamadenu relief figures on the Sumeru base, and the myths of Hinduism appearing on the stone pillars. The Flying Apsaras in the temple were made with the influence of the Indian goddesses flying in clouds and mists, the Greek angels with wings on their backs, and the images of Flying Apsaras in Dunhuang frescoes in China.

相比其他佛教寺庙，泉州开元寺独特的建筑特色让人目眩神迷。大雄宝殿斗拱和铺作间24尊木雕飞天乐伎的形象，多次作为泉州的标志形象之一出现在城市宣传片中。匠人们通过灵巧的双手，把音乐和建筑融为一体，创作出被建筑学家称为"闽南木构古建筑中的一座丰碑"的飞天乐伎。这24尊飞天乐伎象征中国的24个节气，她们或手执文房四宝，或手执管弦丝竹……姿态飘逸，凌空飞舞，令人遐想联翩。

全国佛教寺庙唯有北京戒台寺、杭州昭庆寺和泉州开元寺尚保留着戒坛的建筑规制。开元寺内的甘露戒坛位于大雄宝殿之后。传说，唐朝时，此地常降甘露，僧人行昭遂开挖了一口井，称甘露井。北宋天禧三年（1019年）在井上始筑戒坛，称甘露戒坛。甘露戒坛现存的建筑为清康熙五年（1666年）重建的四重檐八角攒尖式，坛顶正中藻井采用如意斗拱；坛之四周立柱斗拱和铺作间有24尊飞天乐伎，身系飘带，手持乐器，翩翩飞翔，与大雄宝殿的飞天乐伎一样，既是建筑艺术的瑰宝，又是研究闽南古乐南音十分宝贵的形象资料。

甘露戒坛西侧的"桑莲古迹"，即为传说中开白莲的桑树，距今已有一千三百多年，虽老干裂分三枝，但仍枝叶常青，生机盎然。

泉州有句古老的话："站着要像东西塔，躺着要像洛阳桥。"东西塔就位于开元寺内，是中国现存最高的一对宋代石塔。东西塔分别建于唐末和五代，最初都是木塔，后相继更筑为砖塔。南宋绍定元年（1228年）西塔改建为石塔，历十年乃成。南宋嘉熙二年（1238年）东塔开工改建，历时十二年始告竣工。

◎ 开元寺甘露戒坛。（郑文桂 摄）
The Ganlu Altar of Precepts in Kaiyuan Temple. (Photo by Zheng Wengui)

Compared with other Buddhist temples, the unique architectural features of Quanzhou Kaiyuan Temple are dazzling. The images of 24 wood carving Flying Apsaras playing musical instruments in between the bracket sets and the intermediate sets of the Mahavira Hall have repeatedly appeared in Quanzhou's city promo videos as one of the iconic images of Quanzhou. The craftsmen combined music and architecture with their dexterous hands to create the Flying Apsaras, which are called a monument in the ancient wooden architecture of Southern Fujian by architects. These 24 Flying Apsaras symbolize the 24 solar terms of China. They either hold the four treasures of the study, or hold the musical instruments in their hands... All these images with elegant postures flying in the sky draw your imagination out.

The only Buddhist temples in the country that still retain the Ganlu Altar of Precepts include Jietai Temple in Beijing, Zhaoqing Temple in Hangzhou, and Kaiyuan Temple in Quanzhou. The Ganlu Altar of Precepts in Kaiyuan Temple is located behind the Mahavira Hall. According to legend, in the Tang Dynasty, sweet dew often fell here, and the monk Xingzhao dug a well called Ganlu (Sweet Dew) Well. In the year of 1019 in the Northern Song Dynasty, an Altar of Precepts was built on the well, which was called the Ganlu Altar of Precepts. The existing building of the Ganlu Altar of Precepts is a four-eave octagonal pyramidal roof building rebuilt in the year of 1666 of the Qing Dynasty. In the central top of the altar there is the caisson ceiling, which was made of Ruyi-shaped bracket sets. There are 24 Flying Apsaras figures between the bracket sets on the pillars and the intermediate sets. They are wearing ribbons, holding musical instruments as they are dancing trippingly. Like the Flying Apsaras figures in the Mahavira Hall, they are not only a treasure of architectural art, but also very valuable image material for studying Nanyin, the ancient music of Southern Fujian.

Sanglian Historic Site on the west side of the Ganlu Altar of Precepts is the legendary morus tree that blossomed out white lotus. It has been here for more than 1,300 years. Although it is old and cracked with three branches, the branches and leaves are still green and full of vitality.

There is an old saying in Quanzhou: "Stand like the East and West Pagodas, and lie down like Luoyang Bridge." The East and West Pagodas are located in Kaiyuan Temple and are the tallest pair of Song Dynasty stone pagodas in China. The two pagodas were built in the late Tang and the Five Dynasties respectively. They were all wooden pagodas at first, and then re-built as brick pagodas one after another. In the year of 1228 of the Southern Song Dynasty, the West Pagoda (Renshou Pagoda) was converted into a stone tower, which took ten years. In the year of 1238 of the Southern Song Dynasty, the reconstruction of the East Pagoda (Zhenguo Pagoda) started and it took twelve years to complete.

◎ "桑开白莲"成了开元寺中胜境之一。（吴刚强 摄）
Sanglian Historic Site has become one of the most beautiful
places in Kaiyuan Temple. (Photo by Wu Gangqiang)

东西石塔结构紧凑完善，科学合理。东塔高48.24米，西塔高44.06米。东西塔塔心粗壮体实，用横梁、斗拱与外壁相连接，具抗地震和台风能力。东西塔造型宏伟壮丽，石雕工艺精湛古朴。东塔是献给释迦牟尼佛的，象征娑婆世界，现行世界是有等级的，这可以从塔身上80尊人物浮雕看出。东塔共五层，寓意佛教的五乘：人、天、声闻、缘觉、菩萨；西塔是献给西方极乐世界阿弥陀佛的，代表众生平等，所以西塔的80尊佛像是没有等级之分的。

东西塔是刺桐古城的标志性建筑，古城的人们对它们爱护有加。为了让东西塔傲立古城的风姿能轻易为人所见，西街所有建筑的高度均不能超过东西塔。

开元寺除了是泉州最负盛名的佛教三大丛林之一，其在历史上亦是文人荟萃之地。唐朝末年，中原动荡不安，河南光州王潮、王审邦和王审知兄弟领兵南渡，直抵泉州，驻军开元寺，王审邦之子王延彬于此诞生。王延彬长大后，被闽王王审知任命为泉州刺史，其在位二十几年里，励精图治，把泉州海外交通贸易推向高峰，被当时的人称为"招宝侍郎"。发达的海上贸易，云集了各国商人，多元的宗教和文化随之而来，它们在这座城市和睦相处，融合发展。

◎ 东西塔历经1604年明朝最大的地震仍屹立不摇，无言却有力地代表了13世纪中国石构建筑技艺的最高水准。（刘贤涛 摄）

East and West Pagodas stand still high after the biggest earthquake in 1604 in the Ming Dynasty. Standing silently, they powerfully represent the highest level of Chinese stone architecture techniques in the 13th century. (Photo by Liu Xiantao)

The two pagodas are compact and perfect in structure, scientific and reasonable. The East Pagoda is 48.24 meters high, and the West Pagoda is 44.06 meters high. The East and West Pagodas are thick and solid, and they are connected to the outer walls with cross beams and bracket sets, which is capable of resisting earthquakes and typhoons. The two pagodas are magnificent, and the stone carving craftsmanship is exquisite and of primitive simplicity. The East Pagoda is dedicated to Buddha Shakyamuni, which symbolizes the current Sahā world. The current world is hierarchical. This can be seen from the 80 reliefs on the pagoda. The East Pagoda's five floors imply the five vehicles of Buddhism: Human Vehicle, Deva Vehicle, Sound-hearing Vehicle, Enlightened by Conditions' Arhat, and Bodhisattva. The West Pagoda is dedicated to the Sukhavati's Amitabha and represents the equality of all living beings. Therefore, the 80 Buddha statues in the West Pagoda have no hierarchy.

East and West Pagodas are the landmark buildings of the ancient city of Zayton. The people in the ancient city took great care of them. In order to make the beauty of the two pagodas be easily seen, the height of all the buildings on West Street cannot exceed the height of them.

In addition to being one of the three most prestigious Buddhist monasteries in Quanzhou, Kaiyuan Temple is also a place where scholars gathered in history. At the end of the Tang Dynasty, the Central Plains were turbulent. The brothers Wang Chao, Wang Shengui, and Wang Shenzhi in Guangzhou, Henan led the troops to the south and arrived in Quanzhou. They stationed troops in Kaiyuan Temple. Later, Wang Shengui's son Wang Yanbin was born in Quanzhou. After Wang Yanbin grew up, he was appointed as the governor of Quanzhou by Wang Shenzhi, the king of Min State. During his two decades of reign, he worked hard to accelerate Quanzhou's overseas transportation and trade to the peak. Therefore he was called "the governor who brought in wealth and treasure" by the people at that time. The developed maritime trade attracted businessmen from various countries, followed by various religions and cultures. All lived and developed in harmony in this city.

◎ 信众们绕塔礼佛。
（吴云轩 摄）
Disciples were worshipping the Buddhas by walking around the pagoda. (Photo by Wu Yunxuan)

老君岩造像：天人合一、大道至简

　　我国乃至世界著名的古代石雕艺术造像，如巴米扬石窟、龙门石窟、云冈石窟等大多是以佛教为主题的石雕艺术，道教的石雕造像极其罕见，尤其是像清源山老君岩这样的巨型石雕造像，更是难得一见。如果想一睹老子的传世风采，须到清源山老君岩一游。

　　清源山上的老君岩造像，一坐千年，羡煞世人！老君岩露天屹立，与清源山浑然一体，深得老子无为之道！无论是和风细雨抑或飘风骤雨，老子他老人家始终面目如生，须眉皓然，慈祥地注视着山下的芸芸众生！

　　公元618年，李渊建立大唐王朝，中国封建社会空前繁荣。为了李唐王朝千秋万载，大唐的皇帝追认思想影响深远的道教始祖李耳为李家的祖先，并尊奉道教为唐帝国的"国教"。老子被推崇到至尊无上的地位，道教因此风靡全国。赵宋王朝，道教依然十分兴盛。清源山老君岩面世，也就是在此时。

　　这件雕塑到底是谁的作品呢？如今已无史料可查。据清乾隆年间编纂的《泉州府志》记载："石像天成，好事者略施雕琢。"说它原是一块形状肖似老翁的天然巨岩，能工巧匠们赋予他形象和灵魂，把它雕刻成了著名哲学家、思想家、道教开山鼻祖老子的坐像。老君岩雕刻手法写实却又脱俗，只见老君衣褶分明，左手扶膝，右手凭几，神态和蔼可亲，就像一位睿智的老者，与世人毫无距离感。

◎ 老君岩造像高5.63米、厚6.85米、宽8.01米，占地面积55平方米。（李芸生 摄）
The statue is 5.63 meters high, 6.85 meters thick, and 8.01 meters wide. It covers an area of 55 square meters. (Photo by Li Yunsheng)

◎ 老君岩下信众们或烧香，或游赏，或拍照。
（王胜 摄）
Under the Statue of Lao Tze, the faithful burn
incense, admire the scenery, or take photos.
(Photo by Wang Sheng)

Statue of Lao Tze: Unity of Man and Nature; Greatness in Tao's Simplicity

The famous ancient stone sculptures in China and the world, such as those in Bamiyang Grottoes, Longmen Grottoes, Yungang Grottoes, etc., are mostly Buddhism-themed, while Taoist stone sculptures are extremely rare. A giant stone sculpture like the Statue of Lao Tze on Qingyuan Mountain is even rarer. If you want to admire Lao Tze's elegant demeanor over the years, do visit the Statue of Lao Tze on Qingyuan Mountain.

The Statue of Lao Tze on Qingyuan Mountain, sitting there for a thousand years, makes the whole world envious! Standing in the open air and blending into one harmonious whole with Qingyuan Mountain, the statue has presented Lao Tze's philosophy of *wuwei* (inaction)! Regardless of how the weather changes, a gentle breeze and a mild rain, or howling wind and torrential rain, this wise old man is always seemingly alive with snow-white beard and eyebrows, and graciously looks at all the living beings under the mountain!

In 618, Li Yuan established the Tang Dynasty, and China's feudal society was unprecedentedly prosperous. To perpetuate the Tang Dynasty, Li Yuan ratified Li Er (Lao Tze), the first ancestor of Taoism with far-reaching thought, as the ancestor of the Li family, and respected Taoism as the state religion of the Tang empire. Lao Tze was promoted to the supreme status, and Taoism became popular throughout the country. During the Song Dynasty, Taoism was still very prosperous. It was at this time that the Statue of Lao Tze on Qingyuan Mountain emerged.

Whose work is this sculpture? There is no historical data available now. According to the *Local Chronicles of Quanzhou* compiled during the reign of Emperor Qianlong of the Qing Dynasty: "The statue is like a natural stone and someone slightly carved it." That is to say, the statue was originally a natural giant rock shaped like an old man. Skilled craftsmen gave it the image and soul and carved it into a seated statue of Lao Tze, a famous philosopher, thinker, and founder of Taoism. The sculpture is realistic but refined. Lao Tze is in distinctly pleated clothes with his left hand on the lap and the right hand on a small side table. His demeanor was amiable, just like a wise old man with no sense of distance from the world.

据史书记载，早在西晋时期清源山上就有道教寺观出现。北宋年间，罗山脚下建造了北斗殿，武山脚下建造了真君殿，两山之间有元元洞天，建筑规模恢宏，而老君岩雕像大约也完成于这一时期。南宋理学家朱熹曾往清源山游览并瞻仰老子的风范。借宿于道观的朱子，也曾在此领悟道家"顺乎自然，无为而无所不为，修身养性"的道理，对老君岩怀有深厚感情。年移代革，那些恢宏的道观和殿宇早已消逝在历史的烟尘中，而老君岩造像仍完好，成为保留至今的古代石雕艺术瑰宝供人瞻仰。

老君岩的石构山门，窗及门额用盘根错节的枝条装饰，墙体用不同颜色的岩石垒砌，充满山野之趣。山门正前方立一方青石，上书"青牛西去，紫气东来"八个篆字。汉代刘向在《列仙传》中写道："老子西游，关令尹喜望见有紫气浮关，而老子果乘青牛而过也。"这八个字也正是来源于此。

清源山被誉为中华道教名山，景色秀丽，人文荟萃。清源山巨石上的"道教圣地"摩崖石刻和朱红的"玄武"和"朱雀"摩崖为明末四大家之一张瑞图所题刻，是清源山道教文化的最佳注解。除了是道教名山，多元宗教文化荟萃之地的清源山还留有北宋以来各朝各代的大量雕刻，其中宋元时期道教、佛教大型石雕就有7处9尊，历代摩崖石刻近500方，涉及佛教、道教、伊斯兰教等不同宗教，天下的宗教缩影于此，彰显了泉州包容万方的胸怀。

◎ 老君岩山门。（吴幼雄 摄）
The mountain gate of the Statue of Lao Tze. (Photo by Wu Youxiong)

According to historical records, Taoist temples appeared on Qingyuan Mountain as early as the Western Jin Dynasty. In the Northern Song Dynasty, Beidou Palace was built at the foot of Luo Mountain, and Zhenjun Palace at the foot of Wu Mountain, and Yuanyuan Cave Heaven between the two mountains. These buildings were magnificent. The Statue of Lao Tze was also completed around this period. Zhu Xi, a great philosopher in the Southern Song Dynasty, once visited Qingyuan Mountain and admired Lao Tze's demeanor. Staying in the Taoist temple, Zhu Xi comprehended the Taoist principles of "Following nature. Action through inaction. Cultivating one's moral character and behaving ethically", and had a deep affection for the Statue of Lao Tze. Over the years, those magnificent Taoist temples and palaces have long disappeared, while the Statue of Lao Tze is still intact, becoming the ancient stone carving art treasure that has been preserved to this day for people to admire.

The mountain gate of the Statue of Lao Tze is full of wilderness, with the windows and door foreheads decorated with intertwined branches, and the walls built with rocks of different colors. There is a green stone in front of the mountain gate with seal scripts written: "The green cow goes west, and the purple breeze (auspicious sign) comes from the east." Liu Xiang in the Han Dynasty wrote in *Legends of the Immortals*:

◎ 清源山卧佛。（郑文桂 摄）
The Reclining Buddha in Qingyuan Mountain. (Photo by Zheng Wengui)

"Lao Tze travels to the west. The pass control officer Yin Xi is happy to see the purple breeze floating on the pass. As expected, Lao Tze passes by on a green cow." These scripts were derived from this statement.

Qingyuan Mountain is known as a famous Taoist mountain in China, with beautiful scenery and a gathering of various cultures. The stone carvings of Sacred Land of Taoism on the huge rocks of Qingyuan Mountain and the vermilion stone carvings of Black Tortoise and Vermilion Bird were inscribed by Zhang Ruitu, one of the four great calligraphy masters of the late Ming Dynasty. They are the best annotations of the Taoist culture of Qingyuan Mountain. In addition to being a famous Taoist mountain, Qingyuan Mountain, a place where diverse religious cultures gather, has a large number of sculptures from various dynasties since the Northern Song Dynasty. Among them, there are nine large stone sculptures of Taoism and Buddhism in the Song and Yuan Dynasties scattered in seven places, and nearly 500 stone carvings of different dynasties, involving different religions such as Buddhism, Taoism, Islam, etc. The world's major religions are epitomized here, showing the remarkable inclusiveness of Quanzhou.

◎ 清净寺，又名圣友寺、艾苏哈卜大清真寺。（陈英杰 摄）

Qingjing Mosque, also known as Mosque of the Holy Friend or the Great Mosque of Ai Suhab. (Photo by Chen Yingjie)

清净寺：中国现存最古老的伊斯兰教寺院

　　元末明初著名僧人、诗人释宗泐在《清源洞图为洁上人作》一诗中曾对泉州做了这样的描述："缠头赤脚半蕃商，大舶高樯多海宝。"此诗句十分形象地表达了宋元时期穆斯林商人来泉盛况。当时，刺桐港聚集了许多来自阿拉伯、波斯、中亚的穆斯林，伴随他们而来的还有他们的宗教和信仰。泉州成了伊斯兰教在中国传播最早的地区之一，泉州清净寺也成了中国现存最古老的清真寺之一。

　　1992年，在《新华文摘》《河南旅游》评选的"我国的十大名寺"中，清净寺位列榜首。究其原因，除了其历史悠久和保护良好，更重要的是，清净寺鲜活灵动地传递着历史文化信息，力证泉州对世界的重要影响。

　　时至今日，居住在清净寺旁的穆斯林依然传承着伊斯兰风俗习惯，保留开斋节、古尔邦节、圣纪节等节庆活动。每逢开斋节，便有数量众多的教徒到泉州清净寺参加礼拜等活动。开斋节当日，穆斯林们会穿上盛装，到清净寺参加"会礼"和庆祝活动，在泉州的外国穆斯林也会赶来参加，一同庆贺"斋功"胜利完成。清净寺的阿訇会在现场讲经布道，大家互道节日快乐，互赠礼物，节日气氛浓厚，仪式感十足。

Qingjing Mosque: the Oldest Islamic Mosque in China

Zong Le, a famous monk and poet at the end of the Yuan Dynasty and the beginning of the Ming Dynasty, described Quanzhou in his poem as "Half of the merchants are foreign ones with turbans and bare-footed. Big ships are full of overseas treasures". This verse vividly expresses the prosperity of Muslim merchants coming to Quanzhou during the Song and Yuan Dynasties. At that time, many Muslims from Arabia, Persia, and Central Asia gathered in Zayton Port, along with their religion and beliefs. Quanzhou became one of the earliest areas where Islam spread in China, and Qingjing Mosque is one of the oldest extant mosques in China.

In 1992, among Top Ten Famous Temples in China selected by *Xinhua Digest* and *Henan Tourism*, Qingjing Mosque ranked the No. 1. The reason for the status is that in addition to its long history and well-protected situation, more importantly, the mosque conveys historical and cultural information vividly and vigorously, proving Quanzhou's great influence on the world.

To this day, the Muslims living near the mosque still inherit Islamic customs, celebrating festivals such as Eid al-Fitr, Eid al-Adha, and al-Mawlid an-Nabī. On Eid al-Fitr, many followers come to the mosque to participate in worship and other activities. On the day of Eid al-Fitr, Muslims will wear costumes and go to the mosque to participate in eid ul-fitr and celebration activities. Foreign Muslims in Quanzhou will also come to participate and celebrate the successful completion of Zakat (Almsgiving) together. The Akhund of the mosque will preach on the spot, and everyone will exchange happy holiday blessings and give gifts to each other. What a festive atmosphere with a strong sense of ceremony.

◎ 教徒们在清净寺里参加
礼拜。（陈英杰 摄）
Muslims were praying Salah
in Qingjing Mosque. (Photo
by Chen Yingjie)

除了开斋节，平时的清净寺就这么安静地矗立在泉州的古城区。长方形的寺门，葱头形的尖拱门，独特的建筑风格散发着风情浓郁的异国情调，一旦靠近，仿若穿越到中世纪的阿拉伯世界。

始建于北宋大中祥符二年（1009年）的清净寺和广州怀圣寺、扬州仙鹤寺、杭州凤凰寺并称我国沿海地区四大清真寺，同时又和少林寺、寒山寺、白马寺等并列为我国十大名寺。

清净寺的整体建筑风格，延续了阿拉伯世界在中世纪的流行风格。其门楼仿照叙利亚大马士革伊斯兰教礼拜堂的建筑形式建造，门楼整体用加工平整的花岗岩和灰绿岩砌筑，青白两色岩石雕琢出逐层递进的穹形尖拱门。

清净寺第一道尖拱门高10米，宽3.8米，顶部是蜘网穹窿形结构，寓意着宇宙的无限威力。第二道尖拱门顶部是蜂窝状穹窿形结构，由白色花岗岩石拼成，寓意着无上崇高。第三、四道拱门连成一体，构成长方形石门，上面以砖构半球形穹窿覆顶。

高达12.3米、宽达6.6米的清净寺门楼，雄浑素雅。楼顶为平台，四面环形建筑成"回"字形垛子。南垛高1.4米，北垛高1.2米，左右嵌有两方阴刻"月""台"碑石，称"望月台"，是伊斯兰教斋月里阿訇登临望月，以便确定起斋日期的地方。

◎ 清净寺大门穹顶。（成冬冬 摄）
The dome of the gate of Qingjing Mosque.
(Photo by Cheng Dongdong)

Except for the Eid al-Fitr, Qingjing Mosque just stands quietly in the ancient city of Quanzhou at ordinary times. With the rectangular gate and onion-shaped pointed arches, the unique architectural style of the mosque exudes a strong exotic atmosphere. Approaching it, you will feel like traveling back to the medieval Arab world.

Built in the year of 1009 of the Northern Song Dynasty, Qingjing Mosque is listed as one of the four major mosques in coastal areas of China along with Huaisheng Mosque in Guangzhou, Xianhe Mosque in Yangzhou, and Phoenix Mosque in Hangzhou. It is also listed as one of the ten famous temples in China, along with Shaolin Temple, Hanshan Temple, and White Horse Temple, etc.

The overall architectural style of the mosque follows the popular style of the Arab world in the Middle Ages. Its gate tower is modeled after the style of the Islamic House of Worship in Damascus, Syria. The gate tower was made of smoothly processed granites and diabase stones. The green and white rocks were carved out of dome-shaped arches that advance layer by layer.

The first pointed arch of the mosque is 10 meters high and 3.8 meters wide. The top is a dome-shaped structure like a spider net, which implies the infinite power of the universe. The top of the second pointed arch is a honeycomb dome-shaped structure made of white granite stone, which means the supreme sublime. The third and fourth arches are connected together to form a rectangular stone gate with a brick hemispherical dome covering the roof.

The gate tower of Qingjing Mosque, 12.3 meters high and 6.6 meters wide, is majestic and elegant. The top of the building is a platform, and the four-sided circular building forms a stack like a Chinese character "回" in the homocentric square style. The south stack is 1.4 meters high, and the north stack is 1.2 meters high. There are two inscribed steles "月 (Moon)" and "台 (pavilion)" on the left and right sides. Thus it is called Moon Pavilion, where Akhund comes to watch the moon and decide the starting date of the Eid al-Fitr.

◎ 清净寺阿拉伯文墙体。（成冬冬 摄）
The walls with Arabic inscriptions in Qingjing Mosque. (Photo by Cheng Dongdong)

与门楼相连的礼拜大殿又称奉天坛，阿拉伯名叫"麦斯吉德"，即叩拜真主的地方。奉天坛四周墙壁的材质都为白色花岗岩条石。奉天坛西内墙和西墙南北侧壁面（"奎布拉"墙）设有壁龛。壁龛内浮雕有《古兰经》铭文，西墙南侧第二龛所刻"商业不能使他们疏忽而不纪念真主、谨守拜功和完纳天道"，西墙北侧第二龛所刻"船舶在海中带着真主的恩惠而航行，以便指示你们他的一部分迹象，对于每个坚忍的、感谢的人，此中确有许多迹象"。所刻文字向人们宣示着穆斯林严格的教规及其精神追求，也表明了当时来泉的伊斯兰信徒多为远航而来的商人。

明隆庆元年（1567年），奉天坛礼拜殿屋盖倒塌后，立即就建了明善堂，用于教徒礼拜。明善堂仿造当时的闽南古民居建筑，三开间砖木结构，堂前有一只精雕石的香炉，是从奉天坛搬来的旧物。堂前的空旷之地，有一小园圃，花卉竞相开放。花园北墙直对门的楼壁间，有石刻一方，那是明成祖朱棣于永乐五年（1407年）颁发的圣旨，用以保护清净寺及伊斯兰教徒的《敕谕》。

清净寺内也留存了许多宋元时期的伊斯兰式石墓盖，这些石墓盖多由整石雕刻而成，一般分为三至五层不等，底座宽大，逐层缩小，环刻有缠枝花卉纹和覆莲瓣纹等。

一千余年过去，在时光的长河里，清净寺安静地矗立，今人徜徉其中，能感受宗教的肃穆宁静，亦能欣赏建筑艺术之美。

◎ 奉天坛殿内虽仅存数根柱石的残础，却仍然充满了肃穆庄严的气势。（成冬冬 摄）
With only several plinths of pillars remained, the Altar is still full of solemn aura. (Photo by Cheng Dongdong)

◎ 清净寺明善堂。（成冬冬 摄）

Mingshan Hall of Qingjing Mosque. (Photo by Cheng Dongdong)

The worship hall connected to the gate tower is also called Fengtian Altar, whose Arabic name is Masjid. It is the place to worship Allah. The surrounding walls of the Altar were made of white granite strips. There are niches on the west inner wall of the Altar and the north and south sides of the west wall (Kuibula Wall). The niches has the relief inscription of classical texts of *Quran*. The second niche on the south side of the west wall is engraved "Business must not make them neglect to memorialize Allah, keep worshipping and complete the Way of Heaven." The second niche on the north side of the west wall was engraved "The ship sails in the sea with the grace of Allah to show you some of his signs. For every stoic and thankful person, there are indeed many signs." The inscribed text proclaims to people the strict rules and spiritual pursuits of Muslims, and shows the fact that most of the Islamic believers in Quanzhou at that time were merchants who came from a long distance.

In the year of 1567 of the Ming Dyansty, after the roof of the worship hall of Fengtian Altar collapsed, Mingshan Hall was built immediately for its believers to worship. Mingshan Hall imitated the ancient dwellings of Southern Fujian at that time, with three-room brick and wood structure. There is a carved stone incense censer in front of the hall, which is an old relic from the Altar. In the open space in front of the hall, there is a small garden where flowers are blooming. Between the north wall of the garden and the wall directly opposite the door, there is a stone inscription, which is an imperial decree issued by Zhu Di (Emperor Chengzu) in the year of 1407 in the Ming Dynasty to protect the mosque and the Muslims.

There are also many Islamic stone tomb covers from the Song and Yuan Dynasties in the mosque. Most of these stone tomb covers were carved out from whole stones. They are generally divided into three-layer to five-layer ones. The bases are wide and shrink layer by layer. The tomb covers are engraved with interlocking-branch flower patterns, lotus petal patterns, etc.

More than a thousand years have passed. In the long river of time, Qingjing Mosque stands quietly. People walking in it today can feel the solemn and tranquility of religion and appreciate the beauty of architectural art.

灵山伊斯兰教圣墓：世界伊斯兰教的第三圣墓

"求知去吧，哪怕远在中国。"

这是伊斯兰教先知穆罕默德对信徒发出的圣训。大量的穆斯林，不远万里，乘风破浪，通过海上丝绸之路来到中国，当时已崛起为中国四大港口之一的刺桐港成了热门之地。

据说，一千三百多年前，穆罕默德派了两位贤徒来到泉州。他们在泉州传教，在泉州生活，最后，还在泉州获得祥和与安息，泉州在圣贤心中，已然是故土。

据明代史学家何乔远所著的《闽书·方域志》中载："唐武德年间（618—626年），穆罕默德遣门徒大贤四人来华。一贤传教广州，二贤传教扬州，三贤、四贤传教泉州，卒，葬于此。葬后，是山夜光显发，人异而灵之，名曰圣墓，山曰灵山。"

五百多年前，郑和正准备第五次出使西洋，在这之前，他还去了一个地方——泉州的灵山圣墓。他在此处朝谒行香，并留下碑文。此碑文中载："钦差总兵太监郑和，前往西洋忽鲁谟斯等国公干，永乐十五年五月十六日于此行香，望灵圣庇佑。镇抚蒲和日记立。"碑文同时告诉世界，刺桐港是世界海洋大通道的必经之地。浩浩荡荡的郑和船队，远涉重洋，与亚非人民共同见证航海史上的壮举。

◎ 伊斯兰教圣墓位于灵山南麓。（陈英杰 摄）

The Islamic Tombs are located at the southern foothill of Lingshan Mountain. (Photo by Chen Yingjie)

Islamic Tombs in Lingshan Mountain: the Third Holy Tomb of Islam in the World

"Go for knowledge, even if it is in as far as China."

This is the hadith issued by Muhammad, the prophet of Islam, to his believers. After that, a large number of Muslims traveled from afar to China through the Maritime Silk Road. At that time, Zayton Port, one of the four major ports in China, became a hot spot.

It is said that, more than 1,300 years ago, Muhammad sent two sages to Quanzhou. They preached in Quanzhou and settled here. Finally, they found peace and rest in Quanzhou. Quanzhou is already the homeland in the hearts of the sages.

According to the local annals written by Ming Dynasty historian He Qiaoyuan: "During 618 and 626 of the Tang Dynasty, Muhammad sent four great sages to China. One sage preached in Guangzhou, and the second preached in Yangzhou. The third and last sages preached in Quanzhou. When they passed away they were buried here. At the night they were buried the mountain gave off light. People were surprised by seeing this and named the tomb 'Holy Tombs', and the mountain 'Lingshan (Holy Mountain)'."

More than five hundred years ago, Zheng He was preparing for his fifth mission to the West. Before that, he went to a place—the Islamic Tombs of Lingshan

◎ 郑和行香碑。（成冬冬 摄）
The inscription recording Zheng He's pilgrimage to the Islamic Tombs. (Photo by Cheng Dongdong)

Mountain in Quanzhou. Here he paid pilgrimage to the tombs and left a stele. The inscription on the stele says: "The imperial eunuch, Zheng He, went to Ormus and other countries in the West for business. Zheng came here on May 16, the 15th year of Yongle, hoping for the blessing of the Holy Spirit. The inscription was recorded and the stele erected by Pu Heri, a low-ranking military officer." The inscription also tells the world that Zayton Port is a must-pass place of the world's ocean channel. The mighty Zheng He fleet traveled across oceans and witnessed the feats in the history of navigation with the people of Asia and Africa.

泉州灵山原名狮子山，因山体形似猛狮而得名。圣墓就坐落于灵山南麓。灵山伊斯兰圣墓结构独特，由雕琢精细的花岗岩石棺、石亭、石埕、石阶及马蹄形护墓石回廊组成。经历了明朝时的大地震，圣墓回廊和石柱至今保存完整，三层结构的墓体，以莲花瓣为底座，中间是平板石，上面是回字形的墓盖。其他墓石上，刻有祥云或者莲花瓣，象征清净纯洁。回廊中七方石碑分别伫立，其中最著名的便是郑和行香碑和元初重修圣墓的回文碑记。该回文碑是研究泉州伊斯兰教的宝贵资料。回廊正中这方青草石雕琢的回文石碑刻，记载了元至治三年（1323年）有一批阿拉伯穆斯林远渡重洋来到泉州，为圣贤修墓的过程。这些记载圣墓年岁的古老文字，亦记录了当年"东方第一大港"外商云集的盛况。

距圣墓前约百十步间，一块纱帽形巨岩巍然耸立在可容百余人的大磐石上，人若以手撼之，竟会微微晃动，俗称风动石，泉州著名胜境之一"玉毬风动"便是指此。明代泉州知府周道光奇其为神物，于岩上题刻"碧玉毬""天然机妙"以彰之。风动石的传说故事也挺多，回教徒们视其为真主安拉赐予平安的遗物。风动石西侧岩壁尚存朱炳如、李焘二人唱和诗刻。

◎ 马蹄形护墓石回廊半包裹着石亭和其下的石棺。（成冬冬 摄）
Horseshoe-shaped stone cloister half wraps around the stone pavilion and the sarcophagi beneath it. (Photo by Cheng Dongdong)

Lingshan Mountain in Quanzhou was originally known as Lion Mountain, given the fact that the mountain resembled a fierce lion. The Islamic Tombs are located at the southern foot of the mountain. The Islamic Tombs have a unique structure, made of finely carved granite sarcophagi, stone pavilions, stone ridges, stone steps, and horseshoe-shaped tomb-protecting stone corridors. After the great earthquake in the Ming Dynasty, the corridor and stone pillars of the Islamic Tombs survived intact. The three-story structure of the tombs is based on lotus petals, with a slab stone in the middle, and a tomb cover in the shape of a circle on the top. Other tombstones are engraved with auspicious clouds or lotus petals, symbolizing purity and peace. Seven stone steles stand separately in the corridor, the most famous of which are the stele recording Zheng He's pilgrimage to the tombs and a stele in Arabic recording reconstruction of the tombs in the Yuan Dynasty. The stele is a valuable source for the study of Islam in Quanzhou. This Arabic stone inscription carved in lime stone in the middle of the corridor records how a group of Arab Muslims came to Quanzhou in 1323 of the Yuan Dynasty, to repair the tombs of the sages. These ancient texts, which record the age of the tombs, also record the prosperity of Zayton Port (the largest port of the East) where foreigners gathered.

About a hundred steps away from the front of the tombs, a huge veil-shaped rock stands on a big rock that can accommodate more than a hundred people. If a person pushes it with his hands, it will sway slightly. It is commonly known as the wind-moving stone and is one of the places of interest in Quanzhou. Zhou Daoguang, the magistrate of Quanzhou in the Ming Dynasty, wondered at its divine nature and inscribed "Jade Ball" and "Natural Wonder" on the rock to highlight it. There are many legends and stories about this rock. Muslims regard it as a relic of peace given by Allah. The rock wall on the west side of the wind-moving stone still retains the poems carved by Zhu Bingru and Li Tao.

◎ 硕大的"碧玉毬"风动石。（陈英杰 摄）
The giant wind-moving stone is called "Jade Ball". (Photo by Chen Yingjie)

◎ 信徒们前来灵山伊斯兰教圣墓朝拜。（陈英杰 摄）

Muslims are paying pilgrimage to the Islamic Tombs in Lingshan Mountain. (Photo by Chen Yingjie)

　　现在生活在泉州的穆斯林并不算多，但从唐朝开始，很多阿拉伯商人便择泉州而居，并且与当地人通婚，即使死后，也选择留在泉州。泉州除了拥有早期阿拉伯人的墓葬，还有晋江陈埭的丁姓回族祖墓群。泉州曾出土300多方宋元时期的伊斯兰墓碑、墓盖石和建筑构件。碑刻资料显示，宋元时期泉州的穆斯林来自也门、亚美尼亚、波斯等地，其中来自波斯的人数最多。

　　泉州的清真寺在元朝曾一度有六七座之多，而同时期，泉州也涌现出了以蒲寿庚为代表的著名阿拉伯侨民。这些史实资料都是阿拉伯人及伊斯兰文化通过海上丝绸之路进入泉州的历史记载。10—14世纪，随着海洋贸易的发展，众多阿拉伯人、波斯人来到泉州，至元代其人数达到高峰。他们或经商，或传教，或游历，许多人定居下来，聚族而居、繁衍后代，并建清真寺、置墓葬区。

　　如今，灵山上还有很多阿拉伯后裔的墓葬，其前部多融入本地墓葬的传统风格，后半部分多为典型的伊斯兰墓葬墓盖石，体现了中阿文化的交融。作为这些墓葬中的代表，灵山圣墓是我国现存最古老、最完好的伊斯兰教圣迹。伊朗专家阿里·萨哈瓦特和纳岱丽认为，在伊斯兰世界中，除了穆罕默德圣墓和阿里圣墓之外，泉州的三贤墓、四贤墓是历史最久、价值最高的古迹，是"世界伊斯兰教的第三圣墓"。

◎ 元伊斯兰教马哈穆德须弥座式
石墓盖。（成冬冬 摄）
The Islamic Mahmudic Sumerian
stone tomb cover of the Yuan Dynasty.
(Photo by Cheng Dongdong)

There are not many Muslims living in Quanzhou now, but since the Tang Dynasty, many Arab businessmen chose to live in Quanzhou and intermarried with the locals. Even after their death, they chose to be buried in Quanzhou. In addition to the tombs of the Arabs in early times, there are also the tombs of the Hui-nationality ancestors of the Ding clan in Chendai, Jinjiang. Quanzhou has unearthed more than 300 Islamic tombstones, tomb cover stones and architectural components from the Song and Yuan Dynasties. According to inscriptions on the tombstones, Muslims in Quanzhou during the Song and Yuan Dynasties came from Yemen, Armenia, Persia and other places, with the majority of them from Persia.

There were as many as six or seven mosques in Quanzhou during the Yuan Dynasty. At the same time, the famous Arab expatriates, represented by Pu Shougeng, also emerged in Quanzhou. These historical facts recorded the entry of Arabs and Islamic culture to Quanzhou through the Maritime Silk Road. From the 10th to the 14th centuries, with the development of maritime trade, many Arabs and Persians came to Quanzhou, and their number reached a peak in the Yuan Dynasty. They did business, preached, or traveled here. Many of them settled down, lived together, gave birth, and built mosques and burial areas.

Today, there are many tombs of Arab descents on Lingshan Mountain. Usually the front part of them is integrated with the traditional style of local tombs, and the rear is a typical Islamic tomb cover stone, which reflects the integration of Chinese and Arab cultures. As a representative of these, the Islamic Tombs of Lingshan Mountain is the oldest and most intact Islamic holy site in China. Iranian experts Ali Sahavat and Nadali believe that in the Islamic world, except the Holy Tomb of Muhammad and the Holy Tomb of Ali, the tombs of the third and fourth sages in Quanzhou are the oldest and most valuable monuments. "They are the third holy tomb of Islam in the world".

◎ 位于华表山南麓的草庵寺因寺内的摩尼
光佛造像而闻名于世。（田米 摄）
Cao'an Temple, located at the southern
foothill of Huabiao Mountain, is famous for
the Statue of Mani in it. (Photo by Tian Mi)

草庵摩尼光佛造像：明教圣火、世界唯一

　　说起摩尼教，大家或觉陌生，可当摩尼教换一个称呼，成为金庸笔下那个"明教"时，是否就耳熟能详呢？金庸武侠小说《倚天屠龙记》中明教教主张无忌身边的婢女小昭后来当上了明教波斯总坛的教主。小昭从张无忌"婢女"到"顶头上司"的华丽变身，乃是因为明教是由波斯传入中国的。

　　我们当然知道，武侠世界是成人的童话。然而，2004年，金庸先生到访晋江，特地来到华表山南麓的草庵寺。当他参观完这座世界上仅存的摩尼教寺庙遗址后，站在摩尼光佛石像面前凝视许久，连连说道，明教存在是有史迹印证的，绝不是他杜撰的。

　　而早在1987年8月，首届国际摩尼教学术讨论会于瑞典隆德大学召开，"草庵摩尼光佛造像"就作为会议的纪念性吉祥物令世人瞩目。1991年，联合国教科文组织官员来草庵考察，看到保存如此完好的摩尼光佛雕像时兴奋不已。他们认为这是海上丝绸之路考察活动的最大发现、最大成就，这一发现具有世界性和历史性的意义。

　　摩尼教源自公元3世纪的波斯，杂糅佛教、景教和拜火教等教义而成，在中国被称为"明教"，也就是金庸小说《倚天屠龙记》中提到的明教。摩尼教崇拜光明，提倡清净，反对黑暗和压迫。约公元6—7世纪，摩尼教经陆上丝绸之路传入我国新疆地区，后由新疆传入唐朝都城长安。公元9世纪，泉州港海外贸易发展迅速，多有波斯商人来泉州经商，也由此带来他们信仰的宗教——摩尼教。此后的几个世纪，官方对摩尼教时而礼遇时而打压。及至元末，明太祖朱元璋利用明教力量取得天下，并以"明"为国号，却又害怕明教威胁到他的统治，因此下令驱逐信徒、毁坏寺院。盛极一时的明教开始转入秘密活动，融合于道教、佛教的民间崇拜，摩尼教逐渐被其他宗教所融合。

Statue of Mani in Cao'an Temple: the Holy Flame of *Minjiao* (Religion of Light); the Only One in the World

Speaking of Manichaeism, everyone may find it unfamiliar. When the word changes its name and becomes *Mingjiao* in Jin Yong's novels, however, is it familiar? In Jin Yong's Kung Fu novel *The Heaven Sword and Dragon Saber*, *Mingjiao* master Zhang Wuji's servant girl Xiao Zhao later became the leader of *Mingjiao*'s Persian head altar. The magnificent transformation of Xiao Zhao from Zhang Wuji's servant girl to big boss was due to the fact that Mingjiao was introduced to China from Persia.

We certainly know that the world of martial arts is a fairy tale for adults. However, in his visit to Jinjiang in 2004, Jin Yong paid a special visit to Cao'an Temple at the southern foothill of Huabiao Mountain. After visiting the site of the only extant Manichaeism temple in the world, he stood in front of the stone statue of Mani and gazed at it for a long time. He repeatedly said that the existence of *Mingjiao* was confirmed by historical relics, and it was definitely not fabricated by him.

As early as August 1987, the first International Manichaeism Symposium was held at Lund University in Sweden. The "Statue of Mani in Cao'an Temple" was used as the memorial mascot of the meeting and attracted the attention of the world. In 1991, when the officials of the UNESCO visited Cao'an for an investigation, they were very excited when they saw such a well-preserved Statue of Mani. They believed that this was the greatest discovery and achievement of the Maritime Silk Road expedition and this discovery had worldwide and historical significance.

◎ 摩尼光佛造像。（成冬冬 摄）
The Statue of Mani. (Photo by Cheng Dongdong)

Manichaeism originated from Persia in the third century AD, and was formed by a mixture of Buddhism, Nestorianism, and Zoroastrianism. It is called *Mingjiao* in China, which is the *Mingjiao* mentioned in Jin Yong's novel *The Heaven Sword and Dragon Saber*. Manichaeism worships light, advocates purity, and opposes darkness and oppression. Around the 6th and 7th centuries AD, Manichaeism was introduced into Xinjiang via the Silk Road, and then from Xinjiang to Chang'an (now Xi'an), the capital of the Tang Dynasty. In the 9th century AD, the overseas trade of Quanzhou Port developed rapidly. Many Persian merchants came to Quanzhou to do business, bringing with them their religion—Manichaeism. In the centuries that followed, the governments extended courtesies or suppressed Manichaeism from time to time. At the end of the Yuan Dynasty, Zhu Yuanzhang, the first emperor of the Ming Dynasty, used the power of *Mingjiao* to gain the regime, and made "Ming" the dynasty name. Later, being afraid that *Mingjiao* would threaten his rule, he ordered the expulsion of believers and the destruction of temples. With its activities integrated with Taoism and Buddhism folk worship, Manichaeism gradually merged with other religions and became underground with clandestine activities.

如今，晋江草庵寺内的摩尼光佛成了世界上仅存的明教图腾，而和摩尼光佛相呼应的"明教会"碗也在此发现。正是这两样"宝物"让晋江草庵与众不同。

草庵始建于南宋绍兴年间（1131—1162年），初建时为草构，由此得名"草庵"，元朝至元五年（1339年）改为石构，依山崖傍筑，草庵岩壁雕刻出摩尼光佛，配建石室供奉。庵的主体建筑为单檐，置于山顶，建筑的后部则架于山崖之上。

细看草庵寺的这尊摩尼光佛，既有佛教的影子，又有道教的样子，人称"道貌佛身"。因为是在庵内依山石刻而成，所以充分利用了岩石天然的颜色，巧夺天工。摩尼光佛高1.52米，宽0.83米，端坐于莲花坛上，面部呈淡青色，手显粉红色，服饰为灰白色，背有毫光射纹饰。摩尼光佛面相圆润，神态庄严，身着宽袖僧衣，双手相叠，手心向上，置于膝上。其形象与敦煌出土的唐代写本摩尼教重要经典《摩尼光佛教法仪略》中所描述的基本形似，白色的道袍也与新疆吐鲁番发现的摩尼教壁画一致。

看完摩尼光佛，便可前往庵前右边20多米处的摩崖上，那里有摩尼教"四位一体"的"劝念"石刻：清净光明，大力智慧；无上至真，摩尼光佛。

除了摩尼光佛造像和"劝念"石刻，草庵内壁龛上方还有两方纪年具名的记事崖刻，它们共同完整体现了摩尼教的教义和仪轨，以及摩尼教在泉州传播和发展的历程。草庵内摩尼教的光明之火照耀古今，是泉州海丝文化多元包容的又一力证。

◎ 这只刻有"明教会"三个字的黑釉碗为当时明教教徒定烧的食具。（成冬冬 摄）
This black-glazed bowl engraved with the Chinese characters "明教会"(*Mingjiao* Club) was the food utensil ordered by the Mingjiao followers at that time. (Photo by Cheng Dongdong)

Today, the Statue of Mani in Jinjiang Cao'an Temple is the only *Mingjiao* totem in the world, and the "*Mingjiao* Club" bowl that echoes the Mani was also found here. It is these two treasures that make Jinjiang Cao'an Temple unique.

Cao'an Temple was built during 1131 and 1162 of the Southern Song Dynasty. In the early stage, it was a thatched structure, from which it was named Cao'an (Thatched Nunnery). In the year of 1339 of the Yuan Dynasty, the nunnery was converted into a stone structure and built on a cliff, with the Statue of Mani carved into the rock wall and a stone room built for worship. The main building of the temple is a single-roofed structure placed on top of the mountain, and the rear part of the building was erected on top of the cliff.

When we take a closer look at this statue of Mani in Cao'an Temple, we can see the influence of both Buddhism and Taoism. And people usually say it has "the appearance of Taoism and the body of Buddhism". Because it was carved from the rock in the temple, it makes full use of the natural

◎ 摩尼教劝念石刻。（成冬冬 摄）
The "Persuasion" stone carvings of Manichaeism.
(Photo by Cheng Dongdong)

colors in the rock, with exquisite design and ingenious workmanship. The Statue of Mani is 1.52 meters high and 0.83 meters wide. The statue sits on a lotus altar with a light cyan face and pink hands. The clothes are off-white and the back was decorated with light rays. The face of Mani is round and solemn. He dresses in a monk robe with wide sleeves and his hands fold with palms up on the knees. His image is similar to that described in *Manichae Buddhism Laws and Rituals*, the important manuscript of Manichaeism in the Tang Dynasty unearthed in Dunhuang. The white Taoist robe is also consistent with the Manichae frescoes found in Turpan, Xinjiang.

After watching the Statue of Mani, you can go to the cliff more than 20 meters on the right in front of the temple, where there are the quaternary "Persuasion" stone carvings of Manichaeism: purity and brightness, energy and wisdom; supremacy and truth, Mani.

In addition to the Statue of Mani and the stone carvings of the "Persuasion", there are two named memorial cliff carvings above the inner niche of Cao'an Temple, which together fully embody the teachings and rituals of Manichaeism, and the spreading and development of Manichaeism in Quanzhou. The light of Manichaeism in Cao'an Temple illuminates the ancient and modern times, which is another strong proof of the diversity and tolerance of the Maritime Silk Road culture in Quanzhou.

◎ 关岳庙的建筑体现了闽南古建筑的艺术风格。（成冬冬 摄）
The buildings of Guan-Yue Temple show us the artistic style of Southern Fujian ancient buildings. (Photo by Cheng Dongdong)

关岳庙：忠义仁勇、道义化身

关岳庙位于泉州市区涂门街，主祀关圣帝君，附祀岳王以及其他历史名人。关羽和岳飞供奉在一起，并相安无事数百年，这样的庙宇，恐怕只有在泉州才能见到。不仅如此，这座庙供奉的对象还有三国的刘备、张飞、诸葛亮以及明朝的一些名人。虽然庙不大，但此等阵容，简直就是一座英雄堂，足以震慑三教九流。也因此，沐浴着众神光辉的关岳庙成了泉州名气最大、香火最旺的庙宇之一，有泉州第一庙之称，同时是福建省现存规模最大的武庙。

作为海上丝绸之路的重要起点，泉州自古商贸发达。泉州人从事贸易的历史悠久，而做生意的人特别讲究"守信用、重承诺"，他们把道义的化身——关羽奉为"武财神"。在人们的心中，关公取信于人、本领通天、有求必应。

历朝历代对关公的敬慕和尊崇从未间断，上至帝王，下至平民百姓，以至于"汉封侯、宋封王、明封大帝；儒称圣、释称佛、道称天尊"。无论是"桃园三结义""千里走单骑"的武圣关羽，还是忠心爱国的英雄岳飞，都在传扬中华民族引以为傲的品德。在这些品德里，首要品德是"忠"，再由"忠"衍生出其他更多美好的品德——英勇、诚信、仁义……

Guan-Yue (Guan Yu & Yue Fei) Temple: Loyalty, Righteousness, Benevolence, and Courage; Incarnation of Morality

Guan-Yue Temple is located in Tumen Street, Quanzhou, and is dedicated to Guan Yu, Yue Fei and other historical figures. Guan Yu and Yue Fei are enshrined together without any troubles for hundreds of years. Such a special temple can probably only be seen in Quanzhou. Not only that, this temple also enshrines Liu Bei, Zhang Fei, Zhuge Liang from the Three Kingdoms, and some celebrities from the Ming Dynasty. Although the temple is not big, but this lineup is simply a hall of heroes, enough to frighten the three cults and nine schools. For this reason, Guan-Yue Temple, bathed in the glory of the gods, has become one of the most famous temples with the most worshipers in Quanzhou. Known as No. 1 temple in Quanzhou, it is the largest extant Wu (Guan Yu) temple in Fujian Province.

As the important starting point of the Maritime Silk Road, Quanzhou has developed commerce and trade since ancient times. Quanzhou people have a long history of trading, and those businesspersons paid special attention to features such as trustworthiness and keeping promises. They regard Guan Yu, the incarnation of morality and justice, as the God of Fortune. In people's minds, Guan Yu (or called Kuan Kung) is a man of trust, a man of skills, and a man who responds to requests.

The admiration and respect of Guan Yu in the past dynasties has never stopped, from emperors to ordinary people. He was made "Duke in the Han Dynasty, King in the Song Dynasty and Emperor in the Ming Dynasty; Saint of War by Confucianism, Buddha by Buddhism, and Lord of Heaven in Taoism". The legends of the War Saint Guan Yu, such as "the Oath of Brotherhood in the Peach Garden" and "Riding Alone for a Thousand Kilometers", or the loyal and patriotic hero Yue Fei, are all spreading the virtue characters the Chinese nation is proud of. Among these characters, the primary one is loyalty, from which derives other good virtues—courage, honesty, benevolence and righteousness...

◎ 2022年农历五月十三关帝诞辰祭典。（张清杰 摄）
The ritual of the birthday of Guan Yu on the 13th day of the 5th lunar month, 2022. (Photo by Zhang Qingjie)

在泉州这个百步一寺、千步一庙的地方，关岳庙香火鼎盛更胜其他自有其过人之处。人们对于关羽和岳飞的信仰，早已超越了宗教的意义，成为一种心灵的寄托。"忠义仁勇"植根于中华民族几十年传统文化，也长在了泉州悠久而古老的岁月里。

关岳庙正门有朱熹题写的"正气"匾额，大门两侧的对联"诡诈奸刁到庙倾诚何益；公平正直入门不拜无妨"道尽了信仰的要义。关岳庙建筑不是传统的递进院落，而是呈"一"字形的坐落格局，东西并排有武成殿（正殿）、三义庙、崇先殿三座殿堂。正中的武成殿祀关羽和岳飞，面阔三间，进深五间，单檐硬山顶，穿斗式木构架。右为三义庙，祀刘备、关羽、张飞，旁祀诸葛亮。左为崇先殿，奉祀关公三代先祖。庙内保存着明代书法家张瑞图所书"充塞天地"等巨幅名匾，历代泉籍文士名贤之石刻、楹联遍布。殿宇装饰有精美的石木雕和泥塑，屋脊采用闽南传统的剪瓷龙雕。从整个结构看，关岳庙这一"皇宫起"建筑是闽南古民居建筑的宫廷化，深具"帝庙"的形态。

泉州民间传说关岳庙极为灵验，除了遍布闽南的本地信众，其影响更远至我国台湾及东南亚，分灵遍及我国台、港、澳和东南亚地区。每年到此进香的信众有数十万人之多。

◎ 关岳庙正门朱熹所提"正气"匾额。（樊鑫 摄）
The "Righteousness" plaque inscribed by Zhu Xi on the main gate of Guan-Yue Temple. (Photo by Fan Xin)

◎ 关岳庙正门对联。（成冬冬 摄）

The couplet at the main gate of Guan-Yue Temple.
(Photo by Cheng Dongdong)

In Quanzhou, where temples are everywhere, Guan-Yue Temple attracts more worshippers than other places because of its own distinctive features. People's faith in Guan Yu and Yue Fei has long transcended the meaning of religion and become a kind of spiritual sustenance. The characters of loyalty, righteousness, benevolence, and courage were rooted in China's thousand-year traditional culture, and have embedded in Quanzhou's long history.

The main gate of Guan-Yue Temple has a "Righteousness" plaque inscribed by Zhu Xi. The couplet on both sides of the gate reads: "Being deceptive, wily and sly, it is useless for you to worship here, even with all your heart; being fair and upright, you are always welcome to be here, even you don't worship", which profoundly describes the essence of faith. The building of Guan-Yue Temple is not a traditional courtyard with quadrangles, but rather presents a '—(straight-line)'shaped layout, with three halls, namely the Wucheng Hall (the main hall), the Sanyi Hall and the Chongxian Hall, east-westwards and side by side. The main hall is dedicated to Guan Yu and Yue Fei, with a width of three rooms and a depth of five rooms. It is with single eave flush gable roofs and a column and tie-beam wooden construction. On the right of the main hall is Sanyi Hall, dedicated to Liu Bei, Guan Yu, Zhang Fei, and Zhuge Liang. On the left is the Chongxian Hall, dedicated to the three generations of ancestors of Guan Yu. Inside Guan-Yue Temple there is a large plaque inscribed by Zhang Ruitu, a famous calligrapher of the Ming Dynasty, with the words "Filling Heaven and Earth". Besides, stone carvings and couplets of famous celebrities and scholars of Quanzhou origin of various dynasties can be seen throughout the temple. The temple is decorated with exquisite stone and wood carvings and clay sculptures, and the ridge of the roof is carved with the traditional Southern Fujian porcelain dragon carvings. The entire structure of the temple is a mix of the ancient residential architecture of Southern Fujian and imperial court style, and has the form of an imperial temple.

Quanzhou folklore says that Guan-Yue Temple is extremely efficacious. In addition to the local believers all over Southern Fujian, its influence extends to Taiwan at home and even Southeast Asia, and Guan-Yue temples can be found throughout Taiwan, Hong Kong, Macao at home and Southeast Asia. Hundreds of thousands of believers come here every year to pray.

承天寺：闽南古刹里的城市山林

　　不同于其他地方的著名庙宇大多远离城镇，泉州的很多寺庙都与俗世的街巷紧挨着，外面是烟火繁盛的人间，里面便是宁静肃穆的佛门。从俗世到佛门，不过几步台阶。承天寺就是深藏于俗世间的大丛林之一。

　　泉州素有"泉南佛国"之称，"泉南佛国"四字，在清源山、九日山、承天寺都可得见，而承天寺的"泉南佛国"题字最具风骨，是明朝著名书法家张瑞图所书。

　　承天寺的前身是五代清源军节度使留从效的南花园，建寺时间是南唐保大末年至中兴初年（957—958年），初名"南禅寺"。北宋景德四年（1007年）赐名"承天寺"。

◎ 1928年，弘一法师入闽，此后的14年他居留闽南时的户籍就落户在泉州承天寺。1930年，弘一法师移锡泉州承天寺，和性愿法师共同创办"月台佛学院"，讲谈书法，编修佛经。为纪念弘一法师，承天寺重修弘一大师驻锡地"月台别院"，并塑造蜡像供人瞻仰。弘一法师驻锡承天寺期间，也是他一生书法作品最多的时期之一，重修的"月台别院"就是弘一法师赠字处。（成冬冬 摄）

Master Hongyi came to Fujian in 1928, and his household registration was settled in Chengtian Temple in Quanzhou throughout his 14-year-stay in Southern Fujian. In 1930, Master Hongyi moved to Chengtian Temple in Quanzhou, and co-founded Yue Tai Buddhist Academy with Master Xingyuan to lecture on calligraphy arts and compile Buddhist Sutra. In order to commemorate Master Hongyi, Chengtian Temple rebuilt Yue Tai Courtyard where Master Hongyi resided, and made a wax figure for people to admire him. For the period when Master Hongyi was stationed at Chengtian Temple, it was also one of those periods when he wrote calligraphy the most in his life. The restored Yue Tai Courtyard is the place where Master Hong Yi gave his calligraphy to others. (Photo by Cheng Dongdong)

Chengtian Temple: the City Garden in an Ancient Temple of Southern Fujian

Different from the famous temples away from towns and cities in other places, many temples in Quanzhou are close to the streets of the secular world. The outside is a mundane world with hustle and bustle, and the inside is a quiet and solemn Buddhism world. From the earthly world to the Buddhism world, there are only a few steps. Chengtian Temple is one of the great Buddhist monasteries hidden deep in the secular world.

Quanzhou is known as the Quan Nan Buddhism Kingdom. The four characters of "Quan Nan Buddhism Kingdom" can be found in Qingyuan Mountain, Jiuri Mountain, and Chengtian Temple, while the ones in Chengtian Temple are the most vigorous, and were written by the famous calligrapher Zhang Ruitu of the Ming Dynasty.

Chengtian Temple used to be the South Garden of Liu Congxiao, the provincial governor of the Five Dynasties. The temple was built during 957 and 958 in the Southern Tang Dynasty. It was originally named Nanchan Temple. In 1007 of the Northern Song Dynasty, the name "Chengtian" was granted by the emperor.

◎ 承天寺与开元寺、崇福寺并称"泉州佛教三大丛
林"，具有闽南传统建筑风格，环境清幽，是喧
嚣尘世中难得的城市山林。（任嘉雯 摄）
Chengtian Temple, Kaiyuan Temple and Chongfu Temple
are named "the three largest Buddhist monasteries in
Quanzhou". Chengtian Temple adopts the traditional
architectural style of Southern Fujian, and the
environment is quiet and clean. It is a peaceful garden in
the hustle and bustle of the city. (Photo by Ren Jiawen)

弘一法师题写的对联"有无量自在，入不二法门"给承天寺山门平添了几分灵性。此外，弘一法师还为承天寺题写过"此地古称佛国，戒法弘传遍迤"的颂偈，尤为珍贵。承天寺山门匾额楷书横写"月台"二字，白底黑字，沉稳庄重。承天寺又称"月台寺"，由此而得名。

进入寺内，榕阴幽幽，别有一番清凉在心头。百米石铺甬道的右手边墙壁上有弘一法师手迹"南无阿弥陀佛""升无上道 得正法流""善悟无碍 永得大安"等，左手边嵌有"古铸钱遗址"石碑。

承天寺整体建筑气势雄伟。寺院中轴线全长300米，天王殿、弥勒殿、大雄宝殿、法堂、文殊殿依次分布在中轴线两边。禅堂、祖堂、龙王殿和僧舍等建于东侧。

天王殿是第一重殿，殿内两旁供奉四大天王。天王形象虽有时面目可怖，但细看眼神，均是慈悲和祥和。对苍生的悲悯之情，乃宗教大爱所在，是谓"我佛慈悲"。

弥勒殿中的弥勒佛为整块樟木雕刻而成，殿中背后供奉护法神韦驮菩萨，亦由整块樟木雕琢而成，雕工了得，充分凸显闽南木作艺术的高超水平。

承天寺屋顶和房檐的华丽装饰，是一大特色，飞檐在古代是一种吉祥的寓意，形式也很讲究。剪瓷雕塑造的飞龙在天，气势不凡。大雄宝殿内的大柱全用整块大樟木制成，雄伟壮观。昔日民间流行"承天看大佛"，大佛就在大雄宝殿之中。三世佛、迦叶、阿难、护法诸天、十八罗汉、四大菩萨及开山祖师等塑像供奉于大雄宝殿，法相庄严。

◎ 重檐歇山顶五开间的大雄宝殿有匾额"闽南甲刹"。（成冬冬 摄）
The five-*chien* Mahavira Hall with double-eave gable and hip roof has a plaque
"The Best Temple in Southern Fujian". (Photo by Cheng Dongdong)

The couplet "Enjoying infinite freedom; entering the path of one and only" inscribed by Master Hongyi added a bit of spirituality to the mountain gate of Chengtian Temple. In addition, the Buddhist gatha written by Master Hongyi to Chengtian Temple is especially valuable: "This place was called the Kingdom of Buddhism in ancient times, where Buddha Dharma was preached far and beyond." The two characters "Yue Tai (Moon Pavilion)" were written horizontally in regular script on the plaque of the mountain gate, with black characters on a white background, calm and solemn. That is why Chengtian Temple is also known as Yuetai Temple.

Entering the temple, with banyan trees sheltering from the sun, people will have a special feeling of refreshment in their hearts. On the wall on the right side of the hundred-meter stone corridor, there are the handwritings of Master Hongyi: "Nanmu Amitabha" "Ascending the noble way to get the stream of Dharma" "Enlightenment without hindrance and eternal peace", and so on. On the wall on the left side there is a stone tablet showing the Ancient Site of Casting Coins.

The overall architecture of Chengtian Temple is majestic. On the central axis of the temple (a total length of 300 meters), there are the Heavenly King Hall, the Maitreya Hall, the Mahavira Hall, the Dharma Hall, and the Manjusri Hall distributed on both sides. The Meditation Hall, the Ancestral Hall, the Dragon King Hall and monk's dormitories were built on the east side.

The Heavenly King Hall is the first hall, and the four heavenly kings are enshrined on both sides of the hall. Although the images of the heavenly kings are sometimes terrifying, the emotion in their eyes shows compassion and harmony. The compassion for the common people is where the great love of Buddhism lies, which can be called "My merciful Buddha".

The Maitreya Buddha in the Maitreya Hall was carved from a whole piece of camphor wood. The rear of the hall is where the guardian god Skanda is enshrined and the statue was also carved from a whole piece of camphor wood. The carving is superb, highlighting the magnificent art of woodworking in Southern Fujian.

The ornate decoration of the roofs and eaves of Chengtian Temple is a major feature. The flying dragons made of pieces of colorful porcelain look extraordinary. The large pillars in the Mahavira Hall are made of whole large camphor wood, which is majestic. In the past, it was popular among local folks to "see big Buddhas in Chengtian Temple", and these big Buddhas are in the Mahavira Hall. Statues of the Trikalea Buddhas, Kassapa, Ananda, the Protectors of the Heavens, the Eighteen Arhats, the Four Bodhisattvas, and the founder of the temple are enshrined here, with solemn appearances.

承天寺镇寺之宝——隋朝铜铸阿弥陀佛供于法堂内，佛像高达二米，重有一吨多，乃国内罕见。法堂两旁的护廊上彩绘着12幅精美的佛教故事壁画，色彩古朴、栩栩如生，驻足观看，世人各有所悟。

承天寺不仅建筑雄伟，寺内景观也十分雅致。南宋泉州太守王十朋，共写有承天寺十奇诗十首。明天启六年（1626年），书法大家张瑞图用行书体书勒于四块碑石之上，碑石尚存开元寺刷拓部。承天寺自建寺至王十朋任太守时已历经二百余年，王十朋加以总结概括使它成为充满诗意的十奇景。此后又经四百余年，张瑞图书刻于碑石，传之后世。十奇景除"偃松清风""方池梅影"及"章帝朝日"外，尚有"榕径午荫""塔无栖禽""瑶台明月""推蓬雨夜""啸庵竹声""鹦山暮云""石如鹦鹉"。后人在十奇景之外，又在承天寺发现三奇——"月台倒影""一尘不染"及"梅石生香"。

大殿前檐中心两石柱上，刻有清康熙三十三年（1694年）泉州知府蒋毓英题联"悟尽心华早喜心空及地；标来月指共看月涌承天"。蒋毓英后被派任台湾省道台。作为康乾盛世的开创者，康熙深知台湾与泉州的血缘关系，凡是派往台湾任道台的官员，必先派到泉州任知府，等熟谙泉州风俗民情后，再赴台上任，且成为"固定制度"。

据清末进士、著名诗人林骚于1914年撰写的《重修承天禅寺碑记》载："在昔，有清之初，郑氏奉朱明裔，间关百战，规复闽疆。际除夕，驻师兹寺，以元旦受朝臣贺。"碑文中所述的民族英雄郑成功于承天寺活动的事迹，让承天寺增添了更多故事。

◎ 承天寺镇寺之宝——铜铸阿弥陀佛。（成冬冬 摄）
The key highlight of the treasures of Chengtian Temple—the bronze statue of Amitabha Buddha. (Photo by Cheng Dongdong)

◎ 承天寺大悲殿。（任嘉雯 摄）
The Hall of Great Compassion in Chengtian Temple. (Photo by Ren Jiawen)

The Sui Dynasty bronze statue of Amitabha Buddha, the most important treasure of the temple, is consecrated in the Dharma Hall. It is two meters high and weighs more than one ton, which is rare in China. There are 12 exquisite Buddhist story murals painted on the corridors on both sides of the hall. The colors of these murals are primitive and lifelike. Stopping and gazing in awe, every visitor will have their own understanding.

Chengtian Temple not only has grand buildings but also elegant sceneries. Wang Shipeng, the prefect of Quanzhou in the Southern Song Dynasty, wrote ten wonder poems about Chengtian Temple. In 1626 of the Ming Dynasty, Zhang Ruitu, the famous calligrapher, wrote the poems in running script and had them carved on four tablets, which are still preserved in the rubbing department of Kaiyuan Temple. When Wang Shipeng became the prefect of Quanzhou, Chengtian Temple had been built for more than two hundred years. Wang Shipeng summarized the beautiful sceneries, and made them ten poetic wonders. After more than four hundred years, Zhang Ruitu wrote and carved them on the tablets to pass on to later generations. In addition to "Breeze between the Pinus pumila" "Shadow of plum trees over the square pond" and "Curtain facing the sun", there are also "Banyan tree shadow at noon" "Pagodas without birds" "Bright moon over fairyland" "Opening windows to appreciate rainy nights" "Bamboo sounds in Xiao Nunnery" "Evening cloud in Ying Hill", and "Parrot-like stone". In addition to the ten wonders, later generations discovered three more in Chengtian Temple: "Inverted images of Moon Pavilion" "Spotlessness" and "Scent of plum and stone".

On the two stone pillars in the center of the front eaves of Mahavira Hall, there is an inscription by Jiang Yuying, the prefect of Quanzhou in 1694 of the Qing Dynasty. Jiang was later appointed as Taiwan Provincial Daotai (intendant of circuit). As the founder of the High Qing Era of Kangxi and Qianlong, Emperor Kangxi was well aware of the blood lineage between Taiwan and Quanzhou. All officials sent to Taiwan to serve as Daotais must first be sent to Quanzhou as the prefect. Only after they were familiar with the customs of Quanzhou could they go to take office in Taiwan. This has become a "fixed system".

According to the *Reconstruction of Chengtian Temple Stele* written in 1914 by Lin Sao, a scholar and famous poet in the late Qing Dynasty: "In the beginning of the Qing Dynasty, the Zheng family was loyal to the Ming Dynasty and they fought for hundreds of battles to restore Fujian area. On New Year's Eve, Zheng Chenggong (Koxinga) stationed his army in Chengtian Temple and accepted benedictions from his courtiers on New Year's Day." The national hero Zheng Chenggong's activities in Chengtian Temple described in the stele gave more historical stories to Chengtian Temple.

南少林寺：武林圣地、禅武双修

泉州是一个具有浓郁魔幻现实主义色彩的城市，武侠世界里的很多元素在这里都可以寻到踪迹。比如明教在草庵，比如供奉真武大帝的小武当，再比如少林寺里各种高超的武功。

2004年，创作出多部经典武侠小说的金庸先生到访泉州，他为泉州南少林寺题下了"少林武功，源远流长，传来南方，光大发扬"十六字，随后，金庸新版武侠小说里的南少林皆改为泉州南少林。武侠迷们自此知道，在金庸的武侠小说中所提及的南少林，指的就是泉州少林寺了。

始建于唐朝、拥有上千年历史的泉州少林寺，于两宋间兴盛，在三兴三废之后，史迹犹存。经过不断修葺和扩建的泉州少林寺，如今颇具规模，主要由山门、天王殿、观音阁、大雄宝殿和藏经阁五大建筑组成，黄墙橙瓦，庄严肃穆。矗立于凤山之麓的少林寺俯瞰脚下的城市，似乎在默默守护着这座城市。

想起曾救助唐王的十三棍僧，自有一股家国天下的情怀。南宋开禧元年（1205年）晋江进士施梦说所著《鲁东诗集》中记载："少林寺宇筑清源，十进山门万丈垣。百顷田园三岭地，千僧技击反王藩。""十三棍僧"之一的唐朝智空和尚入闽后，建立了泉州南少林寺，他也因此被尊为福建武僧的始祖。

少林南拳世代相传，未曾间断。智空和尚传玄真、玄明等十二门徒，可谓十八般武艺样样精通，在武侠小说中所能见到的功夫都得以传承。据传，十二门徒武艺高超，力大超群，千斤之鼎、千斤之弩不在话下，更可徒手擒虎，不但善舞百节链锤，还可飞檐走壁，令人神往。

◎ "天下少林有二，一在中州，一在闽中"，南北少林同源同宗。北方以嵩山少林寺为正宗，南方则以
　泉州少林寺为代表，南北少林，遥相辉映，名扬天下。（陈英杰 摄）
　"There are two Shaolin Temples in the world, one is in Zhongzhou (Henan) and the other is in Minzhong (Fujian)."
　The North and South Shaolins share the same origin. Shaolin Temple in Songshan Mountain is the orthodox school
　in the north, and Quanzhou Shaolin Temple is the representative in the south. (Photo by Chen Yingjie)

Southern Shaolin Temple: Sacred Place of Martial Arts and Buddhist Meditations

Quanzhou is a city full of magical realism. Many elements in the martial arts can be found here. For example, *Mingjiao* in Cao'an, the Small Wudang (another name of Zhenwu Temple) dedicated to Zhenwu Celestial Lord, and various superb martial arts in Shaolin Temple.

In 2004, Mr. Jin Yong, the author of many classic martial arts novels, visited Quanzhou. He wrote for Quanzhou Southern Shaolin Temple: "Shaolin martial arts, with a long history, spread to the south, and flourished." Then, in the new versions of his martial arts novels "Southern Shaolin Temple" were all changed to "Quanzhou Southern Shaolin Temple". Since then, fans of martial arts know that Southern Shaolin Temple mentioned in Jin Yong's martial arts novels refer to Quanzhou Shaolin Temple.

Founded in the Tang Dynasty and with a history of more than a thousand years, Shaolin Temple in Quanzhou flourished during the Northern and Southern Song Dynasties. After experiencing ups and downs, historical relics of the temple still remain. After continuous repairs and expansion, Quanzhou Shaolin Temple is now quite large. It is mainly composed of five major buildings: the Mountain Gate, the Hall of Heavenly Kings, Kuan Yin Hall, Mahavira Hall, and Sutra Depositary. The yellow walls and orange-colored tiles make the temple filled with a solemn atmosphere. The temple, standing at the foot of Fengshan Mountain, overlooks Quanzhou City below, and seems to be guarding the city silently.

Thinking of the thirteen armed monks who had rescued Li Shimin, a devotion to family and country one will emerge. Shi Mengshuo, a successful candidate in the highest imperial examinations in 1205 of the Southern Song Dynasty, recorded in his work *Ludong Poetry Collection* the legends of the armed monks. After entering Fujian, the monk Zhikong of the Tang Dynasty, one of the thirteen armed monks, established the Southern Shaolin Temple in Quanzhou, and he was therefore revered as the founder of armed monks in Fujian.

Nanquan (Shaolin Fist) has been passed down from one generation to another without interruption. The twelve disciples of monk Zhikong, such as Xuanzhen and Xuanming, were proficient in all kinds of martial arts, and all the *kung fu* that can be seen in martial arts novels was passed down. According to legend, the twelve disciples had superb martial arts skills and strength. Lifting a thousand-*jin* tripod or opening a thousand-*jin* crossbow is not at all a problem for them. They could even catch tigers with their bare hands. They were not only good at playing a chain hammer, but also leaping onto roofs and vaulting over walls, which is really fascinating.

宋时，长老元妙、知客法空、武农法本、武樵法华，腾空穿檐的本领更为精进。至明时，法本以一百三十五岁的高龄，将满身本领传予寺僧志明，志明传艺于晋江东石蔡延赓，蔡延赓又传南安冯安，可谓代代有传人。冯安徒侄包括了清初的五梅、苗显、至善、了凡、了因、胡惠乾等。在历史记录中，胡惠乾与方世玉、洪熙官等人并称为"少林十虎"。

天下武功出少林，想要学武术，来少林寺无疑是最好的选择。少林拳法以洪拳为代表，其代表性人物洪熙官、方世玉、黄飞鸿等早已成为许多热门影视作品演绎的对象。少林拳讲究出拳紧凑，动作实用，在招式上，力求攻防严密，灵活弹性。

如今的少林寺每周末都有公益禅武表演，泉州少林寺希望"以武会友，以禅修心"，以此惠及十方檀越信众，传播南少林禅武文化。走进少林寺，除了在演武厅可以看到武僧们的武术演练，也可以在各处看到孩童或办公室职员在舞剑耍棍。

泉州少林武术是南派少林武术的正宗，广泛流传于福建、广东、浙江、江西四省，泉州、厦门、福州等地则是福建省内的主要流传地。明清以来，少林武术传播至我国台湾、香港、澳门，以及东南亚和琉球等地。南少林武术延绵不绝、薪火相传，经由华侨流传至海外，加深了与海外各民族的文化交流。而其立足中国佛家禅宗思想、拳禅合一的特点跨越了宗教和武术两个领域，体现了古人的包容和智慧。

◎ 南少林武僧练武。（张加陛 摄）
Martial arts practice of armed monks of Southern Shaolin Temple. (Photo by Zhang Jiabi)

In the Song Dynasty, the elder monk Yuanmiao, receptionist monk Fakong, armed farming monk Faben, and armed woodcutter monk Fahua were more sophisticated in their ability to fly through the eaves. In the Ming Dynasty, Faben passed on his mantle skills to monk Zhiming at the age of 135 years old. Zhiming passed on to Cai Yangeng in Dongshi Town, Jinjiang City, and Cai passed on Feng An in Nan'an City. It can be said that there have been heirs from generation to generation. Disciples of Feng An's fellow apprentices included Wumei, Miao Xian, Zhishan, Liaofan, Liao'in, Hu Huiqian, etc. in the early Qing Dynasty. In historical records, Hu Huiqian, Fang Shiyu, Hong Xiguan and others were collectively referred to as the Ten Tigers of Shaolin.

All *kung fu* in China are from Shaolin. If you want to learn martial arts, coming to Shaolin Temple is undoubtedly the best choice. Shaolin fist is represented by Hung Ga, and its representative figures such as Hong Xiguan, Fang Shiyu, Huang Feihong, etc. have long been the protagonists of many popular film and television works. Shaolin fist emphasizes compactness of punching and practicality of movements. In the moves, it strives for rigorousness and flexibility of attack and defense.

Today, Shaolin Temple holds public Zen and martial arts performances every weekend. It hopes to make friends through martial arts and cultivate the minds with Buddhist meditation, so as to benefit the benefactor and believers all around the world and spread the Zen-marital arts culture of Southern Shaolin. Walking into Shaolin Temple, besides the martial arts hall, you can also see children or office staff playing swords and sticks anywhere.

Quanzhou Shaolin martial arts is the authentic southern style of Shaolin martial arts. It is widely spread in the four provinces of Fujian, Guangdong, Zhejiang and Jiangxi. Quanzhou, Xiamen, Fuzhou, etc. are hence the main places in Fujian Province spreading the martial arts. Since the Ming and Qing Dynasties, Shaolin martial arts have been spread to Taiwan, Hong Kong, Macau at home and Southeast Asia and Ryukyu. Southern Shaolin martial arts have been continuously passed down from generation to generation, and spread overseas through overseas Chinese, deepening cultural exchanges with foreign ethnic groups. Based on the Chinese Buddhism Zen ideology, the unity of fist and Zen covers the two fields of religion and martial arts, which reflects the breadth and wisdom of the ancient Chinese people.

◎ 少林功夫。（许师伟 摄）
Shaolin martial arts. (Photo by Xu Shiwei)

◎ 安海龙山寺寺庙不大，名气却不小，是台湾四百余座龙山寺的祖庙。（施清凉 摄）

Though not very large in scale, Longshan Temple is a famous one. It is the ancestral temple of
more than 400 Longshan Temples in Taiwan. (Photo by Shi Qingliang)

龙山寺：闽台同源、法乳一脉

　　龙山寺位于晋江市安海镇的龙山之麓，因此得名"龙山寺"。龙山寺还有其他几个名字，古称"普现殿"，又称"天竺寺"，本地人则更喜欢称其"观音殿"。

　　龙山寺的始建年代至今仍众说不一，但根据《安平镇龙山寺重兴碑记》中记载的"昉自隋"，可推测出龙山寺的建寺时间应不晚于隋皇泰年间（618—619年）。

　　龙山寺虽规模不大，但寺内宝物众多。其一，龙山寺有朱熹、张瑞图、弘一法师、赵朴初等历代名家在寺内的题匾墨宝。朱熹曾题匾"普现殿"，里人榜眼石起崇匾"龙山古刹"，明天启年间御史苏琰重修匾"龙山宝地"；大殿有张瑞图题匾"通身手眼"。

　　除了墨宝，龙山寺还有三宝。第一宝是千手千眼观音。相传隋开皇年间（581—600年），天竺（今印度）僧人一粒沙行至安海，自建茅舍，栖佛度化，并以"天竺"为号，称"天竺寺"。寺中有一水井，井边长着一株巨大樟树。其外形酷似千手千眼观音，且夜发瑞光。人们觉得神奇，就叫画师绘制图像，又让匠人以树为本，雕刻出千手千眼观音，经过几年终于完成。

Longshan Temple: the Buddha Dharma in Fujian and Taiwan Tracing to the Same Origin

Longshan Temple is located at the foot of Longshan Hill in Anhai Town, Jinjiang City. Hence the name Longshan Temple. There are several other names for the temple. In ancient times, it was called Puxian Temple or Tianzhu Temple. Nowadays, locals prefer to call it Guanyin Temple.

The date when Longshan Temple was built is still uncertain, but according to the words "started from Sui Dynasty" recorded in *The Resurrection Stele of Longshan Temple in An'ping Town*, it can be inferred that the construction time of Longshan Temple should not be later than the Huangtai period (618—619) of the Sui Dynasty.

Despite its small scale, Longshan Temple does contain many treasures. First, Longshan Temple has plaques and calligraphy written by famous masters such as Zhu Xi, Zhang Ruitu, Master Hongyi, and Zhao Puchu. Zhu Xi once inscribed the plaque "Puxian Temple"; Shi Qicong, a local runner-up scholar inscribed the plaque "Longshan Ancient Temple"; Su Yan, a censor in the Tianqi period (1621—1627) of the Ming Dynasty inscribed the plaque "The Treasure Land of Longshan" when the temple was repaired; the main hall holds a plaque with Zhang Ruitu's inscription "Hands and Eyes all Over".

In addition the valued pieces of calligraphy, Longshan Temple also has three valuable treasures. The first treasure is Thousand-hand-and-thousand-eye Kuan Yin statue. According to legend, during 581 and 600 of the Sui Dynasty, monk Yilisha from Sindhu (now India) traveled to Anhai, built his own hut, taught and lectured Buddhist scriptures, and named his resident Tianzhu Temple under the name of "Tianzhu". There was a well in the temple, and a huge camphor tree by the well. The appearance of the tree resembled a Thousand-hand-and-thousand-eye Kuan Yin, and it glowed at night. Amazed by its magical appearance, people asked painters to draw the image of the tree, and asked the craftsman to carve the Thousand-hand-and-thousand-eye Kuan Yin statue with the tree as the model, which was finally completed after a few years.

◎ 龙山寺天王殿。（陈钧 摄）
The Hall of Heavenly King of Longshan Temple. (Photo by Chen Jun)

虽然是传说，但它承载着信众们对龙山寺的一种美好想象。实际上龙山寺中的千手千眼观音是明代所雕，与寺内珍藏的木鼓、观音殿大门为同一樟树制作而成，合称"樟树三宝"，是闽南古木雕艺术登峰造极之作。这尊千手千眼观音的珍贵之处不仅在于年代久远、工艺卓绝，而且佛像真有1,008手眼，这区别于多数寺院里供奉的千手千眼观音形象，它们一般仅有40手眼或者是48手眼用以代表千手千眼。

千手千眼观音的千眼意在观世，千手意在济世。龙山寺中的这尊千手千眼观音身披佛教服饰，头顶戴着花冠，站立在莲花座上，高达4.2米，宽达2.5米。在礼冠的正中央还雕刻着一尊坐佛，众多小佛首雕于周围，叠作帽状。在额头正中还雕刻了一只眼。观音的左右手于胸前合十，周身另雕有1,008只手，每只手的掌心雕有一眼。各掌或戴手镯，或持书章、乐器、珠宝、钟鼓、花果等多种物品，状似孔雀开屏。佛像背后为一菱形巨屏，上雕火焰纹和圆日，以示佛光普照。佛像的镂刻工艺，细致生动，于细微处见百态千姿，精妙之功令人叹为观止。佛像在漫长的岁月中仍安然无恙，如此奇迹亦让信众更为崇拜。

The legend is just a legend, carrying a kind of beautiful imagination of the believers about Longshan Temple. In fact, the Thousand-hand-and-thousand-eye Kuan Yin statue was carved in the Ming Dynasty. It was made of the same camphor tree as the wooden drum and the gate of the Kuan Yin Hall in the temple. They are collectively called the Three Treasures of Camphor Trees. The Thousand-hand-and-thousand-eye Kuan Yin statue is the pinnacle of ancient woodcarving art in Southern Fujian. This statue is precious for its long age and excellent craftsmanship, but also the statue really has one thousand hands and eyes. It is totally different from the statues of Avalokitesvara enshrined in most temples, which generally only have forty hands and eyes, or forty-eight hands and eyes to represent a thousand hands and a thousand eyes.

The thousand eyes of Kuan Yin are meant to see the world, and the thousand hands are meant to help the world. This Thousand-hand-thousand-eye Kuan Yin statue in Longshan Temple is dressed in Buddhist costumes and a flower crown on his head. Standing on a lotus seat, it is 4.2 meters high and 2.5 meters wide. In the center of the ceremonial crown there is also a sitting Buddha carved, and many small Buddha heads were carved around it, stacked in the shape of a hat. An eye was carved in the middle of the forehead. The left and right hands of the statue are folded together on the chest, and there are 1,008 hands carved around the body, and the palm of each hand is carved with an eye. Each palm wears bracelets, or holds books, musical instruments, jewelry, bells and drums, flowers and fruits, etc., which look like a peacock displaying. Behind the statue is a giant diamond-shaped screen with a flame pattern and a round sun carved on it to show the Buddha's light. The carving craftsmanship of the statue is meticulous and vivid, and the subtleties can be seen in a variety of ways, and the exquisite work is breathtaking. The statue has survived the long years, and such miracles have also made believers worship even more.

◎ 龙山寺镇寺之宝——千手千眼观音。（成冬冬 摄）
The key highlights among Longshan Temple's treasures—Thousand-hand-and-thousand-eye Kuan Yin. (Photo by Cheng Dongdong)

第二宝就是殿前的一对透雕辉绿石盘龙柱，这一对盘龙柱是清代重修寺庙时配置的，雕工细腻，栩栩如生。龙柱以蟠龙为主要形象、配有云片和人物，比普通的盘龙石柱更有想象空间。令人称奇的是龙爪的一对抓珠，敲之有声，左边似钟声，右边像鱼鼓声。这对被誉为全国古刹四大龙柱之一的宝物，如今用玻璃罩保护起来。

第三宝为整板樟木的大殿大门以及位于钟楼的整木凿空大鼓。钟楼每日清晨撞钟108响，钟声浑厚，经久不息。

龙山寺香火曾随着安平商人和移民海外的闽南先辈传播至我国台湾及东南亚诸岛国侨居地。光台湾的龙山寺分炉就达400多座。晋江沿海在明末清初，有过三次移民潮，目的地均为台湾。为了能够平安横渡台湾海峡，移民们随身携带龙山寺观音菩萨的神像和香火，待到安全抵达后，再于当地建龙山寺，其中最著名的有鹿港龙山寺和台北艋舺龙山寺。台北艋舺龙山寺殿前亦有台湾独一无二的铸铜龙柱，与安海龙山寺的盘龙柱相仿。

安海龙山寺最热闹的是正月初一的燃香祈福。除夕夜，香客从四面八方拥来，只等点上头一炷香，据说能够点上头一炷香的人，新的一年能够交上好运。在台湾的各大龙山寺，这一风俗与安海龙山寺一致。

◎ 龙山寺盘龙柱。（成冬冬 摄）

The stone dragon-wreathed columns in Longshan Temple. (Photo by Cheng Dongdong)

◎ 台北艋舺龙山寺。
（成冬冬 摄）
Taipei Báng-kah Longshan
Temple. (Photo by Cheng
Dongdong)

The second treasure is a pair of open-carved diabase dragon-wreathed columns in front of the temple. This pair of columns were configured when the temple was repaired in the Qing Dynasty. The carvings are delicate and lifelike. The main images of the columns are wreathed dragons, with clouds and characters, which is more imaginative than ordinary dragon-wreathed stone columns. What is amazing is the pair of pearls in the dragons' claws. Knocking on them, the sounds are different: it is like a bell on the left pearl and a fish-shaped drum on the right pearl. This pair of treasures, known as one of the four dragon columns of ancient temples in the country, is now protected by glass covers.

The third treasure is the main hall gates made of camphor wood and the whole wooden hollow drum in the bell tower. The bell rings 108 times every morning, and the sound of the bell is thick and endless.

The practice of Longshan Temple was spread to Taiwan at home and also Southeast Asian countries with An'ping merchants and Southern Fujian ancestors who emigrated overseas. In Taiwan alone, there are more than 400 Longshan Temples. There were three waves of immigrants along the coastal area of Jinjiang during the late Ming and early Qing Dynasties, all destined for Taiwan. In order to cross the Taiwan Straits safely, the immigrants carried the statues and incense of Kuan Yin in Longshan Temple. When they arrived safely, they built Longshan Temples in the local areas. The most famous ones are Lukang Longshan Temple and Taipei Báng-kah Longshan Temple. There is also a pair of cast bronze dragon columns in Taiwan in front of Báng-kah Longshan Temple in Taipei, which is similar to the dragon-wreathed columns of Longshan Temple in Anhai.

The most lively thing in Longshan Temple is the burning of incense for blessing on the first day of lunar January. On Chinese New Year's Eve, pilgrims flooded in from all directions, just waiting to light up the first stick of incense. It is said that those who can light up the first stick of incense will be able to have good luck in the whole new year. In the large Longshan Temples in Taiwan, this custom is consistent with Anhai Longshan Temple.

魅力之城——文化之都的建筑与名人

　　一直以来，泉州之美，常被埋没。它的美，不如厦门那般明丽；它的美，也不如土楼那般具象。但是它的美，很独特。它就像一块璞玉，可由不同的工匠雕琢出不同的美。

　　"地下看西安，地上看泉州。"泉州之美，是等待发现的美，是灿烂的海丝文明对现代人类的馈赠。如果你恰好喜欢怀旧，那么，你可以漫步泉州，去探寻那些老建筑和它的主人们背后的故事。

◎ 亮眼的红是泉州建筑的一大特色。（陈英杰 摄）

The bright red color is a feature of Quanzhou's architecture. (Photo by Chen Yingjie)

◎ 20世纪上半叶，许多下南洋打拼、事业有成的华侨回乡置业，泉州各地散落着不少像景胜别墅这样中西合璧的番仔楼。（茅罗平 摄）

Many overseas Chinese who strove for a success in Nanyang returned to their hometowns to buy properties in the first half of the 20th century. A lot of huan-a-laus like Jingsheng Villa that combine Chinese and Western styles scatter all over Quanzhou. (Photo by Mao Luoping)

A City of Great Charm: Architecture and Celebrities of the Capital of Culture

The beauty of Quanzhou has always been ignored. Its beauty is not as bright as Xiamen, nor as concrete as Fujian Tulou. But its beauty is very unique. It is like a piece of uncut jade, which can be carved with different beauty by different craftsmen.

"Look at Xi'an from those unearthed cultural relics and Quanzhou from cultural relics on the ground." The beauty of Quanzhou is the beauty waiting to be discovered, and the gift of the splendid Maritime Silk Road Civilization to modern mankind. If you happen to like nostalgia, then you can stroll through Quanzhou to find out the old buildings and the stories of their owners.

崇武古城：固若金汤的海防重镇

公元7—14世纪，远在南美洲，一度十分强盛的查查波亚斯王国在秘鲁雨林深处建立了石头古城——卡迦玛瓜拉。遗憾的是，那座石雕石砌都达到巅峰的南美神秘古城随着王国的衰落已然被时间忘却。庆幸的是，万里之外的中国东南沿海还有一座石头城，不仅保存相对完整而且英姿勃发地矗立于世人眼前，它就是崇武古城。

公元10世纪，北宋太平兴国六年（981年），惠安置县，设崇武乡守节里，置小兜巡检寨，后改"小兜"为"崇武"。元丰二年（1079年），朝廷派军于此驻寨，进行防守。明洪武二十年（1387年），江夏侯周德兴根据明太祖朱元璋的决策，在惠安县治东25里的崇武半岛上，建造崇武所城，以此经略海防抵御倭寇。

一千多年来，这里一直是东南海防前线的重要军事设施。这里，曾经鼓点激越。抗倭名将戚继光在此指挥剿倭，平定倭乱。这里，曾经英雄守望。1651年，郑成功以崇武古城为根据地，分兵各海口抵抗清兵，收复台湾时，也有一路人马从此处扬帆出征……这一切，随着时间洪流逝去，仅有古城留下，和大地同生。

◎ 古城一角。（陈莫凡 摄）

A corner of Chongwu Town. (Photo by Chen Mofan)

Chongwu Ancient Town: an Impregnable Key Place for Coastal Defense

From the 7th century to the 14th century AD, in distant South America, the once very powerful Kingdom of Chachapoyas established the ancient stone city Cajamarquilla deep in the rainforest of Peru. Regrettably, the mysterious ancient city of South America, where both stone carving and masonry reached their peak, has been forgotten by time, along with the decline of the kingdom. Fortunately, thousands of miles away, there stands a stone town on the southeast coast of China. It is not only relatively intact but also stands proudly in front of the world. It is the ancient town of Chongwu.

In the year of 981 of the Northern Song Dynasty, Hui'an County was set up, under which there was Shoujie Village, Chongwu Township. The Xiaodou Patrol Inspection Station was there. Later on the name of Xiaodou was changed to Chongwu. In 1079, the imperial court sent troops here to defend. In 1387 of the Ming Dynasty, according to the decision of the Emperor Zhu Yuanzhang, Jiangxia Marquess Zhou Dexing built Chongwu Fortress Town on Chongwu Peninsula, 25 li east of Hui'an County to consolidate coastal defence against Japanese pirates.

For more than a thousand years, this place has always been a key military facility on the front line of coastal defense in the southeast of China. Here, there was once a major hotspot. Qi Jiguang, a famous anti-Japanese-pirate general, commanded the anti-Japanese-pirate wars and defeated the Japanese pirates here. The town was stationed by heroes. In 1651, Zheng Chenggong used the ancient town of Chongwu as his base and sent his troops to seaports to resist the Qing troops. When he was going to regain Taiwan, a group of soldiers set sail from here... When all other things disappeared, only the ancient fortress town where these events occurred was left behind with the eternal earth.

◎ 位于崇武半岛的崇武古城曾是东南海防重镇。（陈英杰 摄）

The Chongwu Ancient Town on Chongwu Peninsula was once a key place for coastal defense in the south-east China. (Photo by Chen Yingjie)

崇武古城位于泉州惠安县东南海滨，全城周长737丈，城基1丈5尺，垛子1,304个，窝铺26座。古城四方设四城门，城门上各建城楼。崇武古城初建时，外墙用石，内墙用土，容易崩塌。后内外墙均用花岗岩块石建筑，石与石之间，牢不可破。善战之师，海洋城堡，多么完美的结合。那些浴血奋战的战鼓声，那些保家卫国的凯歌，都被历史的风吹散，只有石头，依然诉说着曾经的辉煌和伤痛。

崇武古城至今仍然保留着诸多古迹。古城东南角有一座航海灯塔，高达33米，光照射程为15—20海里。此灯塔，在世界航海界，被公认为国际航标。城中有奉祀五代闽将"青山王"张悃的城隍庙，在东门城内有祀青帝的东岳庙，而西门外迎恩亭右的三官庙依然尚存。

另外还有其他的寺宇分布在古城各处，它们历史悠久，别具一格。比较有代表性的，有东门头弘一法师传经的普莲堂、近下田的三教祠，以及位于近城兜的崇山宫、城外西南江口山下的天妃宫、南门城内的关帝庙、城内东南隅诗人黄吾野隐居的云峰庵和祀释迦的海潮庵等。

潮涨潮落，斗转星移，崇武古城的"大岞八景"依然令人神往。这八景指的是"龙喉吼烟""狮石晚照""渔翁撒网""滴水弹琴""军马洞天""玉磬传音""孤屿冬青""白鹤升天"。这八景天然形成，非人力所为。它们的存在，让我们对大自然的鬼斧神工有了更直观的印象。

◎ 俯瞰崇武古城。（田米 摄）
A bird's eye view of the ancient town of Chongwu. (Photo by Tian Mi)

◎ 崇武古城内有多处寺宇宫观。（陈莫凡 摄）
There are many temples and palaces in the ancient town of Chongwu. (Photo by Chen Mofan)

The ancient town of Chongwu is located on the southeast coast of Hui'an County, Quanzhou. The town has a perimeter of 2,432 meters, a wall base of about 5 meters, 1,304 piles, and 26 military camps. There are four gates on the four sides of the town, with towers built on them. In the early stages of the town's construction, stones were used for the outer wall and rammed earth for the inner wall, which was easy to collapse. The inner and outer walls were built with granite blocks later, unbreakable. Brave and skillful armies, and an ocean castle—what a perfect combination. Those bloody battle drums and triumphant songs of defending the country and homes have all been blown away by the wind of history. Only the stones still tell the glories and pains of the past.

The ancient town of Chongwu still retains many historical sites. At the southeast corner of the town, there is a lighthouse for navigation, which is 33 meters high and has a light range of 15-20 nautical miles. This lighthouse is recognized as an international navigation mark in the global navigation cycle. In the town, there is a City God Temple, enshrining Zhang Kun, a Fujian general of the Five Dynasties. In the inner side of the East Gate there is a Dongyue Temple dedicated to Qing Emperor. The Sanguan Temple on the right of Yingsi Pavilion outside the West Gate still exists.

In addition, there are other temples scattered throughout the ancient town. They have a long history and are unique. The most representative ones are Pulian Hall near the East Gate, where Master Hongyi preached, Sanjiao Temple near Xiatian, Chongshan Palace at Jinchengdou, Tianfei Palace at the foot of Jiangkou Hill in the southwest of the town, and Temple of Guan Yu in the inner town of the South Gate, Yunfeng Nunnery where the poet Huang Wuye lived in seclusion in the southeast corner of the town, and Haichao Nunnery where the Sakyamuni was worshipped.

As the tide rises and falls, and the stars move, the Eight Sceneries of Dazuo Village in the ancient town of Chongwu are still fascinating. These eight scenes refer to "Dragon Maw Roaring Mist" "Lion Stone at Sunset" "Fishermen Casting Nets" "Dripping Water Playing Music" "Military Horse Cave" "Jade Chime Transmitting Sound" "Green Winter in the Isolated Island" and "White Crane Ascending to Heaven". These eight sceneries are formed naturally. Their existence gives us a more intuitive impression of nature's extraordinary craftsmanship.

崇武古城因石头坚固的属性得以发挥保家卫国的功能，也得以保存至今。勤劳智慧的崇武人民，也没有辜负大自然的馈赠，他们把石头的实用性和艺术性发挥到了极致，使得惠安石雕名扬天下。

北京人民大会堂的石构件大柱柱础、八一南昌起义纪念塔、井冈山会师纪念碑、鼓浪屿郑成功雕像、厦门集美鳌园人物雕刻均出自惠安工匠之手。惠安的雕刻精品在东南亚华侨聚居之地熠熠生辉，它们装饰寺庙，也装饰着会馆大门。

位于崇武古城景区内的全国最大的岩雕艺术作品——大地艺术，由著名的画家洪世清老先生呕心沥血雕刻而成。他取材于海礁岩崖的原始形态，依形取势，循石造型，创作出形神兼备的各种艺术形象170余件，是惠安成熟的石雕艺术中的一大奇观。

最尖端的科技无法塑造出石雕艺术的细腻和华美，勤劳的双手却能不断带给我们视觉的冲击。一锥一凿的雕镂，传递着人类的文明和智慧。

◎ 崇武古城内的戚继光雕像。（杨婀娜 摄）

The statue of Qi Jiguang in the ancient town of Chongwu. (Photo by Yang E'nuo)

◎ 正在对石雕进行加工的惠安女。（陈英杰 摄）
Hui'an women working on a stone carving. (Photo by Chen Yingjie)

The strong properties of the stone enabled the ancient town of Chongwu to play the function of defending the home and the country, and preserved the town to this day. The hardworking and intelligent people of Chongwu lived up to the gift of nature. They took the practicality and artistry of the stone to the extreme, making the stone sculptures in Hui'an famous all over the world.

The stone pillar foundations of the Great Hall of the People in Beijing, the August 1st Nanchang Uprising Memorial Tower, the Monument of Army Junctions in Jinggang Mountain, the Statue of Zheng Chenggong on Kulangsu, and the figure carvings of Jimei Aoyuan Garden in Xiamen were all made by craftsmen from Hui'an. The exquisite sculptures from Hui'an are shining in the places where overseas Chinese in Southeast Asia live. They decorate the temples and the gates of guildhalls.

Arts of the Earth, the country's largest rock sculpture art work, is located in the scenic area of Chongwu Ancient Town. It was made with the painstaking effort of the famous painter Mr. Hong Shiqing. He created the works based on the original form of the sea reef and rock cliff. There are more than 170 various artistic images with both form and spirit, which are a great spectacle of the mature stone carving art in Hui'an.

The most cutting-edge technology can't create the delicate and gorgeous stone carving art, while hard-working guys can continue to bring us visual impact. The engravings in Hui'an convey the civilization and wisdom of mankind.

五店市：千年地标、盛放乡愁

　　葡萄牙首都里斯本是欧洲大陆最西端的城市，它是欧洲大陆的终点，也是大西洋的起点。为了怀旧，世界各地的人们奔赴它的怀抱。在里斯本，橙红色瓦顶此起彼伏，即使是新盖的楼房，也要覆上标志性的橙红色屋顶。那些建筑在太阳底下，闪着怀旧的光辉，令人沉醉不已。

　　在泉州晋江，也有一片红色的建筑，在城市高楼间显得格外亮眼，那就是五店市。和里斯本一样，五店市拥有一样的沿海怀旧，一样的新旧交汇。五店市，是千年来晋江永不褪色的地标。五店市街区的红砖燕尾脊建筑，在金色的夕阳光辉中，如同华章一般，绵延了一千三百多年的情怀。

　　五店市，从蔡氏五兄弟千年之前开的五间饮食店开始，以一个集市的商号享誉中国。唐开元年间，晋江城区于此发源，市区的青阳和梅岭两个街道，源自五店市的"青梅山"。无论岁月如何变迁，红砖古厝都犹如火炬一样，照亮游子回家的路。

　　五店市如今成为人们怀旧的好去处，也成了晋江的城市会客厅。游客若到晋江来，当地人一定会力推其到五店市去欣赏它的独特之美。五店市以古朴的红色，嵌刻在晋江高度发达的现代建筑中，成为一种对比强烈的诗意。

泉
州

Quanzhou

◎ 五店市传统街区入口的"五店市"三个字，由明代著名书法家张瑞图作品集字而成。（林玉堂 摄）
The three Chinese characters "五店市" at the entrance of Wudianshi traditional blocks are taken from the works of the famous calligrapher Zhang Ruitu in the Ming Dynasty. (Photo by Lin Yutang)

Wudianshi Traditional Blocks: a Millennium Landmark Carrying Home-sickness

Lisbon, the capital of Portugal, is the westernmost city on the European continent. It is the end of the European continent and the starting point of the Atlantic Ocean. For nostalgia, people from all over the world rushed to its embrace. In Lisbon, orange-red tile roofs covered buildings at different heights. Even new buildings are covered with the iconic orange-reddish roofs. Those buildings are under the sun, shining with nostalgic brilliance, which is intoxicating.

In Jinjiang, Quanzhou, there are also some red buildings, which are particularly dazzling among the high-rise buildings in the city. This is the Wudianshi traditional blocks. Like Lisbon, Wudianshi has the same coastal nostalgia and the same intersection of the old and the new. Wudianshi is a landmark in Jinjiang that has never faded for over a thousand years. The red-brick swallow-tailed ridge buildings in Wudianshi traditional blocks, in the golden sunset light, resemble a brilliant work that stretches for more than 1,300 years.

Wudianshi, starting from the five restaurants opened by the five Cai brothers one thousand years ago, is well-known in China as a market brand. During the Kaiyuan period of the Tang Dynasty, city area of Jinjiang originated here. The two streets of Qingyang and Meiling in the city originated from Qingmei Hill of Wudianshi. No matter how time changes, the old red-brick houses are like torches, lighting up the way home for wanderers.

Wudianshi has become a nostalgic place for people, and it has also become the living room of Jinjiang City. When visitors come to Jinjiang, the locals will definitely suggest them go to Wudianshi to appreciate its unique beauty. Wudianshi is carved in the highly developed modern buildings in Jinjiang in a simple red, which has formed a strong poetic contrast.

◎ 位于五店市内的蔡氏家庙。
（杨玉诚 摄）
The Cai Family Temple in Wudianshi.
(Photo by Yang Yucheng)

◎ 五店市传统街区汇集了多种特色建筑，被称为"晋江城市会客厅"。（田米 摄）
Wudianshi traditional blocks have a variety of distinctive architecture and are known as the
"Living Room of Jinjiang City". (Photo by Tian Mi)

　　在五店市，美轮美奂的红砖古厝，星罗棋布。独具闽南特色的古老建筑聚集于此，皇宫起，红砖筑造，小洋楼，中西合璧，更有我们称之为"燕尾脊"的闽南传统建筑艺术。五店市保留了一百多栋明、清、民国、近现代的闽南特色建筑。五店市的房子出砖入石，冬暖夏凉。红砖白石相辅相成，从明清以来，数百年的心血和汗水缓缓流淌，朴实无华的家风一路传唱。

　　一百多处历史建筑如老电影的画面，一帧一帧跃入眼帘，让人欣喜赞叹，为之沉醉。你看那石砌台基雄伟的蔡氏宗祠，状元、进士匾额数十方的庄氏家庙，以及石鼓庙、布政衙等历史建筑，以不同时代的建筑语言向人们展示它们各自的风采。砖镂、石雕、木刻、彩画等丰富色彩，描绘一个个仕宦商贾家族拼搏的生活历程，鲜活地告诉世人这里曾发生过的故事。

　　充满年代感的匾额在古老的墙上演绎着斑斓的故事。五店市的每一户门楣，你都要仔细看，那上面藏着一个个动人的故事；那些鎏金的工艺，是传统工匠们浓缩了中华文明千年的技艺；那些光宗耀祖的门庭，照亮子孙前行的方向。在五店市的门楣里，祖训传芳。逢年过节、初一十五，石埕门口，一群又一群的人进进出出，有海峡对岸的台湾同胞，有东南亚的血亲，他们带着志忑和虔诚，谒祖寻根，跪拜在"公妈厅（祠堂）"前。也许他们心里还在遥想着当年先辈们如何从这里出发，无惧风浪，历尽艰险，去往他乡打拼。

In Wudianshi, the beautiful red-brick ancient buildings are dotted around. Ancient buildings with unique characteristics of Southern Fujian gather here. The local buildings were built with red bricks; the small western-style buildings combined Chinese and Western styles. There are traditional Southern Fujian architecture art—the so-called swallow-ridges. Wudianshi retains Southern Fujian characteristic buildings from the Ming, Qing, Republic of China, and modern times. The houses in Wudianshi were made of bricks and stones, warm in winter and cool in summer. Red bricks and white stones complement each other. After the Ming and Qing Dynasties, hundreds of years of hard work and sweat flowed slowly, and the unpretentious family tradition sang along the way.

The more than one hundred historical buildings, like scenes of old movies, leap into the eyes frame by frame, making people happy, admiring, and intoxicated. Look at the majestic Cai's ancestral hall on the stone base, the Zhuang's family temple with dozens of Number One Scholar's and Advanced Scholar's plaques, as well as other historical buildings such as Shigu Temple and the Governor's Office. They show people in the architectural language of different eras the elegant demeanour. Brick carvings, stone carvings, wood carvings, colored paintings and other rich colors depict hard workings of each official or merchant family and vividly tell the stories that have happened here.

The plaques full of nostalgia interpret colorful and wonderful stories on the ancient walls. You need to look carefully at every door lintel in Wudianshi. There are touching stories hidden on them. Those gilded craftsmanship are the skills of traditional craftsmen who have condensed the Chinese civilization for hundreds of years. Those glorious dooryards illuminate the direction of the children and grandchildren. In the lintel of Wudianshi, ancestors' instructions were handed down from generations to generations. On the big holidays such as Lunar New Year, the first and 15th days of lunar months, a group of people come in and out at the gate of old buildings. Some of them are Taiwan compatriots on the other side of the Taiwan Straits, and some are close relatives from Southeast Asian countries. With perturbation and devotion, they visit their ancestral halls and search for their roots, kneeling in front of the ancestral halls. Perhaps they are still thinking about how their ancestors, without fear of winds and waves, set out from here and went to work in a foreign land by going through all the hardships and dangers.

◎ 五店市建筑中运用了多种传统建筑和装饰工艺。
（杨玉诚 摄）

A variety of traditional building and decorations techniques are applied in the architecture of Wudianshi. (Photo by Yang Yucheng)

在这片老街区里不仅藏着闽南老宅、闽南古物，还有闽南传统记忆。高甲戏、木偶戏、南音及其他富有闽南特色的节目在这里轮番上演，热闹却不喧嚣。一曲南音响起，迤逦的时光中，仿佛穿越了千年。

游人们不仅能在五店市体验传统闽南民俗，还能在这里品尝地道闽南美食。虽然，当年的五间店如今已不复存在，但深扎于此的美食根基依然不朽，几乎所有的闽南传统美食都可以在这里找到：拳头母、土笋冻、壶仔饭、菜粿、面线糊……五店市成了美食店的新集市。漫步其中，街上的铺子散发着生活的气息，咖啡馆、小吃店、书店、火锅店……应有尽有。

这里既可以承载情怀，亦可以承接流行，"小资"的可以在这里寻觅情调，怀旧的也可在这里吟咏。三五好友，徜徉于这一片迥立于高楼大厦间的天地中，细腻地品味别致的生活，俨然成为时尚。情侣们也喜欢到这里来约会，他们或牵手，或私语，或拍照留念，在怀旧中恋爱，在时尚里甜蜜，荷花池畔回响着他们的山盟海誓。

古色古香是五店市的特色，它给晋江这个现代化城市描上非同一般的色彩。红砖古厝，在摩天大楼和玻璃幕墙林立的城市，讲述着独具一格的历史沧桑。不可再生的历史信息和宝贵的文化资源在这里被完整保留，一砖一瓦，透过岁月的沉淀，告诉人们时间的意义。

有幸在这里感受历史的人们，总能找到属于自己的那一隅宁静，慢慢品尝，慢慢回味。在这里，你可以让咖啡静静地变凉，亦可以沉浸在南音的浅唱低吟中。

◎ 夜色里，五店市显得更加璀璨多姿。（苏炳秋 摄）
Wudianshi looks even brighter and more colorful at night. (Photo by Su Bingqiu)

◎ 游客们在五店市欣赏传统戏曲表演。（李雅真 供图）
Visitors enjoy a traditional opera performance in Wudianshi. (Courtesy of Li Yazhen)

In Wudianshi traditional blocks, there are not only the old houses and ancient relics of Southern Fujian, but also the traditional memories of Southern Fujian. Gaojia opera, puppet show, Nanyin and other special Southern Fujian shows are staged here in turn, lively but not hustle and bustle. When a song of Nanyin sounded, people meander through time, as if traveling through a thousand years.

Tourists can not only experience traditional Southern Fujian folk customs in Wudianshi, but also taste authentic Southern Fujian cuisine here. Although the original five restaurants no longer exist, the deep food roots here are still immortal. Almost all the traditional cuisines of Southern Fujian can be found here: fist-shape meat balls, sea worm jellies, pot rice, vegetable kueh, mee sua paste... Wudianshi has become a new market for gourmet restaurants. Strolling through the streets, one will see the shops there exude the breath of life with cafes, snack bars, bookstores, hot pot restaurants...and so on.

Wudianshi can carry feelings, trends and fashions. "Petite bourgeoisie" can find sentiment here, the nostalgic can also chant here. It has become a fashion for several friends to wander in this piece of world standing among high-rise buildings and delicately savor a unique life. Lovers also like to come here for dates. They hold hands, whisper, or take pictures, drowning in love in nostalgia, sweet in fashion, with their vows of love echoed by the lotus pond.

Antique flavor is the characteristic of Wudianshi, which gives Jinjiang an extraordinary color. The old red-brick houses, in a city lined with skyscrapers and glass curtain walls, tell a unique history of the vicissitudes of life. Non-reproducible historical information and precious cultural resources are completely preserved here. Every piece of brick and tile, through the precipitation of years, tells people the meaning of time.

Those who are fortunate enough to experience history here can always find their own quiet corner and taste it slowly. Here, you can let the coffee cool quietly, or immerse yourself in the shallow singing and whispering of Nanyin.

丁氏宗祠：见证回汉民族融合的回族祠堂

陈埭，是晋江的缩影。陈埭以其独有的人文环境和特色经济，成了福建省城镇的翘楚。陈埭丁氏一族，更是创造了诸多传奇。究其原因，阿拉伯商贾的经商基因，大抵是占了些先机的。

宋元时期来泉经商的，有很多阿拉伯人，他们吃苦耐劳，做生意的本事十分了得。他们被泉州的繁华和包容折服，择泉州而永居。

由于种种原因，这些阿拉伯商人的后裔后来又迁居陈埭。宋元时的阿拉伯人，是泉州陈埭丁氏的直接祖先。他们聚集在陈埭繁衍生息，入乡随俗，创造奇迹。

衣冠南渡时期中原文化南传，海洋大通道产生了海洋文化，阿拉伯商贾传入异域美食和阿拉伯文明，开创了回民在泉州的历史。陈埭是三种文化融合的历史产物，丁氏宗祠也具有这三种文化交融的显著特征。

长期的回汉联姻，很多汉族的祖制也早已融入陈埭丁氏一族的生活，由原来的"祀不设主，祭不列器"转变为"拜祖追宗，光宗耀祖"，因而才有了丁氏宗祠。丁氏宗祠里供奉着丁氏的列祖列宗，每年的正月十五和冬至，宗祠会举行盛大的祭祀，不少海内外的丁氏宗亲特地组团回乡参加。

◎ 丁氏宗祠是一座传统闽南风格建筑。（许兆恺 摄）
The Ding's Ancestral Hall is a traditional Minnan-style building. (Photo by Xu Zhaokai)

Ding's Ancestral Hall: an Ancestral Hall of Hui People Witnessing the Integration of Hui and Han Ethnic Groups

Chendai is the epitome of Jinjiang. Chendai has become a leading town in Fujian Province with its unique humanistic environment and characteristic economy. The Ding clan in Chendai has created many legends. The reason is that the business genes of Arab merchants have probably taken advantage of some opportunities.

During the Song and Yuan Dynasties, many Arabs came to do business in Quanzhou. Deeply impressed by the prosperity and toleration of the city, they chose Quanzhou as their permanent residence.

For various reasons, the descendants of these Arab merchants later moved to Chendai. The Arabs in the Song and Yuan Dynasties were the direct ancestors of the Ding clan in Chendai, Quanzhou. They gathered in Chendai, flourished, followed the local customs, and created miracles.

The Central Plains culture spread to the south as the families of elite government officials moved to southern provinces in the Jin Dynasty. The ocean trade corridor produced marine culture. Arabian merchants introduced exotic cuisine and Arab civilization, creating the history of the Muslims in Quanzhou. Chendai is a historical product of the integration of these three cultures, and Ding's Ancestral Hall also has the distinctive feature of them.

In the long-term marriage between the Hui and Han, the ancestral system of many Han people has long been integrated into the life of the Ding clan in Chendai. From the original "worship without the tablets of the ancestors, sacrifice without vessels" to "worshipping the ancestors and seeking roots of the ancestors, glorifying the ancestors". Thus the Ding's Ancestral Hall, where the ancestors of the Ding clan are enshrined. Every year on the fifteenth day of the first lunar month and the winter solstice, the ancestral hall will hold grand sacrifices attended by many Ding clansmen from home and abroad in groups.

◎ 丁氏宗祠见证了几百年回汉融合的过程。（施清凉 摄）
The Ding's Ancestral Hall has witnessed the fusion of Hui and Han ethnic groups in the past centuries. (Photo by Shi Qingliang)

距今已有600多年历史的丁氏宗祠，给人的第一印象是传统的闽南风格建筑——红砖厝、燕尾脊。但走进祠堂，墙面上那些阿拉伯文和隔壁清真寺的诵经声会提醒你，这里延续着一段海丝的阿拉伯情缘。这座位于陈埭岸兜村的陈埭丁氏宗祠，被誉为泉州回族历史教科书。作为福建省历史最悠久、规模最宏大、保存最完整的回族祠堂，丁氏宗祠享有"福建省少数民族第一馆"的美名。丁氏宗祠还被开辟为"回民史陈列馆"。1992年，联合国教科文组织考察团专程到此参观，中外友谊长青的史迹，令考察团深受感动。

陈埭丁氏宗祠建筑规模宏大，形式特别。建筑师将伊斯兰教教堂与泉州古代祠堂建筑形式巧妙结合，成为别具一格的建筑艺术。

从高处看去，丁氏宗祠平面呈十分工整的"回"字形。走进丁氏宗祠，可以看到"陈埭万人丁"的牌匾，在牌匾下面有一只"吉祥鸟"。这只吉祥鸟有孔雀的头、凤凰的尾巴、鸽子的身子，也叫不死鸟，在阿拉伯文化中是吉祥的象征。《古兰经》经文组成的木雕，分布在吉祥鸟的两旁。大殿左右的石刻上，也是阿拉伯文的《古兰经》经文。

◎ 祠堂之中，伊斯兰文化与中华文化相结合的巧思随处可见。（成冬冬 摄）
In the ancestral hall, the ingenuity of the combination of Islamic culture and Chinese culture can
be seen everywhere. (Photo by Cheng Dongdong)

Ding's Ancestral Hall, with a history of more than 600 years, gives people the first impression of traditional Southern Fujian style buildings—red-brick houses and swallow-tailed ridges. But walking into the ancestral hall, the Arabic scripts on the wall and the chanting of the mosque next door will remind you that there is a continuation of the Arabian affection from the Maritime Silk Road. Located in Chendai's Andou Village, the Ding's Ancestral Hall is considered a history textbook of the Hui people in Quanzhou. As the Hui ancestral hall with the longest history, the largest scale and the most complete preservation in Fujian Province, the Ding's Ancestral Hall enjoys the reputation of The First Hall of Ethnic Minorities in Fujian. The Ding's Ancestral Hall has also been used as Hui People's History Exhibition Hall. A UNESCO mission visited here in 1992, and they were deeply moved by the historical sites of everlasting friendship between China and foreign countries.

The Ding's ancestral hall in Chendai is large in scale and special in form. The architect cleverly combined the Islamic mosques and the ancient ancestral halls in Quanzhou into a unique architectural art.

Seen from a bird's eye view, the hall is in a neat homocentric "回" shape. Walking into the hall, you can see the plaque of "A Flourishing Family in Chendai", under which you can see a "lucky bird". This auspicious bird has the head of a peacock, the tail of a phoenix and the body of a dove, and is also called the immortal bird, a symbol of good luck in Arabic culture. The wood carvings composed of the verses of the Quran are distributed on both sides of the auspicious bird. The stone inscriptions on both sides of the main hall are also the verses of the Quran in Arabic.

◎ 丁氏宗祠内景。（施清凉 摄）
The inside view of the Ding's Ancestral Hall. (Photo by Shi Qingliang)

"三开间两护厝"的形式，是这座祠堂主要的建筑格局。正中为三开间，大门设在正中，在同一水平线上设左右两个边门。这种形式，也叫"三千门"。在泉州，古老的祠堂对这一格式情有独钟。正厅位于宗祠正中，先于地面建一座高约二尺的平台，再在平台上建造正厅。围绕正厅，四周廊庑建筑互相连接。中间的正厅即"回"字中的内"口"，四周廊庑即"回"字的外"口"。祠堂外"口"宽达21米，深达36米，总占地面积为756平方米。

　　祠堂的屋顶，采用的是抬梁柱歇山顶砖石木结构，屋顶翘脊，铺瓦盖筒、吊筒、锁筒、斗拱精致华美，花卉、瑞兽、祥云、宝瓶等装饰亦壮观别致，粉金油漆，盛大辉煌。泉州人把这种建筑称为"皇宫式"。

　　陈埭丁氏一族经商能力出众，在仕途上也积极进取，这里是明清时期14位进士、25位举人的故乡。这个家族用祠堂的匾额记载了辉煌和荣耀——"六试七联捷，四闱十登科""兄弟科第""父子进士""三世进士"……

丁拱辰画像

◎ 丁拱辰是丁氏一族的杰出人物，他从一个成功的商人转型为爱国科学家。他自制了象限仪，改造了大炮，其著作《演炮图说》《演炮图说辑要》对当时科技的进步做出重大贡献。他和魏源、林则徐一起被称为"放眼看世界的人"。作为丁拱辰的家庙，丁氏宗祠还保留有丁拱辰的许多遗物。（成冬冬 供图）
Ding Gongchen was an outstanding figure of the Ding clan, who transformed from a successful businessman to a patriotic scientist. He made his own quadrant instrument, modified cannons, and made significant contributions to the advancement of science and technology at the time with his books *Illustration of Cannon Making* and *Essence of Illustration of Cannon Making*. Similar to Wei Yuan and Lin Zexu, he is known as one of "the men who opened minds to reach the world". As the family temple of Ding Gongchen, the Ding's Ancestral Hall still keeps many relics of him. (Courtesy of Cheng Dongdong)

◎ 陈埭丁氏《祖教说》。（成冬冬 摄）

Zujiaoshuo in the genealogy tree of the Ding clan in Chendai. (Photo by Cheng Dongdong)

The form of three *chien* and two guard houses is the main architectural pattern of the ancestral hall. In the middle are three *chien* wide, and the main gate is located in the middle, in the same horizontal line set about two side doors. This form is also called "Sanqian doors". In Quanzhou, ancient ancestral halls have a special preference for this format. The main hall of the ancestral hall is located in the middle. A platform about two feet high was built on the ground first, on which the main hall was built. Around the main hall, the corridors are connected to each other. The main hall in the middle is the inner "mouth (口)" in the homocentric word "回", and the surrounding corridor is the outer "mouth". The ancestral hall is 21 meters wide and 36 meters deep, covering an area of 756 square meters.

The roof of the hall adopted the brick and wood post-and-lintel gable and hip structure. The roof is warped and it is covered by tiles and tubes, with exquisite and gorgeous hanging tubes, locking tubes and brackets. The decorations of flowers, auspicious animals, propitious clouds and precious vases are also magnificent and unique. Quanzhou people call this kind of architecture "palace style".

The Ding clan in Chendai has outstanding business talent and is also active in official career. It is the hometown of 14 advanced scholars and 25 *juren* (successful candidates in the imperial examinations at the provincial level) in the Ming and Qing Dynasties. The clan recorded its glorious history on the plaques of their ancestral hall—"Six Tests and Seven Consecutive Victories, Four Tests and Ten Winners", "Father-and-son Advanced Scholars" and "Three Consecutive Generations of Advanced Scholars"...

永宁——古厝里的时光故事

在泉州石狮，有一个小城上过美国《国家地理》杂志，它的名字叫永宁，寓意"永葆安宁"。版图状若大鳌的永宁小城，还有一个别名叫"鳌城"。在永宁城隍庙里，还可看到清代那幅状若鳌鱼的永宁地图。

永宁在历史上以卫城为世人所知，与北方的天津卫、威海卫齐名。随着时代的变迁，它特殊的地理位置逐渐为世人所淡忘。如今，人们对其念念不忘的是古城里那些风情各异的番仔楼和古朴的老街。

番仔楼是中西合璧的建筑精灵，它们突破了传统的闽南建筑风格，引入了西洋和南洋的石雕、砖雕、彩画、拼砖、灰塑等，使得整栋建筑异域色彩浓厚，再加上番仔楼主人具有的传奇色彩，让建筑本身深藏气质，堪称闽南建筑的瑰宝。

永宁现保存有一百多座番仔楼，每一栋楼都隐藏着一段或感人或励志或发人深省的故事。当现在的女人还在为男人不在房产证上加自己的名字而郁郁寡欢时，永宁有位老华侨，却早已把爱人的名字嵌在了番仔楼里，这栋番仔楼叫"熙宝楼"。

或许是爱意拳拳，岁月眷念，相比其他番仔楼，熙宝楼保存更为完好。熙宝楼是以楼主人夫妻俩的名字命名。二楼阳台上有一副楹联一直见证他俩的爱情，上面写着"焕若宝珠光祖德，熙如珍品霭鸿禧"。这是一副典型的闽南嵌名联，将"焕熙"与"宝珍"二人的名字嵌于联中。一栋有着动人爱情故事的番仔楼总是让人格外温暖。

◎ 永宁卫曾是明代三大卫城之一。（许兆恺 摄）

Yongning Garrison was one of the three garrison towns in the Ming Dynasty. (Photo by Xu Zhaokai)

◎ 见证着楼主人伉俪情深的熙宝楼保存
完好。（李荣鑫 摄）
Xibao Building that witnessed its owners'
love is well preserved. (Photo by Li Rongxin)

Yongning: the Story of Time in Ancient Houses

In Shishi, Quanzhou, there is a small town that has been featured in the US magazine *National Geographic*. Its name is Yongning, which means "keeping peace forever". The small town of Yongning, shaped like a giant legendary turtle, also has an alias called Aocheng (Turtle Town). In Yongning Town God's Temple, you can still see the Qing-Dynasty map of Yongning resembling a giant turtle.

Yongning is known to the world as a garrison town in history, and it is as famous as Tianjin Garrison and Weihai Garrison in the north. With time passed, its special geographical location is gradually forgotten by the world. Nowadays, what people never forget about it is huan-a-lau (Chinese-Western style buildings in Southern Fujian) with different styles and the old streets in the ancient town.

Huan-a-lau is a combination of Chinese and Western architectural works. Breaking through the traditional Southern Fujian architectural style, they introduced Western and Southeast stone carvings, brick carvings, color paintings, brick tiles, gray plastics, etc., making the entire building rich in exotic colors. In addition, the legendary character of the owner of huan-a-lau makes the building itself a treasure of Southern Fujian.

There are more than 100 huan-a-laus in Yongning, and each building hides a touching, inspirational or thought-provoking story. When the women today are still gloomy about men not adding their names on the real estate certificates, there is an old overseas Chinese in Yongning who had already embedded his lover's name in his huan-a-lau, which is called Xibao Building.

Perhaps because of the love, compared with other huan-a-laus, Xibao Building is well-preserved. It is named after the owner of the building and his wife. There is a pair of couplets on the balcony on the second floor that has always witnessed their love. This is a pair of typical Southern Fujian inlaid-name couplets, with the names of Huanxi and Baozhen embedded. A huan-a-lau with a touching love story always makes people extraordinarily warm.

而杨家大楼的主人杨邦俊为我们讲述的则是励志创业故事。杨邦俊为了生计跟随叔伯兄弟"下南洋"讨生活，从一个普通的码头工人做起，在小有所成后，又领着弟兄们在外共同打拼，历经数年，终于能够返乡"起大厝"。这座大厝，占地六十多平方米，称得上是泉州最人的番仔楼，当地人称之为"九十九间"，可见其规模之大。

颍川衍派，是陈家的番仔楼；济阳楼，是蔡氏家族所有；日茂古大厝是鹿港首富林振嵩的……董云阁故居是纯西式的番仔楼；宁东楼是有战争色彩的洋楼……观潮楼、群敬楼、迎薰楼，这些响当当的番仔楼距今已有百年的历史。那些古杉木、花岗岩、红砖、绿栏的巧妙组合，让即使陈旧的建筑都有清新和活泼的感觉。设计师们独具匠心地把中西建筑绝妙糅合，惊艳了时光。

按照闽南传统民居木结构进行技艺性营建，是永宁番仔楼的一大类型。此类番仔楼采用上等木材为建筑原料，利用大木作作为受力结构，凸显闽南古建筑风格。这些番仔楼雕梁画栋、窗棂镂花刻鸟，给人强烈的立体美感，艺术之精湛，手法之绝妙，让人不得不佩服匠人的智慧。另一类则是采用钢筋混凝土所建，其建筑材料几乎都是进口的，如地面花砖、洋灰、钢筋等。

这些番仔楼就像一位位老人，伴随着豪宅的历史变幻，也阅尽了人世沧桑。永宁卫城曾经是热血浇灌的地方，如今成了怀旧的好去处。从一个海防要塞，到一个旅游胜地，其间到底经历了什么？让我们回到"永宁卫"最开始的那段历史。

◎ 杨家大楼还有另一个名字叫"六也亭"，名字取自四书之一《中庸》的"天地之道：博也，厚也，高也，明也，悠也，久也"，合为"六也"。（陈英杰 摄）
Yang Family Building is also called Liu Ye (Six Elements) Pavilion, which is taken from one of the four Confucian classics *The Doctrine of the Mean*: "The way of Heaven and Earth is large and substantial, high and brilliant, far-reaching and long-enduring". Thus the name Liu Ye. (Photo by Chen Yingjie)

The story of Yang Bangjun, the owner of Yang Family Building, is an inspiring entrepreneurial one. In order to make a living, Yang Bangjun followed his uncle and his brothers to "go down to Nanyang (Southeast Asia)" to make a living. He started as an ordinary docker. After making some achievements, he led the buddies to work together in other places. After several years, he was finally able to return to his hometown to build a large house. This large house, covering an area of more than 6,000 square meters, can be called the largest huan-a-lau in Quanzhou. The locals call it Ninety-nine-room Houses, which reflects its huge scale.

Chen family huan-a-lau is represented by the plaque *Yingchuan Yanpai*, Jiyang Building is owned by the Cai family; Rimao Ancient House belongs to Lin Zhensong, the richest man in Lukang... The former residence of Dong Yunge is a pure Western-style huan-a-lau; Ningdong Building is a Western-style building connected with warfare... Guanchao Building, Qunjing Building, Yingxun Building, these famous huan-a-laus have a history of one hundred years. The clever combination of ancient cedar, granite, red bricks and green fences gives even old buildings a fresh and lively feeling. The designers are unique in their ingenuity and skillfully combine Chinese and Western architecture to amaze the time.

It is one of the major types of huan-a-lau in Yongning to carry out technical construction in accordance with the wooden structure of the traditional dwellings in Southern Fujian. This type of huan-a-laus use high-quality wood as the construction material, and use large wood as the force-bearing structure, highlighting the ancient architectural style of Southern Fujian. These huan-a-laus have carved beams and painted buildings, and the window lattices are carved with flowers and birds, impressing people with a strong three-dimensional beauty. The exquisite art and superb technique make people admire the wisdom of the craftsmen. The other type of huan-a-laus were built with reinforced concrete. Almost all of their building materials, such as floor tiles, cement, and steel bars, were imported.

◎ 散落在永宁各处的番仔楼见证了当地侨胞下南洋打拼有成后回乡置业的历史。
（五柳院青年旅舍 供图）
Scattered throughout Yongning, these huan-a-laus witness the history of local expatriates who returned to their hometowns after a successful career in Nanyang. (Courtesy of Wuliuyuan Youth Hostel)

Like old men, these huan-a-laus have experienced the vicissitudes of life along with the historical changes of the mansions. Yongning Garrison was once a place where hot blood was shed, and now it has become a good place for nostalgia. From a coastal garrison to a tourist attraction, what did it experience in the course of history? Let us return to the beginning of Yongning Garrison.

永宁卫设于明朝洪武年间，当时还有泉州卫，这两个卫所为朝廷共同抵御福建沿海的倭寇。建筑于沿海高地上的海防工程，被命名为卫城，它的用途是防御外来入侵。作为卫城的永宁，其将士来自五湖四海，他们落户于此，将近100个姓氏也留了下来。

　　永宁老街横贯卫城东西两端，基于其悠久的历史、特有的建筑风貌、多姿多彩的商号文化，以及沿山势逐步升高的特点，被评为中国历史文化名街。

　　得天独厚的地理位置，让永宁成了旧时闽南与上海及南洋交通的重要通道，常有千吨巨轮于此停泊。许多华侨出洋也从此地出发，有的直抵菲律宾，有的通过我国香港转至越南、缅甸、新加坡、泰国等地。

　　在外漂泊多年的侨胞，通常选择建造一栋番仔楼来表达对家乡的眷念。太阳在哪一个地方都会光辉普照，但是在很多人的心里，总会有一个地方特别温暖，这个地方被称为家乡；也许你会一时贪恋外面的花花世界，也许你会暂时被一个地方牵绊住，但你的心始终都会为一个地方留下位置，这个地方我们把它叫作"故乡"。

◎ 有着600多年历史的永宁城隍庙影响远及我国台湾和东南亚各国。（茅罗平 摄）
With a history of over 600 years, the influence of Yongning Town God's Temple has reached as far as Taiwan at home and Southeast Asia. (Photo by Mao Luoping)

Yongning Garrison was established in the Hongwu period of the Ming Dynasty, and Quanzhou Garrison was also established at that time. These two garrisons were set up by the imperial court to resist Japanese pirates along the coast of Fujian. The coastal defense project built on the coastal highlands was named Weicheng(garrisons), the purpose of which was to defend against foreign invasions. As a garrison, the military officials and soldiers in Yongning were from all over the country. They settled here with nearly 100 surnames remained.

Yongning Old Street traverses the east and west ends of the town. Based on its long history, unique architectural style, colorful business culture, and the characteristics of gradually rising along the mountain, it has been rated as a famous historical and cultural street in China.

The unique geographical location made Yongning an important transportation channel between Southern Fujian, Shanghai and Southeast Asia in the old days. 1,000-ton ships often parked here. Many overseas Chinese also set off from here. Some went straight to the Philippines, and some went to Vietnam, Myanmar, Singapore, Thailand and other places through Hong Kong.

The overseas Chinese who have been wandering for many years usually choose to build a huan-a-lau to express their nostalgia for their hometown. The sun shines everywhere, but in many people's hearts, there will always be a place that is particularly warm. We call this place our hometown. Maybe you will be greedy for the prosperity of the outside world for a while, and maybe you will be temporarily entangled by a place, but your heart will always leave a space for a place, that is, your hometown.

◎ 狭长的永宁老街曾经遍布商号，成为清代大陆对台贸易的重要窗口。（樊鑫 摄）
The long and narrow Yongning old street was once dotted with merchant houses and an important window for the mainland's trade with Taiwan during the Qing Dynasty. (Photo by Fan Xin)

蟳埔：海洋文化的民俗传承

一个女人的一生应该怎么度过呢？即使人类文明已经走到今天，这样的问题依然不会有标准答案。但是，在古城泉州，有一群女子，以顾盼生姿的外在形象，以坚若蚵壳的品性，道出了女子行走于世的独特版本。

宋元时期的泉州，造就中世纪海丝文明的高峰。其造船技术在当时的世界独领风骚；商贸交易以喷薄的张力，让海丝航线成了开阔之地。

蟳埔港是古刺桐港的一部分。数百年前的蟳埔港，迎来送往的都是商贾和他们的商船。今天的人们站在岸边，看着平静的海面，依然会生出一股豪情。如雷贯耳的"东方第一大港"、气象万千的"涨海声中万国商"仿佛就在眼前。

在如此国际化背景下成长起来的女子，是千年海交历史余温的产物，是时代进步超前的缩影。她们似乎雌雄同体，她们似乎无所不能，她们独立，她们志得意满，她们把盛世景象，把对万物的爱，都融入奔腾不息的海洋。

千百年前的泉州大地，吸引外来文化，保留自身文化。古越文化、中原文化、海洋文化，在古泉州城交汇融合，远道而来的海洋文化在蟳埔女子身上独显魅力。她们日出而作，日落而息。她们在外捕鱼劳作，贩卖海鲜，她们在内教养子女，侍奉公婆。她们把五千年来中华民族的传统美德集于一身，她们成了福建最著名的女性群体之一。

◎ 穿着独特服饰、头戴花围的蟳埔村老幼穿行在两旁皆是蚵壳厝的小巷。（王福平 摄）
Old and young people from Xunpu Village, dressed in distinctive costumes and wearing flowery scarves, walk through the alleys lined with oyster-shell houses. (Photo by Wang Fuping)

Xunpu: the Folk Inheritance of Marine Culture

How should a woman's life be spent? Even though human civilization has come to this day, there are still no standard answers to questions like this. However, in the ancient city of Quanzhou, there is a group of women who, with their pretty appearance and strong character as firm as oyster shells, display a unique version of women's life to the world.

Quanzhou in the Song and Yuan Dynasties brought up the peak of maritime civilization in the Middle Ages. Its shipbuilding technology was dominating the world at the time. With commerce and trade developing at top speed, the Maritime Silk Road became an open space.

Xunpu Port is part of the ancient Zayton Port. Hundreds years ago, Xunpu Port welcomed and sent off merchants and their ships. Standing on the shore and looking at the calm sea today, people will still feel a sense of pride. The famous scenes of "the First Port of the East" and the "Emporium of the World in the Sound of the Rising Sea" seem to be right in front of us.

◎ 在中外文化交融之地成长起来的蟳埔女自有一番迥异于其他地方女子的风采。（刘宝生 摄）

Growing up in a place where Chinese and foreign cultures meet, the women of Xunpu have a distinctive style that sets them apart from women of other areas. (Photo by Liu Baosheng)

The women who grew up in such an international background are the products of a-thousand-year history of maritime trade and the epitome of the advancement of the times. Seemingly hermaphrodite and omnipotent, they are independent and full of ambition. They integrate the scene of the prosperous world and their love for all things into the endless stream of sea.

Hundreds of years ago, Quanzhou attracted foreign cultures and preserved its own culture. The ancient Yue culture, the Central Plains culture, and the Marine culture merged in the ancient city of Quanzhou. The Marine culture from afar is represented by the women from Xunpu. They begin to work at sunrise and rest at sunset. They fish, work and sell seafood out of home. They raise their children and take care of in-laws at home. Integrating the traditional virtues of the Chinese nation for five thousand years, they have become one of the most famous female groups in Fujian.

距泉州市区约10千米的蟳埔村子就是一个大海鲜市场，摆摊的多数为女子。她们头戴鲜花，着彩色上衣，黑色裤子，招揽着生意，闲聊着家常。在海蛎剥壳处，亦是清一色的蟳埔阿姨，她们充满活力，灵巧能干。能让人感觉到进入现代社会的，是顺济宫前随着电了舞曲跳着广场舞的衣着鲜艳的女子们。

在海边劳作的矫健女子们，却又极度爱美，她们与花为伴，终日离不开花。蟳埔女每日鲜活地将花园顶在头上，这样的习俗，源自南宋，来自阿拉伯。数百年前，她们头顶上的那些花，据说出自一个阿拉伯商人的私人花园，那个商人叫蒲寿庚，是泉州的提举市舶司。当年富甲一方的蒲寿庚拥有私家别墅，别墅还有个好听的名字叫"云麓花园"。蒲家的花园里有许多从异域移植而来的花卉，惹得附近爱美的女子青眼有加。这个纵横商场的香料大亨，慷慨地把花赠予周边的女子，一朵花，一个祝福。

对于美和祝福，人都是贪心的，女人们巴不得把整个花园都戴在头上。素馨花、含笑花、粗糠花以及应季的小朵鲜花都被扎成整齐的花环，簪在头上。头发上簪着花围，再用筷子固定，成了蟳埔女子特有的爱美仪式。其骨笄头饰是古代"骨针安发"遗风，乃是全国独有的"活化石"。头上的花围和身上鲜艳的大裾衫、宽脚裤交相辉映，形成了独特的风情。

◎ 等待亲人归航的蟳埔女。（苏德辉 摄）
The Xunpu women waiting for their loved ones. (Photo by Su Dehui)

Xunpu Village, 10 km away from the downtown area of Quanzhou, is a big seafood market itself. And most of the stall owners are women. Wearing fresh flowers, colorful shirts, and black pants, they peddle their wares and make small talks. At the sea oyster shelling places, there are aunts without exception, full of vitality, dexterity and ability. What makes people feel that they have entered modern society are the brightly colored women dancing "square dance" to the electronic dance music in front of Shunji Palace.

Working by the sea, strong and vigorous Xunpu women love beauty. They are accompanied by flowers and cannot live without them. Xunpu women put the garden on their heads vividly every day. This custom originated from the Southern Song Dynasty and also from Arabia. The flowers on their heads were said to come from the private garden of an Arab businessman hundreds of years ago. The businessman was named Pu Shougeng, who was the superintendent of Quanzhou Maritime Trade Office. As one of the wealthiest merchants at that time, Pu Shougeng owned a private villa with a nice name Yunlu Garden. There were many flowers transplanted from abroad in this garden, which was admired by the beauty-loving women in the neighborhood. The spice magnate generously gave flowers to women living nearby, a flower being a blessing.

People are greedy for beauty and blessings, and women are eager to wear the entire garden on their heads. Frangipanis, magnolia, chaff flowers and small flowers of the season are all tied into a neat wreath with hairpins on the head. The hairpin is surrounded by flowers, and then fixed with cross sticks, which has become a unique beauty ritual for Xunpu women. The headgear of bones is a relic of the ancient "fixing hair by bone needles", and considered a unique "living fossil" in the country. The flower circle on the head, the big bright shirt and wide-legged pants complement each other, forming a unique style.

◎ 蟳埔女们的日常。（杨建峰 摄）

The daily life portrait of Xunpu women.

(Photo by Yang Jianfeng)

◎ 蟳埔女们盛装打扮参加一年一度的"天香巡境"活动。（许师伟 摄）
Girls and women in Xunpu are dressed up for the annual folklore activity "Tianxiang Xunjing (Mazu Procession)". (Photo by Xu Shiwei)

　　这样的女子，常年在与海浪的搏击中，也被赋予了女神的力量。这位女神，是妈祖娘娘。蟳埔女子不依赖男人，她们信仰同是女性的妈祖林默娘。每年的农历正月廿九日，是蟳埔渔村一年一度大型民俗活动"天香巡境"的日子。女孩和妇女们盛装打扮，头上除了戴着插满鲜花的花围外，已婚女性还把出嫁时陪嫁的金梳、金花、金剑、金钗等金头饰插在花围中。

　　一个又一个的夜晚，古城泉州的蟳埔村，除了有一汪明月倾泻，抑或是满天星辰高挂，还有可能是蟳埔女子一生中最特别的时候。她们的婚礼形式，不同于一般婚礼的大张旗鼓，吹吹打打。蟳埔女子的婚礼是悄无声息的，人们把它称为"夜婚"。这种母系社会流传下来的走婚形式，在这个风情小渔村，至今尚存。在蟳埔，当地的新娘出嫁是在新婚之日的凌晨两到三点，由媒婆将其带到婆家。入门时，婆家须将灯火熄灭，新婚丈夫及婆家的亲朋好友都须回避，新娘才可入门。当日，新娘拜见公婆，向亲人敬茶，行相见之礼，宴请亲戚好友之后，次日凌晨时分，新娘自行悄悄返回娘家，不可在夫家过夜。

Such women are endowed with the power of a goddess in the fight against the waves all the year round. This goddess is Mazu, the sea Goddess. Xunpu women do not depend on men, but they believe in Mazu, who is also a woman. The 29th day of the first lunar month is the day of the annual large-scale folklore activity "Tianxiang Xunjing" in Xunpu Village. Girls and women are dressed up. In addition to wearing wreaths full of flowers on their heads, married women also put golden combs, golden flowers, golden swords, golden hairpins and other golden headpieces in the wreaths.

One night after another, in the ancient city of Quanzhou's Xunpu Village, in addition to bright moonlight pouring down, or the sky full of stars, it may also be the most special time in the life of a local woman—her wedding ceremony. Their wedding ceremony is different from the fanfare of common weddings. The wedding of Xunpu women is silent, and people call it a "night marriage". This kind of walking marriage, which was passed down from matrilineal society, still exists in this small fishing village. In Xunpu, a local bride gets married at two to three o'clock in the morning on the wedding day, and the matchmaker takes her to her husband's house. When entering the house, the in-laws need to put out the lights, and the newlywed husband and the in-laws' friends and relatives need to stay away before the bride can enter. On that day, the bride visits her in-laws, offers tea to the relatives, meets and greets rituals to each other, and treats her relatives and friends. In the early hours of the next morning, the bride quietly returns to her natal home by herself, and is not allowed to spend the night at her husband's home.

◎ 蟳埔村的蚵壳厝和艳丽多姿的簪花围吸引了众多海外游客。（陈英杰 摄）
The oyster-shell houses and the colorful Zanhuawei (Garden on the Head) Headgear in Xunpu attract many overseas visitors. (Photo by Chen Yingjie)

蟳埔村惊动时光的风情除了蟳埔女每日将花园顶在头上，还有遗存的蚵壳厝为我们呈现历史的容颜。经考证，这些古老蚵壳厝的蚵壳并非来自本地，而是从非洲东海岸随着海上丝绸之路的商船返航而来。这些舶来品体积更大，壳也更坚硬，与本地蚝的区别一眼就能看出来。那么它们是如何不远万里而来，成为蟳埔村的一道风景的呢？

蟳埔港位于晋江入海口北岸，是古刺桐港的一部分，也是泉州海上丝绸之路起点的重要港口。当时，从蟳埔起航的商船满载丝绸、瓷器和香料，航行到达南洋，经印度洋到达非洲。返航的时候，船舱已空，可是空船会导致船体重心不稳，对航行不利，船员们就将散落在海边的蚵壳装在船上压舱，返航后便将蚵壳卸在蟳埔海边。勤劳智慧的蟳埔人物尽其用，把这些曾经有生命存在的蚵壳拌海泥建成一座座蚵壳厝。外墙上错落有致地镶嵌着大蚝壳，层层叠叠，分布均匀，呈鱼鳞状；中空的蚝壳垒砌成墙面，墙里隔绝空气多，冬暖夏凉，海风和暴雨也拿它没有办法，所谓千年砖、万年蚵。富有传奇色彩的蚵壳厝，就这样简单直接地把海洋生物的沧海桑田，凝固成建筑奇观。

The time-disturbing charm of Xunpu Village, apart from the fact that Xunpu women put the garden on their heads every day, also includes the remnant oyster-shell houses that present us with the appearance of history. After research, people know that the oyster shells of these ancient houses did not come from the local area, but from the east coast of Africa with merchant ships on the Maritime Silk Road. These imported products are larger in size and have harder shells. Their difference from the local oysters can be seen at a glance. So how did they come from a long distance and become a scene in Xunpu Village?

Xunpu Port is located on the north bank of Jinjiang Estuary. It is a part of the ancient Zayton Port and one of the key ports at the starting point of the Maritime Silk Road in Quanzhou. At that time, merchant ships starting from Xunpu were loaded with silk, porcelain and spices. They sailed to Southeast Asia and then to Africa via the Indian Ocean. When the ships returned, they were almost empty. And the emptiness of ships would lead to unstable center of gravity, which is not good for navigation. The crew then ballasted the oyster shells scattered on the seashore, and unloaded the oyster shells on the shore of Xunpu after returning home. The industrious and intelligent Xunpu people made the best use of the shells and built oyster-shell houses with these shells and sea mud. The outer wall was inlaid with large oyster shells, layered on top of each other, evenly distributed, in the shape of fish scales; hollow oyster shells were built into the walls, making them insulated from air. Such houses are warm in winter and cool in summer. The sea wind and rainstorm also can not do anything to the houses. That is why there is the saying of "a millennium of bricks, ten thousand years of oysters". The legendary oyster-shell houses simply and directly solidified the vicissitudes of marine life into an architectural wonder.

◎ 蟳埔女的发髻活像一座春意盎然的小花园。（张加陞 摄）
The buns of the hair of Xunpu women are like a small garden in spring. (Photo by Zhang Jiabi)

朱熹父子：二朱过化

集理学大成者的朱熹，是继孔子后的又一位伟大的思想家、教育家、文学家。著名的历史学家蔡尚思先生曾这样说过："东周出孔丘，南宋有朱熹，中国古文化，泰山与武夷。"

朱熹，字元晦，号晦庵，晚称晦翁，谥文，世称朱文公。他诞生于南剑州尤溪（今福建三明市尤溪县）。福建人是幸运的，因为有了朱熹，才有了名扬天下的"闽学"。泉州人是自豪的，因为泉州的开元寺天王殿至今还悬挂着朱熹的题联"此地古称佛国，满街都是圣人"。

朱熹父子和泉州结下的不解之缘可追溯到南宋绍兴初年，朱熹的父亲朱松经抚谕东南的胡世将保举，任石井（今晋江市安海镇）镇监。朱松为官期间，除了在政务上颇有建树，对于教育也不曾松懈。在工余期间，他时常召集士子，于官署旁"鳌头精舍"教习"义理之学"，致后人有"谁是当年辟草莱，层轩高栋傍崔嵬"之思。

二十年后，朱熹在泉州同安县任主簿，常往来于相距百余里的泉州、同安之间，也常驻足安海，数度拜访父亲朱松的遗迹。朱熹"见其老幼义理详悉，遂与论说"，所到之处，理学讨论氛围浓厚，在朱熹的带动下，士人学子更加发奋学习。"二朱过化"之后的几十年间，安海就有几十人考中进士。

◎ 朱熹画像。（缘缘 供图）

The portrait of Zhu Xi. (Courtesy of Yuanyuan)

Zhu Xi and His Father: Civilization Brought by the Two Generations of Zhu

Zhu Xi, a master of Neo-Confucianism, is another great thinker, educator, and writer after Confucius. The famous historian Mr. Cai Shangsi once said: "In the history of ancient Chinese culture, Confucius of the Eastern Zhou Dynasty and Zhu Xi of the Southern Song Dynasty are like Mount Tai and Mount Wuyi."

Zhu Xi, with the courtesy name Yuanhui, the pseudonym Hui'an, Huiweng at his old age, and the posthumous title Wen, is called Zhu Wengong by the later generations. He was born in Youxi, Nanjian Prefecture (now Youxi County, Sanming City, Fujian Province). Fujianese are lucky. Because of Zhu Xi, they boast the Min School that is famous in the world. The people of Quanzhou are proud, because the Hall of Heavenly Kings in Kaiyuan Temple in Quanzhou still hangs Zhu Xi's inscription: "This place was called the Kingdom of Buddhism in ancient times, and the streets are full of saints."

◎ 泉州开元寺朱熹所题对联。（成冬冬 摄）

The couplet inscribed by Zhu Xi in Kaiyuan Temple, Quanzhou. (Photo by Cheng Dongdong)

The indissoluble bond between Zhu Xi and Quanzhou can be traced back to the beginning of Shaoxing period (1131-1162) in the Southern Song Dynasty. Zhu Xi's father Zhu Song, recommended by a main official in Southeast China Hu Shijiang, assumed office as the town supervisor of Shijing (now Anhai Town, Jinjiang City). During his tenure in Shijng, in addition to his achievements in government affairs, Zhu Song never slackened on education. During his spare time, he often summoned scholars to teach them the Academic Learning of Righteous Principles at the Aotou Vihāra next to the government office. The later generations missed him by the poem "Who reclaimed the wasteland and built the great house on it, by which we can learn from the great man?".

Twenty years later, Zhu Xi took the post of director in Tong'an County, Quanzhou. He often traveled between Quanzhou and Tong'an, which are more than 50km apart. He also stopped in Anhai several times, visiting the remains of his father Zhu Song. Wherever he went, there was a strong atmosphere for discussion of Neo-Confucianism. Under the leadership of Zhu Xi, scholars and students worked harder to study. In the decades after the "Civilization brought by the two generations of Zhu", dozens of advanced scholars from Anhai emerged.

宋时的同安县隶属泉州府，管辖着今厦门、龙海、金门一带。在任期间，朱熹首创县学，提出了"小学"与"大学"的概念，为我们现在的学制建立了雏形。他建尊经阁，立教思堂，推行教化，使同安成为朱子学的开宗圣地。

　　朱熹在泉州期间，积极讲学、办学。宋时泉州一共有12处书院，几乎所有的书院都和朱熹有着直接或间接的关系。九日山书院和小山丛竹书院是朱熹亲自创建的，石井书院和杨林书院则是朱熹讲过学的地方，文公书院则是为了纪念朱熹而建。朱熹曾多次到杨林书院讲学，四方学士来访求教者络绎不绝，杨子山上还留下"活源""仙苑"等朱熹的题刻。这几处书院中，又以小山丛竹书院和石井书院最具代表性。

　　朱熹曾多次登城北小山纵览，极称泉郡山川之美，为此流连忘返。他认为这里的清源山为"龙首之脉"，应当成为泉州传播正宗儒学的首善之地，即倡议以"不二祠"为场地建设书院，传播儒学。明朝李光缙在《募修欧阳四门祠疏》中写道："朱文公为同安主簿，每抵郡城，必登小山，称其山川之美，为郡治龙首之脉。徘徊数日而后去，自书曰小山丛竹。"如今，书院旧址仅存小山丛竹坊一座，坊额上的"小山丛竹"为朱熹手书，书院旧址一度改为温陵养老院，弘一法师圆寂于此。

◎ 小山丛竹地处泉州城北，唐代为纪念"闽文之祖"欧阳詹，建有祀詹祠堂。（成冬冬　摄）
Xiaoshan Congzhu is located in the north of Quanzhou City. In the Tang Dynasty, an ancestral hall dedicated to Ouyang Zhan was built to commemorate him, the "ancestor of Fujian literature". (Photo by Cheng Dongdong)

In the Song Dynasty Tong'an County was subordinate to Quanzhou Prefecture and governed the areas of Xiamen, Longhai, and Kinmen today. During his tenure, Zhu Xi pioneered county school and proposed the concepts of "primary school" and "university", which established the prototype of our current school system. He built Zunjing Pavilion and Jiaosi Hall. He promoted education and culture all over the area, making Tong'an a sacred place for the founding of Zhuzi School (one of the major philosophical schools of Neo-Confucianism).

During Zhu Xi's stay in Quanzhou, he actively lectured and ran schools. There were a total of 12 academies of classical learning in Quanzhou during the Song Dynasty and almost all of them had direct or indirect relationships with Zhu Xi. Jiurishan Academy and Xiaoshan Congzhu Academy were founded by Zhu Xi himself. Shijing Academy and Yanglin Academy were where Zhu Xi taught. Wengong Academy was built to commemorate Zhu Xi. Zhu Xi has given lectures at Yanglin Academy for many times, and numerous scholars from afar came to listen to his lectures. On Yangzi Hill, there are still inscriptions by Zhu Xi such as Huoyuan and Xianyuan. Among these academies, Xiaoshan Congzhu Academy and Shijing Academy are the most representative.

Zhu Xi has repeatedly visited the hills in the north of the city and admired the beauty of the mountains and rivers in Quanzhou. He believed that Qingyuan Mountain here was "the vein of the dragon head" and should be the best place for the spread of authentic Confucianism in Quanzhou. Thus he proposed to use the Bu'er Hall as the site to build academies and publicize Confucianism. Li Guangjin in the Ming Dynasty once wrote: "Zhu Wengong is the clerk officer of Tong'an. Whenever he arrives in Quanzhou, he always climbs the hills, praising the beauty of its mountains and rivers, and the vein of the dragon head. After staying for a few days, he leaves and writes the words Xiaoshan Congzhu (Little Hill Bamboo Grove) for this place." Today, there is only the Xiaoshan Congzhu archway left on the relic of the academy. The plaque "Xiaoshan Congzhu" on the forehead of the archway was handwritten by Zhu Xi. The former site of the academy was once changed to Wenling Nursing Home, where Master Hongyi passed away.

◎ 朱熹所题 "仙苑"。（成冬冬 摄）
The Chinese characters "仙苑 (paradise)" inscribed by Zhu Xi. (Photo by Cheng Dongdong)

◎ 历史上，石井书院为安海古镇培养了许多人才。（成冬冬 摄）

Historically, Shijing Academy has nurtured many talents for the ancient town of Anhai. (Photo by Cheng Dongdong)

　　石井书院更是与朱家三代人都有关系。南宋乾道年间（1165—1173年），朱熹的学生傅伯成，感念朱氏父子对安海倡教兴学之功绩，于鳌头精舍辟建"二朱先生祠"，绘朱松、朱熹父子画像奉祀。嘉定四年（1211年），当时的安海镇官游绛应好学士民请求，上书邹应龙，在"鳌头精舍"原址，正式筹建"石井书院"。

　　据载，邹应龙"即予批准，拨官帑四十万缗为倡首，并指令漕、舶二司捐助"。同时又调在泉州任通判的朱在（朱熹之子），主持书院营建事宜。南宋嘉定五年（1212年），石井书院建成，与原先的朱子祠合并。书院建成后，又购置许塘、承天等地田亩为学田，使就读的生员"赡养有田，肄业有舍"，成为当时泉州州属建院最早、设备最完整的高级学府。著名文学家留元刚为书院撰写碑文，碑文赞叹道："天下如石井者凡几？"

　　朱熹对泉州书院的勃兴功不可没，在泉州的文化发展史上，朱熹父子是重要的贡献者。泉州开元寺天王殿上悬挂的题联依然在民间父老间相传，脍炙人口。而朱熹在泉州的另一副题联也是闻名天下："事业经邦，闽海贤才开气运；文章华国，温陵甲第破天荒。"这一联题于欧阳祠，祀唐贞元八年（792年）闽南第一个进士欧阳詹。泉州文公巷则因该巷有座奉祀朱文公的庙宇而得名……

　　朱熹的朱子理学，是中国思想史上的一座丰碑。泉州大地，有幸承载其内心思想的虔诚、信仰和孤独，在岁月的淘洗下，朱子理学在泉州从未被遗忘，并随着各种遗存的浮现，越来越为世人熟知。

◎ 南安雪峰寺有朱熹的一副联语："地位清高，日
月每从肩上过；门庭开豁，江山常在掌中看。"
（成冬冬 摄）

Xuefeng Temple in Nan'an has a couplet of Zhu Xi:
"Standing high, the sun and the moon pass over
its shoulder; the gate is widely open, and rivers and
mountains can always be seen in the palm." (Photo by
Cheng Dongdong)

Shijing Academy is even more closely related to the three generations of the Zhu family. During 1165 and 1173, Zhu Xi's student Fu Bocheng, commemorating the achievements of Zhu Xi and his father in advocating education in Anhai, built the Mr. Zhus' Temple in Aotou Vihāra, and painted portraits of Zhu Song and Zhu Xi for worship. In 1211, Youjiang, the then town governor of Anhai, wrote to Zou Yinglong and formally proposed to build Shijing Academy on the original site of Aotou Vihāra at the request of studious scholars and people.

According to records, Zou Yinglong "approved immediately, and led the fund-rising by allocating 400,000 strings of copper coin in official fund, and instructed the Water Transport Office and Maritime Trade Office to donate." At the same time, Zhu Zai (Zhu Xi's son), who served as the general judge in Quanzhou, was in charge of the construction of the academy. In 1212, Shijing Academy was completed and merged with the original Zhuzi Hall. After the academy was completed, fields in Xutang, Chengtian, and elsewhere were purchased as school fields for the students who attended the academy to "be supported by fields and houses", making the academy the first advanced academy with the most complete facilities in Quanzhou at that time. The famous writer Liu Yuangang wrote an inscription for the academy, which is full of praise: "How many academies in the world can be (as great as) Shijing Academy?"

Zhu Xi contributed to the prosperity of academies in Quanzhou. In the history of Quanzhou's cultural development, Zhuxi and his father are important contributors. The well-known inscriptions hanging on the Hall of Heavenly Kings in Kaiyuan Temple in Quanzhou are still passed down among folks. And Zhu Xi's another inscription in Quanzhou also wins universal acclaim. This couplet "A great statesman from Fujian, his honorable career is about the whole country; his articles are of the top level in China, making the breakthrough among the scholars in Quanzhou" was inscribed in the Ouyang Ancestral Hall, dedicated to Ouyang Zhan, the first advanced scholar in Southern Fujian in 792 of the Tang Dynasty. Quanzhou Wengong Lane is named after the temple dedicated to Zhu Xi ...

The Zhu School created by Zhu Xi is a monument in the history of Chinese philosophy. The land of Quanzhou is fortunate to carry the piety, belief and loneliness of his inner thoughts. Over the years, Zhu School has never been forgotten in Quanzhou. On the contrast, with the emergence of various relics, it has become more and more familiar to the world.

紫峰先生：天下第一通

◎ 陈紫峰画像。（吴金鹏 供图）
The portrait of Chen Zifeng. (Courtesy of Wu Jinpeng)

陈埭，原是晋江南岸的一片滩涂，是晋江市唯一以姓氏命名的乡镇，也是晋江以"陈"命名的最高行政级别的地名。五代时，南唐观察使陈洪进率军民围海筑埭后，取名陈埭，俗称陈江。陈埭一开始是军屯，在宋以后，陈、倪、周、谢等诸姓聚居于此。

历史上，陈埭出过许多卓有成就的历史名人。"西滨林氏"人才荟萃，明清两朝科第蝉联，有"四代一品""兄弟尚书""五服八进士"等。据记载，明清以来，"西滨林氏"先后有进士14人、举人33人、序贡生员126人、职官79人、七品以上官员63人，他们清正廉明，名噪一时。其中，著名的有重宴琼林的林云程，广西右布政使林欲厦，兄弟尚书林欲栋、林欲楫，太常寺少卿林洪烈等；"涵口陈氏"以陈腆、陈琛（陈紫峰）、陈让、陈象西四位名宦，号称"四不朽"。清朝军事家、演炮专家丁拱辰盛名远播；当然最有名气的当属拥有"天下第一通"美誉的明代理学家陈紫峰。

陈琛，陈埭涵口人，字思献，明代著名的理学家、教育家。因其曾在泉州紫帽山下结庐讲学，所以又号"紫峰"，人称"紫峰先生"。聪敏好学的陈紫峰，从小拜当代大儒李聪、蔡清等为老师。蔡清是一代大儒，他倾其所有教授陈紫峰。陈紫峰勤奋钻研，终精通理学的精髓和要义。在泉州的水陆禅寺、紫帽山金粟洞等很多地方，都留下了陈紫峰读书的历史遗迹。意境幽远的承天寺内，还有一方现代碑刻，上面刻着"陈紫峰读书处"。

Mr. Zifeng: the No. I Polymath of China

Chendai was originally a tidal flat on the south bank of Jinjiang River. It is the only township named after a surname in Jinjiang City. It is also the highest administrative level place name in Jinjiang named after "Chen". In the Five Dynasties, Governor Chen Hongjin of the Southern Tang Dynasty led the army and the civilians to encircle the sea and build a *dai* (earth dam) and named it Chendai, which was commonly known as Chenjiang. Chendai was originally a military village. After the Song Dynasty, people of Chen, Ni, Zhou, Xie and other surnames lived here.

In history, many outstanding historical celebrities came from Chendai. Xibin Lin family had a wealth of talents, who won excellent grades in the imperial examinations in the Ming and Qing Dynasties. There were "four generations of top-ranking officials""brother ministers""eight-cousin advanced scholars" and so on. According to records, since the Ming and Qing Dynasties, Xibin Lin family has successively had 14 advanced scholars, 33 successful candidates in the imperial examinations at the provincial level, 126 students in the highest academy, 79 officers, and 63 officials of Rank 7 and above. They are honest and upright and famous for the time. The most famous ones among them include high-ranking scholars and officials such as Lin Yuncheng, Lin Yuxia, Lin Yudong, Lin Yuji, Lin Honglie, etc. Famous officials from the Chen clan in Hankou include Chen Tian, Chen Chen (Chen Zifeng), Chen Rang, and Chen Xiangxi. They are known as the "Four Immortals". Ding Gongchen, a military strategist and artillery expert in the Qing Dynasty, is also from Chendai. The most famous among them is by no doubt Chen Zifeng, a Ming Neo-Confucianist with the reputation of "the No. I polymath of China".

◎ 位于陈埭镇涵口村的陈紫峰纪念馆。（庄连白 摄）
The Chen Zifeng Memorial Hall in Hankou Village, Chendai Town.
(Photo by Zhuang Lianbai)

Chen Chen, courtesy named Sixian, was from Hankou Village, Chendai was a famous Neo-Confucianist and educator in the Ming Dynasty. Because he once built a house and gave lectures at the foot of Zimao Mountain in Quanzhou, he was also named "Zifeng (Zi Mountain)" and was known as "Mr. Zifeng". Chen Zifeng, smart and studious, had taken contemporary Confucian masters Li Cong and Cai Qing as his teachers since he was a child. As a guru of his time, Cai Qing taught Chen Zifeng all his knowledge. Chen Zifeng studied diligently and finally mastered the essence of Neo-Confucianism. In Quanzhou's Shuilu Temple, and Jinsu Cave on Zimao Mountain, there are historical relics where Chen Zifeng once studied. Inside the tranquil Chengtian Temple, there is also a modern monument inscribed with the words "Chen Zifeng's Reading Place".

陈紫峰于明正德五年（1510年）中举，十二年成进士，历任刑部山西司主事、南京户部主事、吏部考功郎等职。任职期间，陈紫峰受儒家理学影响，推行放宽政策，讲求实事求是，致力经济繁荣，造福一方百姓。尔后又因"仕不废学"，无意官场利禄，再三乞退归养。离开官场的陈紫峰，心系家乡公益，上书泉州府整修晋江南路，规划晋江水利枢纽工程六里陂。

在泉州，流传着许多关于陈紫峰的智慧故事，如"陈紫峰为泉州说书人挣面子""陈紫峰劝诫文武状元"等。陈紫峰与同时代的泉州名人张岳、林希元三人"汪洋恣肆旁若无人"，被称为"泉州三狂"。"泉州三狂"高谈阔论中闪烁着理学思想的光芒。陈紫峰在明代泉州的才子榜——"温陵十子"和"温陵四杰"均榜上有名。"精研易学，博学思辨，无所不通"是陈紫峰一生的写照。在泉州民间，素有"第一通，陈紫峰"的说法。

陈紫峰一生著有《四书浅说》《易经通典》《正学编》《紫峰文集》，其生平载于《明史儒林》。卒后，泉州府为其建专祠崇祀，以表彰其高尚节操。

◎ 陈埭的陈紫峰故居，保留着浓厚的闽南古厝文化，被称为"紫峰里古厝群"。（庄连白 摄）
The former residence of Chen Zifeng in Chendai retains rich Southern Fujian ancient houses culture and is called Zifengli Ancient Houses Complex. (Photo by Zhuang Lianbai)

Chen Zifeng passed the provincial civil service examination in 1510 of the Ming Dynasty and became an advanced scholar in 1517. He has assumed posts in different ministries in Shanxi, Nanjing and Beijing. Influenced by Confucianism, Chen Zifeng promoted relaxation policies, sought truth from facts, and devoted himself to economic prosperity and benefited the ordinary people during his tenure. Later, because of the thought that "an official should not neglect his studies", he had no intention of profiting from officialdom, and repeatedly appealed for retirement. After leaving the officialdom, Chen Zifeng was concerned about the public welfare of his hometown. He wrote to the Quanzhou Prefecture Government to renovate Jinjiang South Road and proposed Liulibei, Jinjiang River Water Conservancy Project.

In Quanzhou, there are many stories about Chen Zifeng's wisdom, such as "Chen Zifeng earns honor for Quanzhou storytellers" and "Chen Zifeng exhorts the national champions of military arts and literature" and so on. "Extremely forceful and unrestrained as if there was no one else present", Chen Zifeng and his contemporaries in Quanzhou, Zhang Yue and Lin Xiyuan, were called the "Three Maniacs". When they talked freely, the light of Neo-Confucianism was shining. Chen Zifeng was ranked among "Wenling Ten Scholars" and "Wenling Four Masters" in Quanzhou's talent list during the Ming Dynasty. "Intensive study of *I Ching*, erudite and speculative, omnipotent" is the portrayal of Chen Zifeng's life. In Quanzhou folks, there is a saying that "No. 1 polymath, Chen Zifeng".

Chen Zifeng wrote four books in his life as follows: *Elementary Introduction of the Four Books, Encyclopedia Text of I Ching, Compilations of Zheng Xue,* and *Collected Works of Zi Feng.* His life story is contained in *Ming Dynasty Scholars.* After his death, Quanzhou government built a special shrine for him to honor his noble conduct.

◎ 游人可在陈紫峰故居里了解到陈紫峰一生主要成就。（庄连白 摄）
Visitors can learn about the main achievements in Chen Zifeng's life in his former residence in Chendai. (Photo by Zhuang Lianbai)

青史李卓吾：天下奇男子

在泉州，紧挨着天后宫和德济门遗址的，是一处明代大思想家的故居。这座故居夹在一片民宅中，看似不起眼，但其主人的思想却曾经在法制森严的大明王朝发出振聋发聩的声音。他的思想在国际传播不止，他的房子保留至今。这位大思想家的名字叫李贽。

这座故居，是典型的闽南建筑风格民居，三落三开间。前落如今是商铺店面，于正中留一通道，通往中落。中落为正厅，厅中有楹联"两支双名宦，三世四乡贤"。厅口亦有联文"联济南陇西为鼎族，蔚政事文学之名贤"。厅中放置故居主人塑像一座，通高1.8米。

台湾知名作家李敖曾说过，李家出了四个奇男子：李耳、李卓吾、李宗吾、李敖。李卓吾，就是李贽，字宏甫，号卓吾，泉州人，明末杰出思想家和进步史学家。

历史上每一位著名的哲学家，都有其思想成长的沃土。李贽亦然。向海而生的泉州大地孕育了海上贸易的开拓精神，商品经济在海上丝绸之路上应运而生。海丝贸易得以繁荣，有赖于交易契约上的平等关系。刺桐港繁荣的大背景下，多元文化共存、共荣。繁华的世界级大都市留下的辉煌底蕴，让这片土地上萌发的思想独领风骚。李贽的先祖从事海上贸易，泉州海丝文化中的开放性和包容性，赋予李贽自由、开放思想的雏形。李贽提倡自由经商贸易，反对独尊儒学，提出是非标准应该随社会进步而发展变化。他还提倡男女平等、人性解放、追求自由等，这些思想都与海丝文化的精髓高度契合。

◎ 李贽故居位于泉州市鲤城区不起眼的街巷中。（成冬冬 摄）

The former residence of Li Zhi is located in the inconspicuous street of Licheng District, Quanzhou city. (Photo by Cheng Dongdong)

◎ 走进李贽故居可了解其一生之成就与
主张。（许兆恺 摄）
A visit to Li Zhi's former residence provides
a glimpse into his life's achievements and
advocacy. (Photo by Xu Zhaokai)

Li Zhuowu: a Remarkable Man in the History

In Quanzhou, next to Tianhou Temple and Deji Gate there is the former residence of a great thinker in the Ming Dynasty. Interspersed with private houses, the residence seems inconspicuous. But its owner's thoughts have once made a deafening sound in the strong legal system of the Ming Dynasty. His ideas spread internationally, and his house remains till today. The name of this great thinker is Li Zhi.

This former residence is a house typical of Southern Fujian architectural style, three quadrangles and three-*chien* wide. The front quadrangle is now a storefront with an aisle in the middle, leading to the middle quadrangle, the main hall. There are couplets in the main hall, "Two branches with two famous officials; three generations with four distinguished locals". There is also a couplet at the entrance of the hall to praise Li Zhi. A 1.8-meter-high statue of the owner of the former residence was placed in the hall.

The well-known Taiwanese writer Li Ao once said that there are four remarkable men born in the Li family: Li Er (Lao Tzu), Li Zhuowu, Li Zongwu, and Li Ao. Li Zhuowu is Li Zhi, courtesy name Hongfu, pseudonym name Zhuowu. A native of Quanzhou, Li Zhuowu is an outstanding thinker and progressive historian of the late Ming Dynasty.

Every famous philosopher in history has fertile ground for his thoughts to grow. The same goes for Li Zhi. The seaward land of Quanzhou nurtured the pioneering spirit of maritime trade, and the commodity economy came into being on the Maritime Silk Road. The prosperity of the Maritime Silk Road trade depended on the equal relationship in transaction contracts. Under the background of the prosperity of Quanzhou Port, diverse cultures existed and prospered together. The brilliant heritage left by the prosperous world-class metropolis makes the ideas that grow in this land dominate the world at that time. Li Zhi's ancestors were engaged in maritime trade. The openness and tolerance of the Maritime Silk Road culture in Quanzhou gave Li Zhi the embryonic form of freedom and open-mindedness. Li Zhi advocated free business and trade, opposed the exclusive Confucianism, and proposed that the standards of right and wrong should develop and change with social progress. He also advocated equality between men and women, the liberation of human nature, and the pursuit of freedom. These ideas are highly compatible with the essence of the Maritime Silk Road culture.

◎ 位于泉州西湖公园内的李贽雕像。（陈英杰 摄）
The statue of Li Zhi in West Lake Park, Quanzhou. (Photo by Chen Yingjie)

李贽公开反对封建传统教条，认为儒家经典并非"万世至论"；他反对"咸以孔子之是非为是非"，因此被明代的封建统治阶级贴上"异端邪说"的标签。

处于先锋位置的思想斗士李贽，对社会上"男尊女卑、重农抑商、假道学、社会腐败、贪污索贿"等积弊更是大力痛斥和批判，主张"革故鼎新"，反对思想禁锢。这位离经叛道的真心者，看不惯满城腐朽的风气，毅然决然拿起笔杆作为武器。

中国古代思想家对"平等"的讨论和阐发，远远超过同期欧洲思想家，而说到中国古代的平等思想，李贽是当之无愧的第一人。在16世纪，李贽是极其重要的思想家，他的思想对当时的世界产生了难以想象的影响。

"中国通"——意大利传教士利玛窦和李贽私交甚好，在《利玛窦中国札记》中他详尽地介绍了与李贽的交往过程以及李贽的学说。此书被翻译成多国文字，李贽启蒙思想的超前性、深刻性，以及所凸显的自由、批判精神也在国外逐渐传播开来。

日本明治维新，就直接受李贽思想的影响。日本幕府末期的著名汉学家、明治维新运动的先驱者吉田松阴，深受李贽思想的影响和启发。他深入研究李贽的《焚书》和《藏书》等著作，形成自己的创新思想。正是有了明治维新，日本社会才开启了转型和现代化进程。长期以来，日本许多著名学者都对李贽的思想进行深入而广泛的研究，日本现代著名汉学家铃木虎雄著有《李贽年谱》。李贽在日本的影响可谓深远且深刻。

东亚和东南亚国家，如韩国、新加坡，其学术界对李贽的研究也从未停止。在欧美国家，如美国、法国、英国、瑞士、意大利、俄罗斯等国也都有学者对李贽的思想兴趣浓厚，并从事李贽的研究工作。德国汉学家福兰阁在其专著《十六世纪中国之思想斗争》中对李贽的思想及人格魅力赞叹不已，并撰写了有关李贽的研究论文《李贽》《李贽与利玛窦》。

天下奇男子，青史李卓吾。李卓吾在那个时代，以其开拓和进取的斗士精神把沉睡的人们唤醒，对明、清两代以及"五四"时期的思想家、文学家都产生了深远的影响。

Li Zhi openly opposed the traditional feudal doctrines, and believed that Confucian classics were not "the truth of all ages". He opposed "using Confucius' right and wrong as right and wrong", so he was labelled "heresy" by the feudal ruling class in the Ming Dynasty.

In the vanguard position, Li Zhi, an ideological fighter, strongly denounced and criticized the society's long-standing abuse of "men being superior to women, the policy emphasizing agriculture at the expense of commerce, hypocrisy, social corruption, corruption and bribery". Against stifling thoughts, he advocated that the old thoughts must be replaced by the new ones. This rebellious and sincere man disapproved the decayed atmosphere of the whole city and resolutely used his articles as weapons.

The discussion and elucidation of "equality" by ancient Chinese thinkers far surpassed that of European thinkers of the same period. When it comes to the idea of equality in ancient China, Li Zhi is the well-deserved first person. In the 16th century, Li Zhi was an extremely important thinker, and his ideas had an unimaginable impact on the world at that time.

Italian missionary Matteo Ricci, a China Hand, had a very good personal relationship with Li Zhi. In *Matteo Ricci's Reading Notes on China*, Ricci introduced in detail his communication with Li Zhi and Li Zhi's doctrine. This book has been translated into many languages, and the advancement and profoundness of Li Zhi's enlightenment thoughts, as well as the freedom and critical spirit that it highlights have gradually spread abroad.

The Meiji Restoration of Japan was directly influenced by Li Zhi's thoughts. Yoshida Shoin, a famous sinologist at the end of the Shogunate period and a pioneer of the Meiji Restoration Movement in Japan, was deeply influenced and inspired by Li Zhi's thoughts. Based on in-depth study of Li Zhi's *Burning Books*, *Book Collection* and other works, Shoin formed his own innovative ideas. It was by the Meiji Restoration that Japanese society began the process of transformation and modernization. For a long time, many famous Japanese scholars have carried out in-depth and extensive research on Li Zhi's thoughts. The famous modern Japanese sinologist Suzuki Toruo once wrote *Li Zhi's Chronicle*. Li Zhi's influence in Japan can be described as far-reaching and profound.

In East and Southeast Asian countries such as the Republic of Korea and Singapore, the academic research on Li Zhi has never stopped. In European and American countries such as the United States, France, the United Kingdom, Switzerland, Italy, Russia and other countries, scholars are also very interested in Li Zhi's thoughts and are engaged in research work about Li Zhi. In his monograph *The Ideological Struggle in China in the Sixteenth Century*, German sinologist Flange admired Li Zhi's ideological and personality charm, and wrote research papers on Li Zhi such as *Li Zhi* and *Li Zhi and Matteo Ricci*.

A remarkable man, Li Zhuowu stamped his name on the records of history. In his era, Li Zhuowu enlightened the people with his pioneering, enterprising and fighting spirit, and had a profound influence on thinkers and writers in the Ming and Qing Dynasties and during the May 4th Movement period.

弘一法师：缘定泉州、天心月圆

有三位名人这样评价过李叔同——

林语堂说："李叔同是我们时代里最有才华的几位天才之一，也是最奇特的一个人，最遗世而独立的一个人。"

朱光潜曾说，李叔同是"以出世的精神做着入世的事业"。

张爱玲说："不要认为我是个高傲的人，我从来不是的——至少，在弘一法师寺院的围墙外面，我是如此的谦卑。"

李叔同出身天津巨贾之家，弱冠之年便名扬天下。谁也不曾想到李叔同会遁入空门，成为一代高僧。"半生红尘，半生佛门"，用这句话来形容李叔同的一生再合适不过了。红尘滚滚，他是翩翩风流才子，"长亭外，古道边，芳草碧连天……问君此去几时来，来时莫徘徊。"一阕《送别》传唱至今；佛门清净，他师从印光法师，简朴至极，普度众生。他说："纵然有十分福气，也只能享受二三分，其余的留给别人或者留到日后，若能以己之福气，度他人之艰难，便是功德。"

弘一法师遁入空门的24年里，其中有14年是在闽南度过的，他的足迹、墨宝遍布了整个泉州：开元寺、承天寺、温陵养老院、南安灵应寺、雪峰寺、惠安净峰寺、永春普济寺和晋江福林寺、草庵寺、龙山寺、安海水心亭等。

◎ 泉州开元寺内的弘一法师纪念馆。（成冬冬 摄）
Master Hongyi Memorial Hall in Kaiyuan Temple, Quanzhou. (Photo by Cheng Dongdong)

Master Hongyi: Bonding with Quanzhou; a Bright Full Moon Hanging High in the Middle of the Sky

Three famous people have commented on Li Shutong like this—

Lin Yutang said: "Li Shutong is one of the most talented geniuses in our time, and also the most peculiar person, the most independent person standing aloof from the world."

Zhu Guangqian once said that Li Shutong was "naturalizing the world in the spirit of renouncing the world".

Zhang Ailing once said: "Don't think that I am a proud person. I have never been—at least, outside the wall of Hongyi Master's temple, I am so humble."

◎ 泉州承天寺月台别院弘一法师纪念馆内的弘一法师塑像。（成冬冬 摄）

The statue of Master Hongyi in the Master Hongyi Memorial Hall at Yue Tai Courtyard, Chengtian Temple, Quanzhou. (Photo by Cheng Dongdong)

Li Shutong was born in the family of a tycoon in Tianjin, and he became very famous when he was about 20 years old. And no one would have thought that he would become one of the greatest Buddhist monks in that generation. "Half a lifetime spent in the world of mortals, and the other half the Buddhism", this sentence could not be more appropriate to describe Li Shutong's life. In the mortal world, he was a distinguished and admirable scholar. "Outside the long corridor, along the ancient road, the green grass seemed to connect with the sky… To ask my friend, 'When will you be back after we part ways this time?' Please don't hesitate to drop by when you are here again." The song *Bidding Farewell* written by him has been sung to this day. Buddhism world is immaculate. Li Shutong learned from Master Yingguang to save all living beings from sufferings and lived an extremely simple life. He said: "Even if you have great blessings, you can only enjoy 20 or 30 percent of them. Leave the rest to others or in the future. If you can solve the problems of others with your own blessings, it is merit."

During the twenty-four years of Master Hongyi as a monk, fourteen of them were spent in Southern Fujian. His footprints and calligraphy spread throughout Quanzhou: Kaiyuan Temple, Chengtian Temple, Wenling Nursing Home, Nan'an Lingying Temple, Xuefeng Temple, Hui'an Jingfeng Temple, Yongchun Puji Temple and Fulin Temple, Cao'an Temple, Longshan Temple, Anhai Water Heart Temple in Jinjiang, etc.

承天寺是弘一法师最经常驻锡之地。1930年正月十五过后,弘一法师移锡承天寺,和性愿法师共同创办了"月台佛学院",打坐念佛,整理佛经,在他居留闽南的14年里户籍就是落户在承天寺。

由于正是抗战时期,弘一法师亲自书写"念佛不忘救国,救国必须念佛"挂于中堂。据当年承天寺僧人回忆,有一日,弘一法师在用餐之时对身边诸弟子说:"吾人所食中华之粟,所饮为温陵之水,身为佛子,此时此刻,不能共纾国难于万一,为释迦如来张贴体面,自揣不如一只狗子,狗子尚能为主守门,吾人却一无所用,而犹腆颜受食,能无愧于心乎!"众弟子闻言皆泣不成声。

弘一法师曾于1929年和1940年先后两次游住雪峰寺,欢度春节。始建于唐末的闽南名刹雪峰寺依山而建,山门高大巍峨,亭台雨榭层层叠叠。主殿的石柱上有弘一法师手书楹联:寻善意欲洗除惑垢,证无上法究竟清凉。在这佛教圣地,近代佛教三大法师:弘一、太虚、芝峰一度会集。弘一法师与太虚法师所谱《三宝歌》曲调悠扬。1984年,广净法师为纪念弘一法师建造"晚晴亭"于雪峰山竹林边,并题偈赞之:"圣教演心,佛律严身。内外清净,菩提之因。"

开元寺和弘一法师渊源颇深。1933年,弘一法师受邀前往开元寺,长居尊胜院。在尊胜院期间,弘一法师圈点《南山钞记》,编纂《戒本羯磨随讲别录》《南山道宣律组略谱》《梵纲经菩萨戒本浅释》等。除此之外,他还在尊胜院为七百年不传的南山律学圈点、编撰、注释,并总结学研律宗的体验。对此,广洽法师如此评价弘一法师:"他不特集艺术全才于一身,更重要的是继起了七百余年的绝学——南山律宗,并且实践躬行,高风劲节,为世所钦。"

◎ 弘一法师最后居所温陵养老院晚晴室。
（楚鹏 摄）

Wanqing Room of Wenling Nursing Home, the last residence of Master Hongyi. (Photo by Chu Peng)

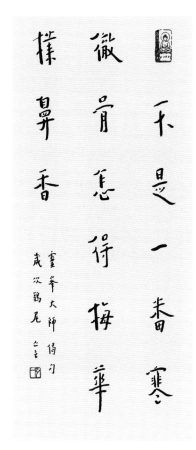

◎ 弘一法师书法作品。（闽人 摄）
A calligraphic work of Master Hongyi.
(Photo by Min Ren)

Chengtian Temple is the place where Master Hongyi was most often stationed. After the 15th lunar January in 1930, Master Hongyi moved here and co-founded the Yuetai Buddhist Academy with Master Xingyuan, where he meditated, chanted and sorted out Buddhist sutras. During his 14 years in Southern Fujian, his household registration was settled in Chengtian Temple.

Because it was during the War of Resistance Against Japanese Aggression, Hongyi personally wrote "Chanting the holy names of Buddha, you can never forget to save the nation. And to save the nation, you must chant the holy names of Buddha" and hung it in the main hall. According to the memories of the monks at Chengtian Temple, Hongyi said to the disciples around him one day while having a meal: "We eat Chinese millet and drink water from Wenling (another name of Quanzhou). As a Buddha, at this moment, we do almost nothing to win honor for Gautama Buddha by warding off the national calamity (caused by Japanese aggression). I think we are not as good as a dog. The dog can guard the door for its owner, but we are useless and thick-skinned enough to be offered food. Do we have a clear conscience?!" Hearing this, all disciples choked with sobs.

Master Hongyi visited Xuefeng Temple twice in 1929 and 1940 to celebrate the Spring Festival. Xuefeng Temple, a famous temple in Southern Fujian, was built on the mountain in late Tang Dynasty. The mountain gate is tall and lofty, and the pavilions and rain-proof pavilions are stacked on top of each other. On the stone pillars of the main hall, there is a couplet handwritten by Hongyi: "Seek kindness to wash away the scumming, and master the ultimate truth of Buddhism to get supreme purity and peace." In this sacred place of Buddhism, Hongyi, Taixu, and Zhifeng, the three masters of Buddhism in modern times, gathered for a time. Master Hongyi and Master Taixu once composed together a melodious tune of *The Song of the Three Treasures*. In 1984, Master Guangjing built Wanqing Pavilion beside the bamboo grove on Xuefeng Mountain to commemorate Hongyi, and he wrote an inscription to commend him.

Kaiyuan Temple has a deep connection with Master Hongyi. In 1933, Master Hongyi was invited to Kaiyuan Temple and lived in Zunsheng House for a long time. During his stay in Zunsheng House, Master Hongyi edited and compiled a number of important Buddhism classics. In addition, in the Zunsheng House, Master Hongyi punctuated, compiled, annotated *Nanshan Vinaya* that had not been preached for 700 years. He also summarized the experience of learning and researching Nanshan Risshū. In this regard, Master Guangqia commented on Master Hongyi: "He not only specializes in all-round arts, but more importantly, he has inherited Nanshan Risshū, the more than 700 years of fascinating knowledge, and practiced them himself. His exemplary conduct and nobility of character are remembered and admired by the world."

◎ 位于清源山弥陀岩西侧的弘一法师舍利塔。（吴寿民　摄）
The stupa of Master Hongyi on the west side of Mituo Rock, Qingyuan Mountain. (Photo by Wu Shoumin)

　　1933年，弘一法师偶然于泉州西门外潘山发现晚唐诗人韩偓墓道碑后，便命弟子编著《韩偓评传》，又附文《香奁集辩伪》。1938年，弘一法师在尊胜院连续讲解《心经》三天。

　　1942年9月1日的温陵养老院晚晴室，弘一法师亲笔书下"悲欣交集"四字，并自注"见观经"。三日后，弘一法师安详往生，世寿63，僧腊24。

　　为了纪念弘一法师与泉州的特殊缘分，1982年，开元寺尊胜院设为"弘一法师纪念馆"。中厅陈列法师的佛学研究作品；东侧一室展出法师出家前的艺术成就，包含了文学和戏曲；东侧二室展示法师出家后的书法成就；晚期手迹陈列于西侧一室；生前的卧室位于西侧二室，陈列的生活用品十分简朴。

　　尤为珍贵的是，纪念馆的条幅、中堂、对联等均为法师弘法时留下的真迹。作为一位著名的书法家，其在闽地留下大量墨宝，纪念馆内共计收藏弘一法师书法作品60余件，篆刻41件。

In 1933, after Master Hongyi accidentally discovered the tombstone of the poet Han Wo in the late Tang Dynasty in Pan Mountain outside the west gate of Quanzhou, he ordered his disciples to compile *Han Wo Critic Biography* with an accompanying article *Xiang Lian Ji: True or False*. In 1938, Master Hongyi lectured on *The Heart of Prajna Paramita Sutra* for three consecutive days in Zunsheng House.

In Wanqing Room of Wenling Nursing Home on September 1, 1942, Master Hongyi wrote "悲欣交集(Mixed Emotions of Grief and Joy)" in his own handwriting, and annotated the writing as *See the Sutra on Contemplation of Amitayus*. Three days later, Master Hongyi passed away peacefully, with a lifetime of sixty-three and a monkhood of twenty-four years.

To commemorate the special fate of Master Hongyi and Quanzhou, Zunsheng House in Kaiyuan Temple was set as Master Hongyi Memorial Hall in 1982. The main hall displays the master's research works of Buddhism. The first room on the east side displays the master's artistic achievements before the monkhood, including literature and opera. The second room on the east side displays the master's achievements in calligraphy during the monkhood. The handwriting in his late years is displayed in the first room on the west side. The bedroom before his death is located in the second room on the west side, and the household items on display are very simple.

What is particularly precious is that the banners, central scrolls and couplets in the memorial hall are all authentic works left by Master Hongyi when he was propagating the Dharma. As a famous calligrapher, he left a lot of calligraphy in Fujian, and the memorial hall boasts a total collection of more than sixty pieces of calligraphy and forty-one pieces of seal carvings.

◎ 弘一法师舍利塔左侧岩石上刻有其遗墨"悲欣交集"。（任嘉雯 摄）
"悲欣交集(Mixed emotions of grief and joy)", written by Master Hongyi, was carved on the rock to the left of his stupa. (Photo by Ren Jiawen)

非遗之城——千年古城的独特底蕴

　　非物质文化遗产是一个地区历史底蕴、文化根基和传统积淀的体现，被誉为历史文化的"活化石"和"民族记忆的背影"。泉州处处皆文脉，这个城市的独特之处，绝不仅仅来源于山水之间，也不仅仅来源于文物史迹，更来源于其非物质文化遗产的独特魅力。

　　在泉州，任何一样非遗，都可以让人流连忘返，赞不绝口。听一曲悠悠南音，观一出高甲戏，看一段木偶戏，沉浸其中，慰藉旅人的疲乏，给心灵以暂歇。

　　泉州的无可取代、泉州的独一无二，皆在于其深厚的文化积淀，而品类众多、类型多样的泉州非遗是其中的重要组成部分。

◎ 泉州提线木偶亮相2021年央视戏曲春晚。（陈英杰 摄）

Quanzhou marionettes in 2021 CCTV New Year's Opera Gala. (Photo by Chen Yingjie)

The City of Intangible Cultural Heritage: the Profound Cultural Background of a Thousand-year-old City

Intangible cultural heritage is the embodiment of the historical background, cultural foundation and traditional accumulation of a region, and is known as the "living fossil" of history and culture as well as the "back view of ethnic memory". Quanzhou is full of cultural heritage. The uniqueness of this city is not only derived from the mountains and rivers, cultural relics and historical sites, but also from the unique charm of its intangible cultural heritage.

In Quanzhou, any intangible cultural heritage would make people linger and praise. Listen to a slow and elegant Nanyin performance, watch a Gaojia opera or a puppet show. They can ease away the fatigue of travelers and give the soul a rest.

Quanzhou is irreplaceable and unique because of its profound cultural antecedents. The intangible cultural heritage in many categories and types is an important part of it.

◎ 被人们戏称为"东方迪斯科"的拍胸舞。（陈英杰 摄）
Chest-slapping Dance is jokingly referred to as Oriental Disco. (Photo by Chen Yingjie)

南音：唐宋遗音、宫廷雅乐

汉代张衡的《南都赋》最早出现"南音"一词，里面写道："于是齐僮唱兮列赵女，坐南歌兮起郑舞。"南歌，取南音以为歌也。古乐南音在古城泉州传唱了千年。千年后的我们，听到的是唐宋遗音，亦是音乐活化石。

古代乐人对南音的巧思妙想，在时光中行走，来到我们面前。在许多古老音乐都已逐渐与历史剥离的漫长遗憾中，南音节步缓行，与人类不离不弃。

"中国的音乐是全世界最古老的音乐，而中国音乐之中，则以南音为最古。"这是音乐界权威人士通过研究得出的结论。泉州地方戏曲研究社社长郑国权曾指出："南音有着'严谨的规制、成熟的体系，艺术上精雕细刻、精益求精，传承上师道尊严、训练有素'，因此，可以认为，这只能是由那些有权有势有财力的宫廷教坊或王侯贵族家班造就的。否则，如果只是纯粹跑江湖卖艺糊口的民间戏曲，往往是土生土长、自生自灭，不可能有那么深厚的艺术积累和文化含量。"

南音、智化寺京音乐、西安古乐等之所以被人们称为中国传统音乐的活化石，是因为它们有史记载，而且仍鲜活地存在。它们可视可听，通过它们流淌出来的音符，我们得以和先人共享历史的吟唱。

◎ 2009年10月1日，南音（泉州弦管）正式被联合国教科文组织列入《人类非物质文化遗产代表作名录》。（刘宝生 摄）
On October 1, 2009, Nanyin (Quanzhou string/wind musical instruments) was officially included in the Representative List of the Intangible Cultural Heritage of Humanity by the UNESCO. (Photo by Liu Baosheng)

Nanyin: Legacy of the Tang and Song Dynasties, and Elegant Imperial Court Music

The word "Nanyin" appeared the first time in Zhang Heng's *Rhapsody of the Southern Capital* in the Han Dynasty, which reads: "So Qi slave servants sang and Zhao dancers dance, Zheng Dance was performed with Nange." Nange here refers to Nanyin. The ancient music Nanyin has been played in the ancient city of Quanzhou for hundreds of years. What we hear now is the legacy of the Tang and Song Dynasties, the living fossils of music.

Ancient musicians' ingenuity about Nanyin came to us after so many years. In the long regret that many other ancient music have gradually been separated from history, Nanyin is inseparable from us in steady stroll.

"Chinese music is the oldest music in the world, and among Chinese music, Nanyin is the oldest." This is the research conclusion drawn by authoritative figures in the music industry. Zheng Guoquan, the president of Quanzhou Local Opera Research Association, once pointed out: "With a rigorous regulation and a mature system, Nanyin is meticulously carved and refined art. The dignity of the Nanyin teachers are fully respected, and the players are well-trained. Therefore, it can only be created by those powerful and wealthy palace Jiaofang (music academy) or noble families. If the folk artists just purely travell around to perform the folk opera to make a living, their music is often native and self-perpetuating and it is impossible to have such profound artistic antecedents and cultural content".

The reason why Nanyin, Jing Music from Zhihua Temple, and Xi'an Ancient Music are called the living fossils of traditional Chinese music is because they have historical records and still exist freshly. They are visible and audible, and through their flowing notes, we can share the historical singing with our ancestors.

中国的音乐尤其是宫廷音乐，灿烂辉煌，至唐，宫廷音乐达到顶峰。杨贵妃和唐玄宗的《霓裳羽衣曲》似乎犹在耳畔，盛唐传奇，透过一首舞曲亦能窥之。

唐末及五代十国，中原连年战乱，士族大举南迁，唐玄宗时期形成的"大曲"，也随之来到闽地，共载悲欢离合。南音就是以唐代"大曲"为基础，在广泛流传和不断演绎中，受到元曲、昆曲、弋阳腔、佛曲以及地方戏曲的影响，逐渐形成独特的完整体系。

南音至今仍保留唐朝"琵琶惯用拨子、横抱姿势"的遗风。腹大颈细的南琶被横抱用于南音之中。泉州开元寺内的飞天乐伎及敦煌壁画上的飞天造型都是横抱琵琶，五代南唐顾闳中名作《韩熙载夜宴图》中人物弹琵琶也是横抱姿势。在唐代的乐队中，琵琶相当于乐队的指挥，南音亦如此。

在其他古乐种中消失不见的拍板，还保留于南音中，延续着千年前汉代相和歌"丝竹更相和，执节者歌"的古老音乐传统。敦煌壁画中的伎乐图完美呈现了古代南音所用"拍板"以及演奏方式。拍板是南音不可或缺的拍击乐器，又称"拍"或"撩"，材质是檀木、荔木等硬木，用绳索将五片木板串联而成，中间三块板规格相同，外形平整，外侧两板稍长，两端均呈弧形。

◎ 南音由古代的御前清音到现在泉州民间的音乐，传承不息。（林建祥 摄）

The endless legacy of Nanyin, from the ancient imperial music to the current folk music of Quanzhou, continues.
(Photo by Lin Jianxiang)

◎ 开元寺甘露戒坛的飞天手持南音
　　乐器。（陈英杰 摄）
Flying Apsaras at the Ganlu Altar of
Precepts of Kaiyuan Temple holds
Nanyin instruments. (Photo by Chen
Yingjie)

Chinese music, especially the court music, was magnificent and glorious. In the Tang Dynasty, court music reached its peak. The *Melody Of White Feathers Garment* by Concubine Yang and Emperor Xuanzong of the Tang Dynasty seems to be still in our ears, and the legend of the prosperous Tang Dynasty can be known through this dance music.

At the end of the Tang Dynasty, and the Five Dynasties and Ten Kingdoms, the Central Plains had wars over the years, and large amount of gentry moved south. The "Daqu" formed during the Emperor Xuanzong period of the Tang Dynasty also came to Fujian, carrying joys and sorrows together. Nanyin is based on the "Daqu" of the Tang Dynasty. It has gradually formed a unique and complete system under the influence of Yuanqu Opera, Kunqu Opera, Yiyang Opera, Buddhist music and local operas in the wide spread and continuous interpretation.

Nanyin still retains the legacy of pipa's habitual picking and holding posture in the Tang Dynasty. Held horizontally, the Nanpa (Nanyin Pipa) with a big belly and a thin neck is used in Nanyin performances. The flying Apsaras in Quanzhou Kaiyuan Temple and Dunhuang murals all hold their pipas horizontally. In the famous painting *Han Xizai Attending an Evening Banquet* by Southern Tang Dynasty painter Gu Hongzhong, the performer also plays pipa horizontally. In the orchestra of the Tang Dynasty, pipa player is equivalent to the conductor of the orchestra, and the same is true for Nanyin.

The clappers that have disappeared in other ancient music genres still survive in Nanyin, carrying on the ancient music tradition "singers beating time on a drum to the accompaniment of string/wind musical instruments" of the Han Dynasty Xianghe Song thousands of years ago. The relief fresco musicians in Dunhuang murals perfectly presents the "clappers" and the way of performance used by ancient Nanyin. The clapper is an indispensable slap musical instrument of Nanyin, also known as "beat" or "slap". The clappers are made of hardwoods such as sandalwood and litchi wood. The five boards are connected in series with ropes. The three boards in the middle are of the same specifications and have flat appearance. The two outer boards are slightly longer, and both ends are curved.

在泉州开元寺镇国塔、大雄宝殿、甘露戒坛所雕刻的南音古乐器有37件，包含有拍板、琵琶、尺八、二弦、三弦、唢呐、品箫和双铃等，一应俱全，而且还有较少见的竽及扁鼓等，它们广泛应用于吹、拉、弹、拍等演奏形式。

承袭汉唐古韵的南音，在乐器、造型和演奏方式上，以其古朴和原生态的魅力，在苍茫岁月中，演绎历史沧桑。唐宋遗音，传唱至今。南音名曲《摩诃兜勒》《阳关》《汉宫秋》《后庭花》《三台令》《梁州曲》《甘州曲》《婆罗门》《太子游四门》等被载入汉唐文献之中，而《沁园春》《念奴娇》《浪淘沙》等则为宋词曲牌。

至明清，南音空前繁盛。康熙帝六十寿典，内阁大学士、泉州安溪人李光地选派了五位南音高手前往御前演奏。康熙帝听到南音逸韵雅致，龙颜大悦，要加封五人留京，他们便唱《远望乡里》，奏大谱《百鸟归巢》以表思乡之情。皇帝终于感悟，赐他们"御前清客，五少芳贤"匾额，同时赐赠曲柄黄凉伞和金丝宫灯，准许他们"传驿荣归"。"御前清曲"的雅号从此成了南音的又一荣耀。

从大唐宫廷雅乐到"御前清曲"，南音在泉州肥沃的土壤中滋长，无论街巷之中，抑或平常人家，都能听见南音的吟唱。对于泉州人来讲，南音不仅是一种艺术形式，也是一种生活方式。

◎ 每到夜晚，人们都能在泉州府文庙南音传习所里欣赏到南音乐团的表演。（颜家蔚 摄）
Every evening, people can enjoy the performance of the Nanyin Ensemble in the Nanyin Education Center in Confucius Temple in Quanzhou. (Photo by Yan Jiawei)

There are 37 ancient Nanyin musical instruments carved in Zhenguo Pagoda, Mahavira Hall, and Ganlu Altra in Quanzhou Kaiyuan Temple, including clappers, pipa, shakuhachi, two-string fiddles, three-string fiddles, *suona* horns, *pinxiao* and double bells, and four treasures. And there are also *shengs* (reed pipe wind instruments) and flat drums, which are rarely seen. All these instruments are widely used in performance formats of blowing, bowing, plucking, and clapping.

Nanyin, which inherits the ancient rhyme of the Han and Tang Dynasties, interprets the historical vicissitudes in terms of instruments, styles and performing methods, with its primitive simplicity and original ecological charm. The legacy of the Tang and Song Dynasties has been performed to today. Nanyin's famous songs *Mahadur, Yangguan, Han Palace Autumn, Flowers in the Back Garden, Santai Lyric, Liangzhou Song, Ganzhou Song, Brahman, The Prince's Tour of the Four Gates*, etc. were included in the Han and Tang literature. *Qinyuanchun, Niannujiao* and *Langtaosha* are names of the tunes to which *qu* are composed in the Song Dynasty.

In the Ming and Qing Dynasties, Nanyin was unprecedentedly prosperous. The cabinet scholar Li Guangdi from Anxi, Quanzhou, selected and sent five Nanyin masters to perform in the imperial palace at the 60th birthday ceremony of Emperor Kangxi. The Emperor Kangxi was so pleased to hear the beautiful and elegant Nanyin and he wanted to keep the five masters in Beijing. They then sang *Looking Hometown from Afar* and played *Hundred Birds Returning* to *the Nests* to show their homesickness. The emperor finally realized they would like to go home instead of staying in Beijing. So he gave them the plaque of *The Imperial Qing Visitors, the Five Young Scholars*, and at the same time gave them a crank yellow umbrella and a golden silk palace-lantern, allowing them to "get the post stage's help to return home". The elegant title of "imperial music" has since become another glory of Nanyin.

From the court music of the Tang Dynasty to the imperial music, Nanyin has grown in the fertile soil of Quanzhou. You can hear Nanyin's singing everywhere from streets or ordinary households. For the people of Quanzhou, Nanyin is not only an art form, but also a way of life.

◎ 南音清唱《王昭君》。（刘宝生 摄）
The Nanyin cappella *Wang Zhaojun.* (Photo by Liu Baosheng)

◎ 江加走大师木偶头作品。（杨湘贤 摄）
Puppet head carvings by Master Jiang Jiazou. (Photo by Yang Xiangxian)

掌中木偶、提线木偶：指出风云动、掌中弄乾坤

"生如素纸长如花，毛钢铅蜡笔来画。木偶脱线安能存，人若傀偏性难发"，这四句诗，活灵活现地描写出人类掌控木偶来演绎人世间的悲欢离合。从平淡无奇的木头到形神兼具的木偶头，需要工匠们非比寻常的智慧和无比灵巧的双手。

制作木偶头，先要找到合适的木头，用斧头劈粗坯，量好尺寸锯定位，着手雕刻，再用桂花土研磨加胶水搅拌滤出土浆，以保证在上粉彩之前将存在的裂缝或间隙填平。同时，在木头表面裱上一层棉纸，等木头阴干以后，再重新用刀开脸，使用鲨鱼皮磨平，竹篾修整成型，而后用手工研磨的颜料在作品上进行描绘……整个过程，绝不能操之过急，讲究的是精细的手工和持久的耐心。

国家级非物质文化遗产项目——木偶头雕刻，因"江加走"这个名字而誉满全球。

被国际木偶界誉为"木偶之父"的江加走，出生于泉州。他雕刻的木偶头，称为"加走头"或"花园头"，是国家一级文物，亦被世界各大博物馆视为珍宝收藏，在许多台湾同胞心目中更是当之无愧的民间国宝。江加走的代表作《媒婆》享誉国际，有"东方艺术珍品"的美名。这位世界级的大师，让泉州的木偶倍添光彩。江派木偶头制作技艺，如今已传承到了第四代。

泉
州

Quanzhou

Hand Puppets and Marionettes: Making Things Happen in the Palm

"**B**orn like white paper and grown like a flower, drawn with brushes, pens, pencils, and crayons. Puppets cannot survive without strings, and puppet-like people cannot be themselves." The poems vividly describe the human control of puppets to interpret the joys and sorrows of the world. The generation of puppet heads with both form and spirit from plain wood is based on craftsmen's extraordinary wisdom and extremely dexterous hands.

To make a puppet head, you must first find a suitable wood, split the rough blank with an axe, measure the size of the saw and position, start carving, and then use osmanthus soil to grind and glue to filter out the soil slurry, which is to fill up existing cracks or gaps before the pastel is applied. At the same time, a layer of tissue paper is mounted on the surface of the wood. After the wood dries in the shade, the face is re-opened with a knife, smoothed with shark skin, and bamboo strips are trimmed, and then hand-grinded paint is used to paint the work. One must not be rushed and need to pay attention to fine handwork and have long-lasting patience through out the whole process.

Puppet head carving, a national intangible cultural heritage project, is famous all over the world because of the name Jiang Jiazou.

Jiang Jiazou, known as the "father of puppets" by the international puppet circles, was born in Quanzhou. The puppet heads he carved, called "Jiazou heads" or "Garden heads", are national first-class cultural relics and also regarded as treasures in the collection of major museums around the world. They are well-deserved national folk treasures in the eyes of many Taiwan compatriots. Jiang's masterpiece *Matchmaker* is internationally renowned and has won the reputation of "Treasure of Oriental Art". This world-class master makes Quanzhou's puppets even more splendid. The craftsmanship of Jiang School puppet heads has been passed down to the fourth generation.

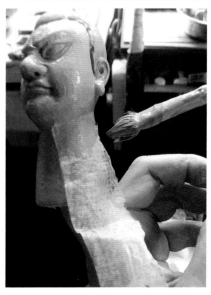

◎ 艺术家在制作木偶头。（黄雪玲 供图）
An artist was working on puppet head carving. (Courtesy of Huang Xueling)

传承千年的泉州木偶有提线木偶和掌中木偶两种表演形式。

走出泉州，走出福建，走出中国，让世人看看泉州木偶的艺术水平，是泉州几代木偶人的心声。无论是在北京奥运会开幕式上，还是在央视舞台上，抑或是在国际文化艺术交流舞台上，泉州木偶独特的表现手法总能让世人连连称赞。即使观众听不懂闽南话，但看到木偶或走或跳或书写或舞蹈，总是目不转睛。

泉州的提线木偶，古称"悬丝傀儡"或"线戏"，在民间被俗称为"嘉礼"。"嘉礼"是我国古代的五礼之一，祭祀之事为吉礼，丧葬之事为凶礼，军旅之事为军礼，宾客之事为宾礼，冠婚之事为嘉礼。闽南语"傀儡"的发音和"嘉礼"发音相同。何为"傀儡"？就是表演者掌中的提线木偶。

每个木偶身上有16条至30多条细若发丝的提线，表演者依靠对这些提线的熟练控制进行表演。简单一点的木偶，提线分布在其手部、腿部、肩部、耳部以及脊骨底部。而复杂的提线木偶更为细致，因为精密的提线分布，使得它们能够模仿人类和动物几乎所有的动作。

泉州提线木偶戏有专属于自己剧种的音乐——傀儡调，这在中国其他传统木偶戏中未曾有过。这种古老的戏种，至今仍完整地保存了下来。在将近300支曲牌的旋律曲调中，我们得以了解到诸如南鼓、拍板、压脚鼓、钲锣等古乐器。

◎ 泉州木偶剧团表演。（施维猛 摄）
A puppet show performed by Quanzhou Puppet Troupe. (Photo by Shi Weimeng)

Quanzhou puppets, which have been passed down for hundreds of years, have two performance forms: marionettes and hand puppets.

Out of Quanzhou, out of Fujian, out of China, showing the world the artistic level of Quanzhou puppets is the aspiration of generations of Quanzhou puppeteers. Whether at the opening ceremony of the Beijing Olympics, or on the stage of CCTV, or on the stage of international cultural and artistic exchanges, the unique performance of Quanzhou puppets are always praised by the world. Even if the audience does not understand Minnan dialect, they always keep their eyes on seeing the puppets walking or jumping, writing or dancing.

◎ 泉州提线木偶剧团表演的木偶戏《闹元宵》。（刘宝生 摄）
Celebrating the Lantern Festival, a marionette show performed by Quanzhou Marionette Troupe. (Photo by Liu Baosheng)

The marionettes in Quanzhou were called "hanging silk *kuilei* (puppets)" or "line play" in ancient times, and were commonly called "*Jiali*" in the folks. "*Jiali*" is one of the five rites in ancient China: Sacrifices are fortune rite, funerals are misfortune rites, military affairs are military rites, guests affairs are guest rites, and wedding ceremonies are "*Jiali*". The pronunciation of "puppet" in Minnan dialect is the same as "*Jiali*". What is a "puppet"? It is the marionettes performed in palms.

Each puppet has 16 to more than 30 hair-like threads. The performer relies on the skillful control of these threads to give the performance. The simpler puppets have thread lifts on their hands, legs, shoulders, ears, and the bottom of their spine. The complicated marionettes are more sophisticated, because the precise string distribution allows them to imitate almost all the movements of humans and animals.

Quanzhou marionettes have its own style of music—puppet tune, which has never been seen in other traditional Chinese puppet shows. This kind of ancient drama is still intact. In the melody of about 300 *qupai* (the generic term for a fixed melody used in traditional Chinese music) , we were able to learn about ancient musical instruments such as Nangu, Clapper, Foot Drum, Zhengluo, and so on.

木偶的另一种表演形式——掌中木偶戏，俗称"布袋戏"。拥有数百年历史的布袋戏，从明清到今天，始终流传于闽南的民间。

掌中木偶的形象是小巧的木偶头联结着造型各异的衣服。衣服的造型像个开口的布袋。表演者将手伸进木偶的衣服，食指套在头腔内，大拇指和另三个指头则套在两个衣袖里，靠着灵活自如的手指，把各种木偶角色表演得活灵活现，栩栩如生。泉州掌中木偶戏的代表性作品有传统剧目《大名府》《雷万春打老虎》等。

《人民日报》曾经如此报道过掌中木偶："掌中木偶扮饰人物，以说唱讲故事，木偶动作涵化戏曲身段，木偶表演与语言艺术相生相融，技术性、文学性、音乐性和趣味性兼具。因受傀儡戏、梨园戏、南音等的滋养，'唱南曲，依傀儡调，做梨园科'被认为是南派掌中木偶戏的剧种特点，而细腻优雅的表演风格，则成为南派掌中木偶戏区别于其他偶戏剧种的重要标识。"

本没有生命的木偶被泉州艺人的巧手赋予了灵魂，从而有了动人的故事。清人蔡鸿儒在《晋水常谈录》如此评价："傀儡，木偶也，今俗之线戏……泉人最工此技。"

◎ 提线木偶和掌中木偶表演。（陈英杰 摄）
Hand puppet and marionette shows. (Photo by Chen Yingjie)

Another form of puppet performance—hand puppets—are commonly known as "puppet show". The puppet show, with a history of hundreds of years, has been popular among the folks in Southern Fujian from the Ming and Qing Dynasties to today.

The image of hand puppets is a small puppet head connected with clothes of various shapes. The shape of the clothes is like a sack with its mouth wide open. The performer puts his hand into the puppet's clothes, his index finger in the head cavity, and thumb and the other three fingers in two sleeves. Relying on his flexible fingers, he performs various puppet characters vividly. The representative works of Quanzhou puppet show include the traditional plays *Daming County* and *Lei Wanchun Beats the Tiger,* among others.

People's Daily once reported on the hand puppets: "The hand puppets dress up as characters, tell stories with rap, and the movements of puppets imitate and integrate the body movements of operas. Blended with language arts, puppet performances are technical, literary, musical, and interesting. With the nourishment of Puppet Play, Liyuan Opera, Nanyin, etc., 'singing Nanqu, following the puppet tune, and moving as the Liyuan performers' is considered to be the characteristic of the puppet show of Southern School. The delicate and elegant performance style has become an important sign that distinguishes hand puppets from other types of puppet shows."

The lifeless puppets are endowed with soul by Quanzhou artist's skillful hands, and thus have moving stories. Cai Hongru from the Qing Dynasty commented in his works *Jinshui Chang Tan Lu* : "*Kuilei* are puppets, and are commonly referred to as marionettes... Quanzhou people are the best at this skill."

◎ 泉州府文庙前的掌中木偶表演。
（许师伟 摄）
Hand puppet performance in front of Confucius Temple in Quanzhou.
(Photo by Xu Shiwei)

梨园戏、高甲戏：文化瑰宝、历史传承

从宫廷来，到民间去，这是"梨园"的宿命。公元714年，大唐天子李隆基在皇宫中设立了第一座国立戏曲学校，史称"梨园亭"。梨园，从此成了后世演艺界的别称。

在玄宗皇帝的注脚里，除了杨贵妃，还有他的音乐才华。戏曲界至今仍供奉唐玄宗为祖师爷，又因其善用羯鼓指挥乐队，后代的戏曲仍保留司鼓板为乐队的指挥，尊其为打鼓佬，位于舞台九龙口。

梨园因其宫廷血缘，注定了表演程式典雅，唱曲法度严谨。我们现在所说的梨园戏诞生于南宋，发源于泉州，又称宋元南戏，与浙江的南戏共为"搬演南宋戏文唱念声腔"的"闽浙之音"，被誉为"古南戏活化石"。

南宋时的泉州，经济繁荣，是文化丰饶之地，梨园戏亦蓬勃发展。梨园戏的语言基础为泉州方言，在音韵上保留诸多古语，但方言土腔一律以泉州音为准，同时杂糅了部分汉族民间音乐，因不同人物身份与地方色彩，保留了地方土音和古音。

在梨园戏的一出戏里，可用一种宫调中的曲牌连缀表演，也可用不同宫调中的曲牌组套表演。每一出传统剧目都配有一套专属的曲牌，形式包含集曲、慢、引、小令等。梨园戏还可细分为三种：第一种是小梨园，演绎才子佳人的故事；第二种是下南流派，主要演绎家庭邻里故事；第三种是上路，主要演绎宫廷戏。梨园戏的乐律和乐器沿袭唐代旧制，采用琵琶、洞箫、二弦、三弦、唢呐等伴奏，打击乐器以鼓、小锣、拍板为主。

◎ 梨园戏《陈三五娘》。（吴刚强 摄）
Liyuan Opera *Chen San and Wu Niang*. (Photo by Wu Gangqiang)

Liyuan Opera and Gaojia Opera: Cultural Treasures and Historical Heritage

From the palace to civil society, this is the fate of Liyuan Opera. In 714 AD, Li Longji, Emperor Xuanzong of the Tang Dynasty, established the first national opera school in the imperial palace, known as "Liyuan Pavilion" in history. Liyuan has become another name for the show business ever since.

In the footnote of Emperor Xuanzong, besides Concubine Yang, there is also his musical talent. The opera circle still enshrines Xuanzong as the ancestor master. In addition, because of his good use of *Jiegu* (an ancient hour glass drum popular in the Tang Dynasty) to conduct the orchestra, subsequent generations of opera retain the *Siguban* as the orchestra conductor, respecting him as a drummer, and locating it at *Jiulongkou* (the point where performers make their debut) of the stage.

Because of its relation with the imperial palace, Liyuan Opera was destined to perform elegantly and rigorously in singing. The Liyuan Opera we are talking about here was originated in Quanzhou in the Southern Song Dynasty, and is also known as the Southern Opera of the Song and Yuan Dynasties. As one of the "Sounds of Fujian and Zhejiang", i.e. "a performance of the Southern Song Dynasty opera with singing and reading voices", Liyuan Opera is known as the "Living Fossil of Ancient Southern Opera" along with the Southern Opera of Zhejiang.

In the Southern Song Dynasty, Quanzhou was prosperous in economy and rich in culture, and Liyuan Opera flourished. The linguistic foundation of Liyuan Opera is Quanzhou dialect, which retains many ancient languages in terms of phonology. However, the dialect is always based on Quanzhou accent. At the same time, it blends part of Han folk music. Due to different character identities and local colors, the local dialect and ancient tones are preserved. Every Liyuan Opera can be played consecutively using one *qupai* of *gongdiao* (modes of ancient Chinese music), or by combining different *qupai* from different *gongdiao* into sets. Each traditional repertoire is equipped with a set of exclusive *qupai*, in the form of Qu, Man, Yin and Xiaoling. Liyuan Opera can be subdivided into three types. The first is Small Liyuan, which interprets the story of gifted scholars and beautiful ladies. The second is the Xia'nan School, which mainly interprets stories of families and neighborhoods. The third type is Shanglu, mainly performing court dramas. The rhythm and instruments of Liyuan Opera follow the old system of the Tang Dynasty, accompanied on Pipa, Dongxiao, Erxian, Sanxian, and Suona. Percussion instruments are mainly drums, small gongs, and clappers.

◎ 梨园戏《高文举》。（吴云轩 摄）

Liyuan Opera *Gao Wenju*. (Photo by Wu Yunxuan)

梨园戏最特别之处是有传统的压脚打鼓。有别于其他剧种的锣鼓，梨园戏的鼓用音色浑厚的"南鼓"，伴奏时将左脚压在鼓面上，进行不同位置的移动，配合鼓槌打出几十种轻重不同的鼓点。

　　梨园戏表演细腻，有自己传统且严谨的艺术演绎程式，所以流传不甚广。中华人民共和国成立之前，闽南各地散落着一些戏班，中华人民共和国成立后统一成一个梨园戏团——福建省梨园戏实验剧团。2006年，梨园戏经国务院批准列入第一批国家级非物质文化遗产名录。

　　泉州梨园戏的艺术家们，既有传承又有创新。如今，他们不仅面向全国，还面向欧洲开拓市场。虽然多数外国人听不懂唱词，但他们静下心来看着角色的表演，都会沉浸其中，继而喜欢上这典雅的唱腔和表演。台上低吟浅唱，台下穿越时空，八百年前的南戏遗响，饱经岁月，历久弥新。

◎ 说到泉州梨园戏，就不得不提曾静萍。曾静萍在戏曲界光芒闪耀，为泉州梨园戏的领军人物。她的粉丝们如朝圣一般，从四面八方拥来泉州看她的戏。《陈三五娘》《节妇吟》《董生与李氏》《康王告状》等经典曲目，不但让她囊括了业界的诸多大奖，也让她声名远扬。看曾静萍的戏是不可多得的艺术享受，堪称视听盛宴。（陈英杰 摄）

When it comes to Quanzhou Liyuan Opera, Ms. Zeng Jingping cannot be ignored. Ms. Zeng shines in the world of opera and is a leading figure of the field. Her fans, like pilgrims, came to Quanzhou from all directions to watch her plays. *Chen San and Wu Niang, Reply of a Chaste Wife, Mr. Dong and Ms. Li, Kang King's Lawsuit* and other classic plays, not only won her many awards, but also made her famous. Zeng Jingping's plays are rare artistic enjoyment, and they can be called audio-visual feasts. (Photo by Chen Yingjie)

The most special feature of Liyuan Opera is the traditional press-foot drumming. Not like other types of gongs and drums, Liyuan Opera adopts the thick-sounding South Drum. When accompanying the opera performance, drum players press their left foot on the drum surface and move it in different positions to create dozens of different light and heavy drum beats with the drumsticks.

The delicate performance and traditional and rigorous artistic interpretation program of Liyuan Opera limit its wide popularity. Before 1949, there were some theater troupes scattered all over Southern Fujian. After the founding of the People's Republic of China, all troupes were unified into one Liyuan opera troupe—Fujian Liyuan Opera Experimental Troupe. Approved by the State Council in 2006, Liyuan Opera was included in the first batch of National Intangible Cultural Heritage list.

The artists of Quanzhou Liyuan Opera have both inheritance and innovation. Today, they are not only facing the audience of the whole country, but also developing markets in Europe. Although most foreign audience don't understand the lyrics, they calm down and watch the character's performance. They will be immersed in it, and then they will like the elegant singing and performance. The opera performs on stages and travels through time and space. The relics of the Nanxi Opera 800 years ago are heard over the years, long-lasting with never-fading charm.

◎ 梨园戏传统的压脚打鼓。（陈英杰 摄）

The traditional press-foot drumming of Liyuan Opera. (Photo by Chen Yingjie)

每行每业都有其业界翘楚，身在业内，知其翘楚乃为常识。就像说起高甲戏的代表，就不得不说高甲戏丑王柯贤溪。

柯派丑角，以一个男演员来扮演开朗泼辣、诙谐有趣的女角，在体现和表达人物时，超越了性别，使得角色独具一格，无可取代。柯贤溪老先生自成一派的柯派高甲戏《金魁星》《闹茶馆》《骑驴探亲》等融入了京剧、梨园戏、木偶戏的表演元素，甚至借鉴了国际喜剧大师卓别林的表演技巧。

高甲戏，古称宋江剧，也叫戈甲戏，是清代闽南农村一种假扮梁山英雄的武打游行，距今有两百多年的历史。2006年5月20日，高甲戏被列入第一批国家级非物质文化遗产名录。高甲戏的表演形式兼容开放，在国内戏剧界屡获大奖。

20世纪20至40年代是高甲戏发展的黄金时期，整个泉州差不多有四百个戏班，戏班之间各显神通，出现了"十大虎班"的繁盛景象，但最好的戏班叫做"龙班"，也叫"金莲升"，因此有"一龙破五虎"的说法。

20世纪30年代，高甲戏开始走出国门表演，东南亚诸国都有其巡演的足迹。中华人民共和国成立以来，高甲戏从草台转入剧场。在角色方面，原先只有生、旦、丑，后又拓展了净、贴、外、末和北。其中丑最为突出。

"戏如人生，人生如戏"，这八个字道尽了戏剧和人生的关系。在台上演绎的种种故事，映射百态人生，人人都可寻得一丝代入感，大抵是这样的缘由，使得世人千百年来对戏剧都趋之若鹜。

◎ 高甲戏《昭君出塞》。（陈英杰 摄）
Gaojia Opera *Lady Zhaojun Going out of the Frontier*. (Photo by Chen Yingjie)

◎ 高甲戏丑角表演。（陈英杰 摄）
Harlequin performance of Gaojia Opera. (Photo by Chen Yingjie)

Every industry has its own leaders, and it is common sense to know the leaders in the industry. For Gaojia Opera, the representative is Ke Xianxi, the King of Clown of Gaojia Opera.

Ke School Harlequin refers to an actor playing a cheerful, humorous and interesting female character. When embodying and expressing characters, it transcends gender, making the role unique and irreplaceable. In his special Ke School Gaojia Operas scuh as *Golden Kuixing (the four stars in the bowl of the Big Dipper), Stirring up Troubles in a Tea House, Riding a Donkey to Visit Relatives*, etc, Mr. Ke incorporated the performance elements of Peking Opera, Liyuan Opera, and Puppet Show, and even draw on the performing skills of international comedy master Charles Chaplin.

Gaojia Opera, also known as Songjiang Opera or Gejia Opera in ancient times, is a martial arts parade with players pretending to be the heroes of Liangshan Mountain. It was originated in Southern Fujian since the Qing Dynasty and has a history of more than two hundred years. On May 20, 2006, Gaojia Opera was included in the first batch of National Intangible Cultural Heritage list. With compatible and open performance forms, Gaojia Opera has won many awards in the domestic theater industry.

The period from the 1920s to the 1940s was the golden age of the development of Gaojia Opera. There were almost 400 troupes in Quanzhou, and the troupes showed their own magical powers respectively. The prosperous scene of "ten tiger troupes" appeared. However, the best troupe was called "Dragon Troupe", also the name "Jinliansheng". Thus the saying went that "one 'dragon' beats 'five tigers'". In the 1930s, Gaojia Opera performers began to perform abroad and left their touring footprints in Southeast Asian countries. Since the founding of the People's Republic of China, Gaojia Opera was played in theaters rather than those simple temporary stages. In terms of roles, originally there were only Sheng (male role), Dan (female role), and Chou (clown), but later Jing (painted face), Tie, Wai, Mo and Bei were added, among which the clown is the most prominent.

"Drama is like life, while life is like a drama." This saying fully explains the relationship between operas and life. The various stories performed on stage reflect all kinds of life, and everyone can find a sense of substitution. This is probably the reason why people have been eager for operas for thousands of years.

拍胸舞：东方迪斯科

我国古代诗歌理论著作《毛诗序》写道："情动于中而行于言，言之不足故嗟叹之；嗟叹之不足故咏歌之；咏歌之不足，不知手之舞之足之蹈之也。"舞蹈，通过肢体语言表达出人类的各种情感。中国人早在五千年前就有了舞蹈，从最开始的求欢，表达情爱，到后来的祭祀、庆典、娱乐等，舞蹈未曾缺席过文明的发展。

泉州的拍胸舞，是闽越族的遗存。这种以男性为主的舞蹈里，我们看到了高高盘蛇的舞者，热情洋溢，以赤膊之姿，展示男性最原始的雄浑。舞者头上的蛇，是古闽越族的图腾崇拜，保留在拍胸舞中，使得千年以后的我们仍然可以领略古闽越图腾祭祀舞蹈的遗风。

拍胸舞被誉为闽南民间舞蹈活化石，于2006年被列入首批国家级非物质文化遗产保护名录。拍胸舞风格古朴，舞者全情投入，如痴如醉，壮硕的男子们把裸露的上身拍得"啪啪"作响，全身通红。伴随着音乐节奏，舞者以蹲裆步为主，双手依次击掌，拍击前胸、两胁、腿部，也叫"打七响"。

◎ 热情奔放的拍胸舞。（吴刚强 摄）

Passionate and spirited Chest-slapping Dance. (Photo by Wu Gangqiang)

Chest-slapping Dance: Oriental Disco

According to *Preface to the Book of Songs*, a poetic theory book written in ancient China: "Emotions in the heart will be reflected by words, and if words are not enough, people will sigh; if sighs are not enough, people will chant; if chants are not enough, people will unconsciously dance with hands and feet." Dances express various human emotions through body language. The Chinese danced as early as five thousand years ago. In occasions of seeking pleasure and expressing love, sacrifices, celebrations, and entertainment, dance has never been absent.

Chest-slapping Dance in Quanzhou is the remains of the Minyue people. In this male-dominated dance, we saw the enthusiastic dancers with images of snakes on their heads, showing the most primitive vigor of the male in a shirtless posture. The snake on the dancer's head is the totem worship of the ancient Minyue people, and it is retained in the dance, giving us the chance to appreciate the legacy of the ancient Minyue dance for totem sacrifice after thousands of years.

The Chest-slapping Dance is known as the living fossil of Southern Fujian folk dance and was included in the first batch of National Intangible Cultural Heritage Protection list in 2006. The style of the dance is quaint and simple. The dancers are fully engaged and intoxicated. The sturdy men pat their naked upper body with pops, and the whole body is flushedly red. Accompanied by the music rhythm, the dancers mainly squat their crotch steps, with their hands in turn giving high-fives, slapping their chests, two sides, and legs—also called "make seven beats".

◎ 拍胸舞不仅是一项非遗传承项目，更是老少皆宜的运动项目。（张清杰 摄）

The Chest-slapping Dance is not only an intangible cultural heritage item, but also a sport suitable for young and old alike. (Photo by Zhang Qingjie)

◎ 拍胸舞既可以在正式的舞台上表演，也可以在民间活动中表演。（吴云轩 摄）
The Chest-slapping Dance can be used for formal stage performances and folk activities. (Photo by Wu Yunxuan)

被称为"东方迪斯科"的拍胸舞极具感染力。在道具謦鼓（一种用竹筒做成的圆形长鼓）和钱鼓的带动下，场面气氛很是热烈。在无音乐伴奏的情况下，钱鼓的作用就更为重要。

宋元时期，新生的地方戏曲与拍胸舞相互融合，互相影响。宋元南戏《郑元和与李亚仙》中加入拍胸舞，使得南曲《三千两金》成了拍胸舞的标配。拍胸舞在泉州流传范围广泛，但直到今天，各地跳的拍胸舞绝大多数都配以《三千两金》的音乐。因为《三千两金》讲述的是郑元和迷恋歌伎李亚仙，上京赶考的三千两盘缠散尽，沦为街头乞丐的故事，因此"乞丐舞"也成为拍胸舞的又一别称。

拍胸舞得以传承千年，得益于泉州发达、开放的经济文化环境。"市井十洲人"的泉州，歌舞升平，百戏兴盛。再加上泉州人"事死如生"，对丧事极为重视，凡有丧事必有拍胸舞辟邪祛灾纳吉，使得拍胸舞从古至今，传承不断。

Known as "Oriental Disco", the Chest-slapping Dance is very contagious. Driven by Pi drums (a long round drum made of bamboo tubes) and tambourines, the atmosphere of the scene is very warm. In the case of no musical accompaniment, the role of tambourines is more important.

During the Song and Yuan Dynasties, the newly born local operas and Chest-slapping Dance merged and influenced each other. The addition of Chest-slapping Dance in the Southern Opera of the Song and Yuan Dynasties *Zheng Yuanhe and Li Yaxian* made the Nanqu *Three Thousand Liang* (1 *liang*=50g) *Gold* a standard part of the Chest-slapping Dance. The dance is widely spread in Quanzhou, but until today, most of the dances performed in various places are accompanied by the music of *Three Thousand Liang Gold*. According to the story, Zheng Yuanhe's obsession with sing-song girl Li Yaxian cost him all three thousand *liang* gold, the travelling fare for imperial examination, and Zheng thus became a beggar. So "Beggar Dance" has become another nickname of Chest-slapping Dance.

The Chest-slapping Dance has been passed on for thousands of years, thanks to Quanzhou's developed and open-minded economic and cultural environment. As a city where "people from ten continents lived", Quanzhou is peachy and all kinds of operas are flourishing. Coupled with the local custom to "serve the death as they are alive", Quanzhou people attach great importance to funerals. Whenever there is a funeral, there must be a Chest-slapping Dance to ward off evil and calamity and receive good luck. This custom has kept the Chest-slapping Dance alive from ancient times to the present day.

◎ 如今拍胸舞在泉州对外文化交流中发挥着重要的作用。（吴云轩 摄）
Nowadays, the Chest-slapping Dance plays an important role in Quanzhou's international cultural exchange. (Photo by Wu Yunxuan)

赏灯猜谜：传统文化嘉年华

若要说起哪个节日在中国的文化史上，既有情怀又有情调，既有传统风俗又有艺术氛围，那元宵节可以算一个。西风渐进，很多古老的传统似乎都消失了，好在泉州古城用"赏灯猜谜"锁住了岁月的快速流转，传承至今的手工造灯技艺，令世人铭记历史的多彩璀璨。

元宵节始于秦朝，汉文帝时，正月十五被定为元宵节。汉武帝时，司马迁创"太初历"，元宵节被定为重大节日。缺乏娱乐活动的古人，对元宵节翘首以盼，尤其是未婚青年男女。在古代，未婚的女子轻易不出门，而在元宵节当天她们却可以出门去看灯，猜谜，游乐，顺便找寻如意郎君。礼法森严的封建时代，男女授受不亲，更别提自由恋爱了，于是可以尽兴踩街游玩的元宵节便成了自由恋爱的最好时机。

如果说西方的情人节传说具有浪漫的悲剧色彩，那么中国的情人节就喜庆热闹多了。泉州传统梨园剧剧目《陈三五娘》中，主人公陈三和五娘亦是在元宵佳节赏花灯时一见倾心的。据说南北朝时陈国公主乐昌和驸马徐德言也是在元宵之夜破镜重圆……这些缠绵悱恻的动人故事为元宵节增添了柔情万种的魅力，使元宵节成为中国的"情人节"。

在元宵节，除了欣赏各种新奇耀眼的花灯，猜灯谜也是一项必不可少的活动。在文学创作上把花灯和灯谜结合在一起的是《春灯谜》。《春灯谜》是一部传奇作品，其作者为明末清初戏曲家阮大铖，故事主要描述男主人公宇文彦与女主人公韦影娘在元宵节灯会上因灯谜而结缘的爱情故事。

◎ 万人空巷赏花灯。（陈英杰 摄）

Everyone comes out to admire lanterns. (Photo by Chen Yingjie)

Admiring Lanterns and Guessing Riddles: Traditional Culture Carnival

◎ 每年正月十五，晋江东石镇的嘉应庙吸引了泉台两地的同胞
一起来数宫灯。（许兆恺 摄）

Every year on the 15th day of the first lunar month, Jiaying Temple in Dongshi Town, Jinjiang, attracts compatriots from both Quanzhou and Taiwan to come together to count lanterns. (Photo by Xu Zhaokai)

If you wonder which festivals in the history of Chinese culture are with feelings, sentiment, traditional customs, and artistic atmosphere, then the Lantern Festival must be one of them. With Western customs gradually coming into China, many ancient Chinese traditions seem to have disappeared. Fortunately, in the ancient city of Quanzhou, the fast passage of time has been locked by admiring lanterns and guessing riddles. The hand-made lantern craftsmanship that has been passed down to this day has made the world remember the colorful and brilliant history.

The Lantern Festival began in the Qin Dynasty. Under the reign of Emperor Wen of the Han Dynasty, the 15th day of the lunar January was designated as the Lantern Festival. During the reign of Emperor Wu of the Han Dynasty, Sima Qian created the Taichu Calendar and the Lantern Festival was designated as a major festival. The ancients who lacked entertainment activities, especially those unmarried youths, looked forward keenly to the festival. In ancient times, unmarried girls did not go out in normal times. However, on the Lantern Festival they were allowed to go out to watch lanterns, guess riddles, have fun, and find the ideal husbands by the way. With strict rules and regulations in the feudal era, men and women had no dealings with each other, not to mention free love. Thus the Lantern Festival, when people could enjoy shopping and entertainment on the street, became the best time for free love.

While the legend of Western Valentine's Day has a romantic and tragic color, Chinese Lovers' Day is much more festive and lively. In Quanzhou's traditional Liyuan play *Chen San and Wu Niang*, the protagonists Chen San and Wu Niang fell in love at first sight during the Lantern Festival. It is said that during the Northern and Southern Dynasties, Princess Lechang and her husband Xu Deyan of the Kingdom of Chen also reunited on the night of the Lantern Festival…These lingering and moving stories added tenderness and charm to the Lantern Festival, making it the Valentine's Day of China.

In the Lantern Festival, in addition to admiring all kinds of novel and dazzling lanterns, guessing lantern riddles is also an essential activity. In literary works, lanterns and lantern riddles are combined together in *Spring Lantern Riddles*, a legendary work written by Ruan Dacheng, a dramatist from the late Ming and early Qing Dynasties. The story mainly describes the love story between the hero Yu Wenyan and the heroine Wei Yingniang at the Lantern Festival.

谜语这种古老的文化，从神话时代的问答形式孕育而来。至宋代，谜语和传统的灯彩艺术相互融合，别具一格的"灯谜"文化从此诞生。当花灯和谜语在一起的时候，璀璨的文明之火通过这种古老的仪式传递出来。

汉字的博大精深，在灯谜的世界里被发挥得淋漓尽致。制谜、猜谜、制灯、观灯、赏灯成了元宵节最核心的狂欢。无论是平头百姓还是文人雅士都可参与的广泛性，使得中国出现了诸多谜语之乡。比如广东澄海、福建石狮、福建晋江、福建漳州，这几地的灯谜历史可以追溯到宋代。

泉州深厚的文化底蕴使之成为灯谜的一方热土。唐代欧阳詹、宋代吕惠卿、明代郑成功等历史名人均与灯谜结下不解之缘。近现代享誉厦坛的谜家有谢云声、邱春木等。

2018年福建高考揭榜后，获得文科第一名的黄亦陈瞬间刷爆朋友圈。而和她同时出现的关键词，还有"灯谜"二字。她坦承，灯谜对她帮助很大。当时光倒回到2016年元宵节，那时候中央电视台《中国谜语大会》（第三季）正举行决赛，黄亦陈和她的小伙伴最终以绝对的优势战胜对手，登上了最高领奖台，那是泉州灯谜之光。

泉州盛大的元宵赏灯活动推动了花灯制作技艺的发展！根据南安丰州傅姓、黄姓族谱记载："唐僖宗年间，傅实以尚书左仆射衔带兵入闽，驻于武荣（今南安市），在桃源建唐王宫，按长安结灯的礼仪祝圣天子万年，于是有了桃源点灯的开始。"泉州花灯制作由此开始，于宋元炽盛，延续至今，誉满华夏。

◎ 制作无骨花灯。（陈英杰 摄）

Making frameless lanterns. (Photo by Chen Yingjie)

The ancient culture of riddles was borne out of the quiz of mythological age. In the Song Dynasty, riddles and traditional lantern art were integrated together, generating the unique culture of lantern riddles. When lanterns and riddles come together, the sparkling fire of civilization is transmitted through this ancient ritual.

The extensiveness and profoundness of Chinese characters are brought to the fullest in the world of lantern riddles. Making riddles, guessing riddles, making lanterns, watching lanterns, and admiring lanterns have become the core carnival of Lantern Festival. The wide range of participation, whether it is ordinary people or literati, has made many homes of riddles throughout China. For example, the history of lantern riddles in Chenghai of Guangdong, Shishi of Fujian, Jinjiang of Fujian, and Zhangzhou of Fujian can be traced back to the Song Dynasty.

Quanzhou's profound cultural heritage makes it a hot spot for lantern riddles. Historical celebrities such as Ouyang Zhan in the Tang Dynasty, Lyu Huiqing in the Song Dynasty, and Zheng Chenggong in the Ming Dynasty all had an indissoluble bond with lantern riddles. Xie Yunsheng and Qiu Chunmu are famous riddle makers in the riddle industry.

After the university entrance examination results were unveiled in 2018, Huang Yichen, who ranked first in liberal arts in Fujian, instantly blasted her circle of friends. And the key word that appeared at the same time with her was "riddle". She confided that lantern riddles helped her a lot. When the time went back to the 2016 Lantern Festival, the finals of CCTV's *Chinese Riddles Conference* (season 3) was held. Huang Yichen and her friends finally defeated their opponents by absolute advantage and boarded the highest podium. That is the highlight of Quanzhou lantern riddles.

The grand lantern appreciation activities in Lantern Festival in Quanzhou promoted the development of lantern making skills! According to the genealogies of the Fu and Huang in Fengzhou, Nan'an: "During the reign of Emperor Xi in the Tang Dynasty, Fu Shi led his troops into Fujian under the title of prime minister and stationed in Wurong (now Nan'an City). He built the Tang Palace in Taoyuan, and blessed the longevity of the emperor according to the light etiquette in Chang'an (now Xi'an). This was the beginning of the Taoyuan lighting." Lantern production in Quanzhou began from then, flourished in the Song and Yuan Dynasties, and continues to this day, famous in China.

◎ 花灯制作技艺传承人教授孩子们如何制作花灯。（陈英杰 摄）
A lantern-making inheritor teaches children to make lanterns. (Photo by Chen Yingjie)

◎ 泉州特色花灯：刻纸料丝灯、彩扎灯和针刺无骨灯。（许兆恺 摄）
Unique lanterns in Quanzhou: carved paper and glass silk lanterns, colorful patterned lanterns, and needle pierced frameless lanterns. (Photo by Xu Zhaokai)

泉州花灯品种俱全，明末清初文学家张岱所著《陶庵梦忆》中记载了"杭州抚台委托泉州府尹和南安知县雇人精制花灯"的史实，并夸其灯"穷工极巧"。

清乾隆年间编修的《泉州府志》如此描述泉州的奇巧灯品："周围灯火，缘以练锦，缀以流苏，鼓鸣于内，钟应于外""灯火三层，蘸沉檀其上，香闻数里矣！"泉州花灯工艺之精湛由此可见。"春光结胜百花芳，元夕分华盛泉唐""天下上元，灯烛之盛，无逾闽中"——泉州赏灯氛围之浓，由此可见。

泉州的花灯分为刻纸料丝灯、针刺无骨灯、锡雕宫灯、彩扎灯等，每一盏灯集绘画、书法、刀刻、裱糊、彩扎等于一身，如流光坠，盏盏生春晖。刻纸料丝灯和针刺无骨灯更是泉州花灯的集大成者，冠绝全国。

清朝末年，泉州刻纸大师李尧宝融合刻纸工艺和古典图案纹样，创造性地把刻纸技艺应用到料丝灯造型图案中，创作出如梦幻般优美典雅的刻纸料丝灯。

泉州老艺人蔡炳汉是首批国家级非物质文化遗产项目代表性传承人。他创作的针刺无骨灯，只用厚片，不用骨架支撑，经缝衣针刺出精美花纹图案，按所需造型裁剪、折叠和粘贴，再饰上花边，造型小巧玲珑。灯光在内亮起时，华美透亮。

我们追赶不了时光，也留不住岁月，但是古老的赏灯猜谜习俗和制灯技艺一路传承，在一定程度上修复了时间列车过快的轮转，折射出古老温婉的文化内涵。

◎ 泉州花灯制作技艺传承人林守明。（吴云轩 摄）

Lin Shouming, the inheritor of Quanzhou lantern making technique. (Photo by Wu Yunxuan)

Quanzhou has a wide variety of lanterns. In his *Tao An Dreaming Memory*, Zhang Dai, a writer in the late Ming and early Qing Dynasties, recorded the historical facts that "The governor of Hangzhou commissioned the governor of Quanzhou and Nan'an County magistrate to hire skilled craftsmen to make refined lanterns". In addition, the lanterns were made with "extreme skillfulness".

The *Local Chronicles of Quanzhou* compiled during the reign of Emperor Qianlong of the Qing Dynasty described Quanzhou's exquisite lanterns as follows: "The surrounding lights are decorated with brocades and tassels; drums ring inside, and bells echo from outside." "The lanterns are of three layers dipping with eaglewood and sandalwood on them; the fragrance can be smelt for several miles away!" This shows the exquisite craftsmanship of Quanzhou lanterns. "The beauty of spring lights wins over hundreds of flowers, and Lantern Festival was in its peak time in the Tang Danasty." "In Lantern Festivals all over China, the beauty of lanterns in Quanzhou is the number one." This reflects atmosphere of lantern admiring in Quanzhou.

The lanterns in Quanzhou are divided into paper-cut silk lanterns, needle-punched boneless lanterns, tin-carved palace lanterns, colored tie lights, etc. Each lantern integrates art and techniques of painting, calligraphy, knife-cutting, paper-pasting, and festoon. Every piece of them shines as a shooting star. The paper-cutting silk lanterns and the needle-punched boneless lanterns are comprehensive synthesizers of Quanzhou lanterns, which are the best in the country.

At the end of the Qing Dynasty, combining paper-cutting techniques with classical patterns, Quanzhou paper-cutting master Li Yaobao creatively applied paper-cutting techniques to the pattern of the filament lantern. By doing this, he created dreamlike and elegant paper-cutting filament lanterns.

Cai Binghan, an old craftman from Quanzhou, is the representative inheritor among the first batch of national intangible cultural heritage projects. The needle-punched boneless lanterns he produced adopt only thick slices and need no frame support. The sewing needles are used to pierce exquisite patterns according to needs. The shape is cut, folded and pasted, and then decorated with lace, which is small but exquisite. When the lights are on inside, the lanterns are gorgeous and bright.

We can't keep up with the time, nor can we keep it, but the ancient lantern-admiring and riddle-guessing customs and lantern-making skills have been passed down all the way. These facts make up for the fleeting time to a certain extent and reflect the gentle ancient cultural connotation.

◎ 制作福船模型。（陈英杰 摄）

Making a model of a Fu junk. (Photo by Chen Yingjie)

水密隔舱福船制造技艺：扬帆万里的船舶技术保障

在古代，海上船只的远航能力，是大国繁荣昌盛的标志。中国古代海上丝绸之路上，最令人赞叹的就是具备远洋航行能力的大型船只——福船和广船，亦即福建制造的船和广东制造的船。

被誉为"海上兵马俑"和"海上敦煌"的"南海I号"，是福船的巅峰之作，其船体在不同部位使用了六种不同的木材，如马尾松木、福建柏、海南榄仁木等，木质优良，保存完好。

1974年夏天，在泉州后渚港发掘的一艘南宋晚期木帆船，其船身残长24.2米，残宽9.15米，复原长度达34米，宽11米，船重200吨。沉船出土物和科学考证揭示出，这是一艘13世纪泉州造的三桅远洋商船，运载着大量香料、药物及其他商品从东南亚归来。古沉船内部结构和轮廓造型指向了13世纪最尖端的造船工艺。

古船上的水密隔舱技术表明，在宋代，中国的造船业和航海业十分发达，而造船技术在那一时代遥遥领先于世界的，便是泉州。泉州后渚港发掘的这一艘宋代木帆船，亦是福船的代表作，而福船最核心的技术就是水密隔舱工艺。

通过古船本身和古船上的文物，我们得以和千年前的造船工匠们对话。12道隔舱板将全船分成13个舱，舱壁钩联严密，水密程度很高。13个水密隔舱增加了船舶海上航行的存活率和安全性。平时用来存放货物的水密隔舱，最核心的功能是保证船只安全。倘若船体发生碰撞导致开裂，也只有破损部位的隔舱会进水，哪怕有几个隔舱同时进水，船只依然能够保证安全。

The Craftsmanship of Watertight Fu Junks: the Technical Guarantee of Sailing for Thousands of Miles

In ancient times, the long-distance sailing ability of marine vessels was a sign of the prosperity of a great country. On the ancient Chinese Maritime Silk Road, what are most amazing are the large ships with ocean-going capabilities— Fu junks and Guang junks, that is, ships made in Fujian and Guangdong respectively.

The *Nanhai I*, known as the Terracotta Warriors and Horses at Sea and Dunhuang at Sea, is the pinnacle of the Fu Junks. Six different types of wood were used to made different parts of its hull, such as masson pine, Fujian cypress, and Hainan terminalia, and so on. The wood is fine and well preserved.

In the summer of 1974, an ancient junk was excavated at Houzhu Port in Quanzhou. Its residual hull was 24.2 meters long, 9.15 meters wide, 34 meters long, 11 meters wide, and 200 tons in weight. It was made in late Southern Song Dynasty. The unearthed objects of the sunken ship and scientific research revealed that it was a triple-mast ocean-going merchant ship built in Quanzhou in the 13th century. It returned from Southeast Asia carrying a large number of spices, medicines and other commodities. Its internal structure and contour modeling indicated the most edge-cutting shipbuilding craftsmanship in the 13th century.

The watertight compartment technology on this junk shows that in the Song Dynasty, China's shipbuilding and navigation industries were highly developed, and the shipbuilding technology in Quanzhou in that era was far ahead of the rest of the world. This ancient junk unearthed in Houzhu Port of Quanzhou is also a masterpiece of Fu Junk, whose core technology is that of watertight compartment.

Through the ancient ship itself and the relics on it, we were able to talk to the shipbuilders thousands of years ago. The 12 bulkheads divide the ship into 13 cabins, and the bulkheads were tightly coupled, generating a high degree of watertightness. Thirteen watertight cabins increase the survival rate and safety of ships at sea. The core function of the watertight compartments used to store cargoes is to ensure the safety of the ship. If the hull crashes due to a collision, only the compartments in the damaged part will be flooded. Even if several compartments are flooded at the same time, the ship can still be safe.

◎ 惠安小岞造船场景。（成冬冬 摄）
Boat building scene in Xiaozuo, Hui'an. (Photo by Cheng Dongdong)

用牢固的铁钩和钉钩连在一起的隔板和船壳，其两旁还有形似"肋骨"的装置，用来增加船体强度，船体本身具有多重木板结构，尾舵可以升降，桅杆使用转轴。龙骨、肋骨结构与榫挍方式，使得古船具有很强的抗击风浪能力。无论是驭风缓行，还是全速前行，一艘又一艘的福船，都在向世界彰显着宋王朝的海上实力。

古人用"一叶扁舟"来形容船在水中的飘逸之姿，而泉州出土的这艘福船，造型十分流畅，呈现"V"字形，在现代动力学上来讲，属于流线型设计，船舶航行在海面上，具有叶子的形状与轻盈。

刺桐古城在公元6世纪就有了与南海诸国进行商贸往来的记载。唐代，泉州港名列中国四大名港之一，水密隔舱技术业已开始应用。宋元时期，泉州港发展为"东方第一大港"，水密隔舱技术更加成熟。西方历史上同等规模的船舶使用水密隔舱技术，还要等到18世纪。

彼时的泉州港，波澜壮阔，千帆竞发，帆樯林立，商贾云集，梯航万国。这艘出土的泉州古沉船，让古代泉州开放与繁荣的具象逐渐清晰起来，再次令世界瞩目。

我国造船史上两项重要创新——隔舱板和肋骨，都在福船上得以完美应用。2010年1月15日，泉州"水密隔舱福船制造技艺"被联合国教科文组织列入急需保护的非物质文化遗产名录。

宋元时期的闽商，以水密隔舱技艺造就的福船为利器，打造海洋经济的宏大经略，为亚非欧人民架起了商贸与文明交流的通道，缔造了一部海上丝绸之路的传奇。

◎ 新制的福船。（田米 摄）

A newly-made Fu junk. (Photo by Tian Mi)

◎ 航行在晋江出海口的小型福船。（陈英杰 摄）
A small Fu junk sailing at the mouth of Jinjiang River.
(Photo by Chen Yingjie)

The bulkheads and the hull are connected by strong iron hooks and nail hooks, and ribs-shaped devices were placed on both sides to increase the strength of the hull. The hull itself adopts a multi-plank structure. The rudder can be raised and lowered and the masts use a rotating shaft. The keel and rib structure and the mortise joint method enable the ancient ship to resist wind and waves effectively. Either driving the wind slowly or moving forward at full speed, one after another Fu junk showed the world the maritime strength of the Song Dynasty.

The ancients used "a small boat roaming on the water" to describe the elegant posture of a ship in the water. This Fu junk unearthed in Quanzhou has a very smooth V shape. In terms of modern dynamics, it is of a streamlined design. The ship sailed over the sea with the shape and softness of leaves.

In the sixth century AD, the ancient city of Zayton stored records of business dealings with various countries in Southeast Asia. In the Tang Dynasty, Quanzhou Port was listed as one of the four famous ports in China, and the watertight compartment technology was applied. During the Song and Yuan Dynasties, Quanzhou Port developed into "the largest port in the East", and the watertight compartment technology became more mature. In Western history, the application of watertight compartment technology in ships of the same size did not appear until the 18th century.

At that time, Quanzhou Port was magnificent with thousands of sails waiting for departure, merchants gathered, and voyaged to many countries of the world. The unearthed ancient shipwreck in Quanzhou gradually clarified the openness and prosperity of ancient Quanzhou, and once again attracted the attention of the world.

Two important innovations in the history of this country's shipbuilding, bulkheads and bottom frames, have been perfectly applied on Fu junks. On January 15, 2010, Quanzhou's watertight compartment Fu junk manufacturing technique was included in the List of Intangible Cultural Heritage in Need of Urgent Safeguarding by the UNESCO.

During the Song and Yuan Dynasties, Fujian merchants used the watertight compartment technology as a tool to create a grand strategy for the marine economy, setting up a channel for commerce and communication of civilization for the people of Asia, Africa and Europe, and creating a legend of the Maritime Silk Road.

美食之城——海丝起点的舌尖旅行

对于泉州人来说，"吃饭皇帝大"。美食是泉州除了丰富多样的文化之外另一张闪亮的名片。乐于向生活致敬的泉州人，在三餐里，重新定义了"幸福"和"满足"，让很多人不由得感叹，生活在泉州真乃"人间值得"。

泉州的美食基因里，除了有山海融合，兼容并蓄，还有难得的古早味——那是古越族的遗韵，是魏晋士族的做派，亦是"涨海声中万国商"那万种风味的交融。独具风格的烹饪手法加上物产丰饶的绵长海域，使得泉州的"舌尖之旅"更为广阔辽远。曾经的"东方第一大港"，把美食的基调定在了"开放融合"的国际格局上，既立足本土又融合海内外。

在烟火气十足的泉州，食客们最为津津乐道的是，哪里还藏着美食。他们以发现美食的藏身之所为荣。毕竟，在泉州的每一条大街小巷里，都可能藏着一段与美食有关的传奇故事。

曾经的繁华在饮食文化中得以呈现，来自异域的风味糅合于本土风味及中原风味之中，蒸煮炖卤煎炸，样样都有代表性美食。海鲜白灼或酱油水，讲究的是本味、新鲜；多元的肉类做法，迥异于中华美食版图上的其他地域；最令人无法抗拒的则是各类小吃——面线糊、土笋冻、海蛎煎、牛肉羹、烧肉粽、润饼等牵动游子乡愁的味道，如今早已搅动味蕾江湖。

与古迹不期而遇，与美食悄然邂逅，这就是泉州，一座一生至少要来一次的城。

◎ 泉州丰富的海产资源使得海鲜占据本地美食的重要部分。（吴刚强 摄）
Quanzhou's rich marine resources make seafood an important part of local cuisine. (Photo by Wu Gangqiang)

Gourmet City: a Bite of Quanzhou, the Starting Point of the Maritime Silk Road

There is a saying among Quanzhou people that "Eating is more important than the emperor". Delicious food is another shining card of Quanzhou besides its rich and diverse culture. Quanzhou people, who are willing to pay tribute to life, redefine happiness and satisfaction in their daily meals. Many people can't help but admire that living in Quanzhou is truly "worthy on earth".

In the genes of Quanzhou's cuisine, in addition to the fusion and inclusiveness of mountains and seas, there is also a rare taste of ancient times—the legacy of the ancient Yue people, the style of the Wei and Jin gentry, and the blend of flavors from all over the world in the "Emporium of the World in the sound of the rising sea".

The unique cooking techniques and the long and fertile sea areas make Quanzhou's "trip to the tip of the tongue" even more expansive. The once "largest port in the East" sets the keynote of the cuisine on the international pattern of "openness and integration", a combination of local taste and that from all over the world.

◎ 泉州多样而美味的小吃吸引着越来越多的国内外游客。（郑朝阳 摄）
Quanzhou's diverse and delicious snacks are attracting more and more tourists from home and abroad. (Photo by Zheng Chaoyang)

In Quanzhou, a city full of hustle and bustle, what diners talk about most is where are the delicacy hidden. They are proud of finding a hiding place for good food. After all, in every street and alley in Quanzhou, there may be a legendary story related to delicious food.

The prosperity of the past is presented in the dietary culture. The flavors from the exotic are blended with the local flavors and the Central Plains flavors. Steaming, cooking, stewing, stewing in soy sauce, deep frying and frying, all these methods have representative delicacies. Seafood, boiled or in soy sauce, highlights the original and fresh taste. Diversified methods of cooking meat are very different from other regions on the Chinese cuisine map. What are most irresistible are all kinds of snacks—mee sua paste, sea worm jelly, oyster omelet, beef strip soup, *zongzi* with meat stuffing, and *runbing* (spring rolls). All these are the flavors of homesickness and have already stirred one's degustator.

Let's have an unexpected encounter with historical sites and quiet encounter with food. This is Quanzhou, a city that everyone must visit at least once in his/her lifetime.

面线糊：暖心温情的家乡味

何为美食？在美食界恐无定论，但是在泉州人心中，那一碗暖心温情的面线糊是当之无愧的家乡味。无论身在何处，心中总有念想！

传说中，面线糊被乾隆誉为"龙须珍珠粥"，其最大的特点是呈糊状，面细，汤荤，汤由猪骨或虾糠熬成，糊是地瓜粉调制而成，爽滑细腻，鲜美纯醇，入口即化。

作为古早味的经典美食，以泉州为发源地的面线糊早已成了泉州的特色之一。泉州人一般将面线糊作为早餐食用，就着油条或马蹄酥吃，当然也可以当作点心和夜宵。泉州人喜欢在面线糊里加入各种各样的配料，比如醋肉、虾仁、海蛎、卤蛋、煎蛋等。

面线糊独树一帜的口感，蕴含了泉州当地的饮食习惯和文化背景，也让每一位来到泉州的人，都以舌尖的味蕾开启探索泉州的旅程。

◎ 一碗好吃的面线糊除了汤底要好，面线也是关键。（刘宝生 摄）
For a bowl of delicious mee sua paste, in addition to the good soup base, the quality of the noodle is also a key. (Photo by Liu Baosheng)

◎ 面线糊与油条的搭配是许多泉州人的选择。（陈英杰 摄）
The combination of mee sua paste and deep-fried dough sticks is the
choice of many people in Quanzhou. (Photo by Chen Yingjie)

Mee Sua Paste: a Warm Hometown Flavor

What is delicacy? There is no consensus in the food industry. However, in the hearts of Quanzhou people, a bowl of warm-hearted mee sua paste is a well-deserved taste of hometown. No matter where they are, they always miss it in their hearts!

Legend has it that mee sua paste was hailed by Emperor Qianlong as "dragon beard pearl porridge". Its biggest characteristic is that it is a paste with slim noodles in meaty soup. The soup is made from pork bones or shrimp bran, and the paste is made from sweet potato powder. Smooth and delicate, delicious and pure, it melts in the mouth.

As a classic delicacy of ancient times, mee sua paste born in Quanzhou has long been one of Quanzhou's characteristics. People in Quanzhou generally eat mee sua paste for breakfast, with deep-fried dough sticks or Beh Teh Sor, and of course it can also be used as a snack and supper. People in Quanzhou like to add a variety of ingredients to mee sua paste, such as vinegared pork, shrimp, sea oysters, braised eggs, fried eggs, etc.

The unique taste of mee sua paste contains the local eating habits and cultural background of Quanzhou. It also allows every visitor to Quanzhou to start a journey of exploration with the taste buds.

很多人说泉州是一座来了就不想走的城市，在泉州混迹久了，就和各色美食混熟了，混得有感情了。深谙泉州美食的人，对美食存在的各个角落了然十心，对品尝美食的最佳时间也了然于心，资深食客们如数家珍，以此为荣。

泉州府文庙附近有一面线糊摊，摊主是一个清瘦却很有精神的短发女人，有几个人帮忙打下手。人来人往的人气聚集，使得整条路在凌晨仍显得熙攘热闹，这种热闹让人很舒服，空气和气温都恰到好处。黎明时分，气温微凉，但这位女摊主的面线糊和猪血汤喝起来总是令人温暖惬意。对于真正的食客来说，味道是一种幸福的感觉。一个泉州的女人，摆出一个以她的名字命名的面线糊摊，成就了这个城市别样的温情。

类似这样的面线糊小店或摊点，毫不起眼地散落在泉州的大街小巷，几十年如一日，用它们独特的高汤、面线和品种多样的配料，不仅温暖古城居民和四方来客的胃，也温暖他们的心！

泉州这个城市的味道，从各个小摊小贩勤劳的双手里散发出来，带着芳香，带着细腻，带着风情，带着温情，让人"吃"迷不已……

◎ 吃面线糊可以随意挑选多种配料。（陈英杰 摄）
You can choose as many ingredients as you like for mee sua paste. (Photo by Chen Yingjie)

Many people say that Quanzhou is a city that you don't want to leave once you've been here. Moreover, if you've been in Quanzhou for a long time, you've become acquainted with the various types of food and become attached to them. Those who know Quanzhou's food well know every location of the food and the best time to try them, and veteran diners are proud to know all about the delicacy.

There is a mee sua paste stall near the Confucius Temple and School in Quanzhou. The stall owner is a thin but energetic woman with short hair. There are also a few helpers. The gathering of people makes the whole road still bustling in the early morning. This kind of bustle is very comfortable, and the air and temperature are just right. At dawn, the temperature is slightly low, but mee sua paste and pig blood soup of the female stall owner are always warm and cozy. For real diners, nice taste is a feeling of happiness. A Quanzhou woman put up a mee sua paste stall named after her and made this city a special kind of warmth.

Small shops or stalls like this are scattered inconspicuously in the streets and alleys of Quanzhou. For decades, they use their unique soup, noodles and a variety of ingredients to warm not only stomachs of the residents of the ancient city and visitors from all over the world, but also their hearts!

The taste of the city of Quanzhou radiates from the industrious hands of various stall vendors, with fragrance, delicacy, amorous feelings, and warmth, making people fascinated in "eating"…

◎ 曾经上过美食纪录片《舌尖上的中国》的后城面线糊是许多游客慕名打卡的泉州小吃店之一。（陈英杰 摄）

Houcheng Mee Sua Paste, which has been featured in the gourmet documentary *A Bite of China*, is one of the most popular Quanzhou snack restaurants for tourists. (Photo by Chen Yingjie)

肉粽、牛肉羹：完美搭配，爽口筋道

有华人的地方，米和面几乎是不可或缺的主食。在泉州，大米做成的美食不在少数，光特色主食就有咸饭、萝卜饭、壶仔饭和肉粽等。

端午节是中国传统节日之一，人们在这一天吃粽子，观龙舟赛。而在泉州，粽子并非只在端午节才吃，而是几乎天天都能吃。外地游客到泉州必吃美食名单上有肉粽和牛肉羹。这两样美食看似普通，但对于那些既想有口感又有饱腹感的食客们来说，那简直是人间美味，至尊搭配。

泉州的特色肉粽历史久远，和南宋大诗人陆游颇有渊源。传说当年陆游到福州为官，带来了"艾香粽子"。陆游离任后，在陆家当过差的泉州人，便把"艾香粽子"的制作方法带回泉州，并根据泉州人的口味，进行了改良，成了现在我们在泉州许多小吃店里常见到的"烧肉粽"。

"烧肉粽"的重点在"烧"这一字，意即趁热吃热乎乎的粽子。食客剥开粽叶，蘸上喜欢的酱汁，食指大动，满口留香。泉州肉粽的材料似乎可以包罗万物，虾米、芋头、栗子、五花肉、鸡蛋、香菇、干贝、莲子等和爽滑的糯米包裹在一起，拌上卤汤和葱油，配上沙茶酱、蒜蓉和甜辣酱等调料，是单纯包糯米的粽子无法企及的美味。

◎ 包肉粽。（王福平 摄）
Wrapping zongzi with meat stuffing. (Photo by Wang Fuping)

Zongzi with Meat Stuffing and Beef Strip Soups: Perfect Match, Refreshing and Chewy

Where there are Chinese, rice and noodles are almost indispensable staple food. In Quanzhou, quite a lot of delicacies are made of rice. The specialty staple foods include salted rice, radish rice, pot rice and *zongzi* with meat stuffing.

The Dragon Boat Festival is one of the traditional Chinese festivals when people eat rice dumplings and watch dragon boat races. In Quanzhou, people eat rice dumplings not only on the Dragon Boat Festival, but almost every day. For visitors, there must be *zongzi* with meat stuffing and beef strip soup on the list of must-eat foods in Quanzhou. These two delicacies seem ordinary, but for those diners who want to have both taste and satiety, they are quite delicious, a supreme match.

The special *zongzi* with meat stuffing in Quanzhou has a long history and has a lot to do with the great poet Lu You in the Southern Song Dynasty. Legend has it that when Lu You took his office in Fuzhou, he brought Aixiang *Zongzi* (*zongzi* with fragrance of Artemisia) with him. After he left, some Quanzhou people who had worked in the Lu family brought back the production method of Aixiang Zongzi to Quanzhou, and made improvements according to the tastes of local people. They are *zongzi* with meat stuffing that are commonly available in many snack bars in Quanzhou.

◎ 热乎乎的"烧肉粽"常引得食客们食指大动。（陈剑 摄）
The steaming-hot *zongzi* with meat stuffing often attract a lot of diners since it is finger-licking yummy. (Photo by Chen Jian)

The focus of *zongzi* with meat stuffing is on the word "steaming-hot", which means to enable the diners to eat them while they are hot. The diners peeled off the leaves, dipped them in their favorite sauce, and left their mouths full of fragrance. The ingredients of *zongzi* with meat stuffing in Quanzhou seem to be all-inclusive: shrimp, taro, chestnuts, streaky pork, eggs, mushrooms, scallops, lotus seeds, etc. They are wrapped with smooth glutinous rice, mixed with stewed soup and scallion oil, and served with Satay sauce, garlic condiments and sweet chili sauce, making a delicacy unmatched by glutinous *zongzi*.

吃肉粽，要配羹汤，牛肉羹、鱼丸汤等都是不错的选择。牛肉羹顾名思义就是用牛肉煮羹，让牛肉的香味散发在羹汤里。泉州的牛肉羹是用木棒将牛肉碾碎，再经反复捶打，表面裹一层地瓜粉，加入水、酱油、味精、生姜等不断揉拌而成。吃的时候，把牛肉捏成不规则的条状放入锅中，约10分钟后牛肉浮出水面即可。牛肉羹汤里加入些许姜丝和香菜，既可去腥，也可暖胃。

用料实在的泉州牛肉羹，保留了泉州人爱食牛肉的传统。"古早味"的牛肉羹配上肉粽，既让本地人的饮食习惯得以传承，也满足了外乡人对美味的渴求。

纪录片《舌尖上的中国》所讲述的故事中，阐明了一个道理：一种饮食传承的是一种文化。泉州人对于肉粽和牛肉羹的钟爱，在于味道，也在于生活。对于所有的人来说，家乡的味道，等同于秘制，只在故土，别无他寻。

◎ 姜丝和香菜让牛肉羹更美味。（陈海平 摄）
Shredded ginger and cilantro make beef strip soups more delicious. (Photo by Chen Haiping)

◎ 在泉州街头，你可以轻易地找到做牛肉
羹的店，其中有些店还是经营多年的老
字号。（李铭炎 摄）

On the streets of Quanzhou, you can easily
find stores that make beef strip soups, some
of which have been in business for years.
(Photo by Li Mingyan)

Zongzi with meat stuffing are usually associated with soups. Beef strip soups and fish ball soups are both good choices. As the name suggests, beef strip soups are boiled with beef, so that the aroma of beef is diffused in the soup. Quanzhou beef strip soups are made by beef crushed with a wooden stick and beaten repeatedly. Then the beef will be covered with a layer of sweet potato powder and constantly kneaded with water, soy sauce, monosodium glutamate, and ginger, etc. For eating, knead the beef into irregular strips and put them in the pot. After about 10 minutes, the beef will surface. Add a little ginger and cilantro to the beef broth, which can remove the fishy taste and warm the stomach.

Quanzhou beef strip soups, full of ingredients, retain the tradition of Quanzhou people's love of eating beef. The "old taste" beef strip soups along with *zongzi* with meat stuffing not only allow the local people's eating habits to be passed on, but also satisfy the desire of outsiders for delicious food.

The story in the documentary *A Bite of China* clarifies a truth: a kind of food inherits a kind of culture. Quanzhou people's love for *zongzi* with meat stuffing and beef strip soups lies in the taste and life. For all people, the taste of hometown is equivalent to the secret recipes which can only found in the homeland, nowhere else.

◎ 润饼是许多泉州人的心头好。（陈剑 摄）
Runbing is the apple of many Quanzhou people's eye. (Photo by Chen Jian)

润饼：一卷思乡菜

杜甫在《立春》一诗里写道："春日春盘细生菜，忽忆两京梅发时。盘出高门行白玉，菜传纤手送青丝。"古书《岁时广记》中也有记载："在春日，食春饼、生菜，号春盘。"

据载，泉州人吃春饼的习俗，自宋开始。古人所食，今日仍存。泉州的春饼也叫润饼，清明节吃春饼是泉州人过节的仪式之一。当然，即使不是清明节，人们也喜欢买点润饼过过嘴瘾。

润饼对泉州人意味着什么？

有人说是思乡的味道。在泉州，润饼又叫思乡菜，那些在外的游子，每年清明回来祭祖扫墓，心心念念的都是家乡地道的润饼。扫完墓，拜祭完祖先，一家老小，一起包润饼吃，那是过节的氛围，也是家族凝聚的象征。润饼皮和红馅，有"包金包银"的招财寓意；润饼圆，寓意家人团团圆圆。

也有人说，润饼代表的是泉州的包容。润饼，用一张薄面皮，把诸多关于春天的食材都包裹在一起，胡萝卜丝、豆芽、肉丝、海蛎煎、芫荽……润饼，老少咸宜，包容一切，极好地表达了泉州开放的饮食文化。

Runbing: a Roll of Homesickness Dish

The Chinese famous poet Du Fu once wrote in his poem *Start of Spring*: "On a spring day, small fresh vegetables fill gift food baskets. Abruptly, memory flashes of plum blossoms in two capitals. Baskets from mansions are delivered over white-stone lanes. These vegetables are held in hands of maidens." There is also a record in the ancient book *Sui Shi Guang Ji* (a book on the ancient traditions in festivals and solar terms): "On spring days, (people) eat spring rolls and lettuce, which is called the spring plate."

It is recorded that Quanzhou people's custom of eating *Runbing* began in the Song Dynasty. What was eaten by the ancient still exists today. Spring rolls in Quanzhou are also called *Runbing*. Eating *Runbing* on Qingming Festival is one of the rituals of Quanzhou people. Of course, even in days other than Qingming Festival, people also like to buy some *Runbing* for a good meal.

What does *Runbing* mean to the people of Quanzhou?

Some people say it is the taste of homesickness. In Quanzhou, *Runbing* is also called homesickness dish. Those wanderers who come back to sweep tombs of their ancestors during Qingming Festivals miss *Runbing* in their hometown. After sweeping the tombs and paying homage to the ancestors, the whole family will make and eat *Runbing* together, an atmosphere of the festival and a symbol of family cohesion. The wrappers of *Runbing* and the red filling have an implied meaning of bringing fortune while the round shape of *Runbing* implies family reunion.

It is also said that *Runbing* represents Quanzhou's inclusiveness. *Runbing* is made of a thin wrapper wrapped together with many spring-related ingridents: carrot shreds, bean sprouts, shredded pork, oyster omelet, coriander... It is suitable for all ages, includes everything, and expresses perfectly Quanzhou's open food culture.

◎ 润饼皮由匠人手工制作而成。（林瀚森 摄）
The wrappers of *Runbing* are handmade by artisans. (Photo by Lin Hansen)

润饼，制作起来很是讲究：先摊开润饼皮，撒上一层吸油解腻的海苔；再依次撒上花生粉末、胡萝卜丝、豆芽等时令菜，配以自己喜爱的其他食材，最后包成圆筒状，小心翼翼握着吃。

润饼好不好吃，润饼皮非常关键。皮太薄，容易破；皮太厚没有口感。润饼的皮，在泉州人不断改良的岁月中，渐渐吸收了中原面食中饼皮的功能，同时适应闽南水土的温润。

改良以后的饼皮不再干燥，而是脆香。泉州人在制作的过程中，人为控制饼皮的火候，这样既保证饼皮熟透，又保留了饼皮中一部分的柔韧性和水分，再利用饼皮的延展性来包住食物，让其更好入口。

每年清明排长队买润饼皮的泉州人，为的是那一口思乡的滋味，以及儿时对家乡小吃的特殊记忆。这种感情，让润饼保留至今，同时也使其成为泉州饮食版图中不可或缺的一角。

《舌尖上的中国》倾情记录过的西街百年老店——亚佛润饼店，吸引着几代泉州食客们的味蕾。那个从1961年用到现在的印尼老锅，如今还在为所有慕名而来的人们制作着美味的润饼皮。尽管一年有九个月的淡季，但店主亚佛仍然坚守着祖传的手艺。他说想让想吃润饼的人，随时都可以吃到他家的润饼。如今，亚佛润饼已传承至第四代。

◎ 位于西街的亚佛润饼店吸引了众多游客的驻足。（陈英杰 摄）
Yafo *Runbing* Shop in West Street attracts many visitors. (Photo by Chen Yingjie)

*R*unbing is made very delicately: first spread the wrapper, sprinkle with a layer of seaweed that absorbs oil; and then sprinkle with peanut powder, carrot shreds, bean sprouts and other seasonal vegetables in turn, with other favorite ingredients; finally wrap it into a cylindrical shape and hold it carefully to eat.

Whether *Runbing* is delicious or not, the wrapper of it is the key. If too thin, the wrapper breaks easily; if too thick, the wrapper would be tasteless. In the years of continuous improvement by the people of Quanzhou, the wrapper of *Runbing* has gradually absorbed the functions of the wrapper in the Central Plains pasta, while adapting to the warmth of the water and soil in Southern Fujian.

The improved wrapper is no longer dry, but crispy and fragrant. In the process of making, Quanzhou people artificially control the heat of the wrapper to not only ensure that the wrapper is fully cooked, but also retain part of the flexibility and moisture in the wrapper. They then use the ductility of the wrapper to wrap the food and make it even tastier.

Every year during the Qingming Festival, Quanzhou people wait in long queue to buy *Runbing* for the taste of homesickness and the special memory of their hometown snacks when they were children. This feeling has kept *Runbing* to this day. At the same time, it also makes it an indispensable part of Quanzhou's food map.

Yafo *Runbing* Shop, the century-old shop on the West Street recorded in *A Bite of China*, has attracted the taste buds of generations of Quanzhou diners. The old Indonesian pot used since 1961 is still in use for making delicious wrappers for all admirers. Although there is a nine-month off season in a year, the shopkeeper Yafo still sticks to the ancestral craft. He said that he wanted people who love his *Runbing* to be able to eat them at any time. Today, Yafo *Runbing* has been passed down to the fourth generation.

◎ 人们可以根据自己的饮食喜好在润饼中加入各种食材。（林瀚森 摄）

People can add various ingredients to the *Runbing* according to their dietary preferences. (Photo by Lin Hansen)

牛肉文化：异域风味、本土气息

一个地方的饮食和一个地方的文化息息相关。泉州的饮食文化里带着中原、海洋、古越三种文化的多元特点。海上丝绸之路上来来往往的人，带来了各自的饮食习惯，在泉州汇成一幅巨大的美食版图，而牛肉，在这美食版图里占了大片疆土。

泉州人爱吃牛肉，起源于刺桐港的繁盛时期。千年之前，世界上最爱吃牛肉的那群人（欧洲人、波斯人、阿拉伯人、蒙古人……）因为商贸聚集到了泉州，泉州的牛肉文化便也异常兴盛。

如今走在泉州的大街小巷，牛肉馆几乎随处可见。更有意思的是，很少有什么地方像泉州这样，在吃这件事上，把牛身上的部位分得这么细致，这么丰富。

先说牛排，泉州做牛排的方法和全世界其他地方都不同。泉州的牛排，不是西餐的牛排，而是指牛的排骨。取牛的排骨一两根，剁成宽厚适宜的块状，牛排块块带骨，入沸水焯掉血水，洗净；油锅放入姜蒜爆香，下牛排，加入料酒、咖喱、辣椒、八角、桂皮、当归等，爆炒三分钟，加入酱油，加水没过牛排；焖三四个小时后开锅，香味扑鼻，夹一块入口，肉质嫩滑。这样的做法据说是宋元时期由伊斯兰教民传入并融合了中式做法。

接着说说牛肉面。一碗热气腾腾的牛肉面端上来，天然的香气沁人心脾，让人瞬间口水直流。吃面先喝汤，泉州牛肉面的汤味鲜美无敌，面条本来的劲道和浓汤混合的香味，让人欲罢不能。最值得一提的就是碗中的片片牛肉，嫩而不柴，香而不腻，味道穿透在上下牙床之间，余留在牙缝间。

◎ 泉州街头遍布着各种牛肉店。（罗嘉蓓 摄）
Quanzhou streets are dotted with various beef restaurants. (Photo by Luo Jiabei)

Beef Culture: Exotic Flavors, Local Colors

The food of a place is closely related to its culture. The food culture of Quanzhou carries the diverse characteristics of the three cultures of Central Plains, Ocean, and Ancient Yue. The people who came and went on the Maritime Silk Road brought their own eating habits and formed a huge food "map" in Quanzhou. Beef occupies a large area on this food "map".

◎ 泉州每家牛肉店都有自己的独门秘方，让自己家的牛肉具有独特的风味。（童佳欢 摄）

Every beef restaurant in Quanzhou has its own unique recipe to give its own beef a unique flavor. (Photo by Tong Jiahuan)

Quanzhou people's love of beef originated in the prosperous period of Zayton Port. Hundreds of years ago, the group of people who love beef most in the world (Europeans, Persians, Arabs, Mongolians...) gathered in Quanzhou because of commerce and trade, making Quanzhou's beef culture extremely prosperous.

Today, beef restaurants can be seen almost everywhere in the streets and alleys of Quanzhou. What's more interesting is that few places like Quanzhou, in the matter of eating, divide the parts of cows so carefully and so richly.

Let's start from steak. The method of making steak in Quanzhou is different from other places in the world. The steak in Quanzhou does not refer to a Western steak, but a rib of beef. Take one or two beef ribs and chop them into chunks of appropriate breadth and thickness. The steaks are with bones. Blanch the blood in boiling water, and wash them. Add ginger and garlic in a frying pan until smells fragrant, then the steak, cooking wine, curry and pepper. Stir-fry star anise, cinnamon, angelica, etc. for three minutes. Add soy sauce, and water to submerge the steak. Simmer for three or four hours, then the aroma is tangy. Put a piece in the mouth, the beef is tender and smooth. This practice is said to be introduced by the Islamic people during the Song and Yuan Dynasties and combined with Chinese methods.

Then have a look at beef noodles. When a bowl of steaming beef noodles is served, the natural aroma is refreshing, which make people drool in an instant. Drink the soup first when you eat noodles. The soup of Quanzhou beef noodles is delicious and invincible. The original strength of the noodles and the aroma of the thick soup mix to make you crave for more. What is most worth mentioning is the slices of beef in the bowl, which are tender but not woody, fragrant but not greasy. The taste penetrates between the upper and lower gums and remains between the teeth.

再来说一下牛肉火锅。牛肉火锅讲究"炼汤"，而各家店主都有自己的独特做法。有些讲究养生的店主是以祖传汤底加上名贵中药以及龙骨、番鸭，用炭火炖制而成，汤既滋补养生，又甘甜不油腻，令人口齿留香。牛肉汤锅端上来，加热至沸腾，顿时香气四溢，令人食指大动，先喝一碗热乎乎的汤，再捞大块美味的牛肉，让人觉得"大口吃肉"的感觉真好。泉州人吃牛肉火锅的派头，透着一股豪气。

牛肉的味道好，首先得益于新鲜的牛肉。很多店家每天所需的牛肉产品，都是由屠宰场直接送过来的。更有挑剔者，需要每天早起亲自去市场选料，因为"料好"才能味道好。

等到牛肉买回来，开始用炭火熬上三四个钟头，这个过程称为"炼汤"。有些牛肉店外会有大炉灶，那就是所有美味的来源。那些让人念念不忘的味道把控者们，秉承着每天早上六七点就起来"炼汤"的功夫，每日清晨用炭火大锅，花上至少三四个小时，把牛的整根龙骨慢慢熬成汤底。到了午饭时间，客人就可以喝到"原汤原味"。

泉州牛肉店能让人回味无穷的原因，是因为美味，也是因为讲求缘分。万千食客所能喝到的原汤原味，经常一天只此一锅，卖完了就卖完了，如果卖不完，追求美味传统的店家们也是一定要倒掉的，绝不过夜。

牛肉在泉州的做法和吃法，不像西餐那般精致，但那股子带着古人豪爽的原始感却广为流传。

◎ 令人垂涎欲滴的泉州牛肉。（七桃生活 摄）

Mouth-watering Quanzhou beef. (Photo by Qitao Shenghuo)

Now let's talk about beef hot pot. Beef hot pot is very particular about "refining soup", and each restaurant owner has his own unique method. Some shopkeepers who pay attention to health care treat the ancestral soup base with precious Chinese medicine, keel bones, and Muscovy duck, stewed with charcoal fire. The soup is nourishing, healthy, sweet, and not greasy, which makes the mouth fragrant. The beef soup pot is brought up, heated to boiling, and the aroma is finger-licking good. First drink a bowl of warm soup, and then fish a large piece of delicious beef. People will feel good about "meat eating". Quanzhou people eat beef hotpot with a sense of grandeur.

The good taste of beef owes first to the fresh beef. The beef products that many stores need every day are delivered directly from slaughterhouses. People that are more meticulous need to get up early every day to go to the market to select beef in order to make sure that the beef tastes good.

When the beef is bought, it is boiled over charcoal fire for three to four hours. This process is called "refining soup". There are large stoves outside some beef restaurants, which are the source of all delicious food. Those unforgettable taste controllers, adhering to the habit of getting up at six or seven o'clock every morning to "refine soup", use a large pot of charcoal fire every morning and spend at least three or four hours to simmer the entire keel of the cow slowly into the soup base. At lunchtime, clients can enjoy the original soup flavor.

The reason why Quanzhou beef restaurants are so memorable is that the dishes are delicious and also because of timing and bonding. The original soup that thousands of diners would like to drink is often only one pot a day for a restaurant. When the soup is sold out, it is sold out. If it is not sold out, the owners who stick to the traditional deliciousness must discard it and never keep it overnight.

The way beef is prepared and eaten in Quanzhou is not as refined as Western food, but the primitive feeling with the heroism of the ancient people is widely spread.

◎ 咸饭、牛排和牛肉丸汤是许多泉州人常点
的"三件套"。（七桃生活 摄）
Salty rice, steak and beef ball soup are the
"three-piece meal set" that many Quanzhou
people often order. (Photo by Qitao Shenghuo)

醋肉：外酥里嫩、犒赏味蕾

在泉州的饮食地图里，有一种叫做"醋肉"的地道美食，让人回味无穷。

中国的饮食文化里，时间往往也是一种重要的"配料"，许多美食需要时间的酝酿。这在醋肉的制作上得到了印证。醋肉，如果要做得好，可不是那么容易，单是腌制这一步骤，对于精益求精的人来讲，就需要三天的等候。

上好的醋肉要选择三层肉而不是纯瘦肉，如此方可肥中带瘦，瘦中带肥。把大块的三层肉切成大小适中的小肉块，加醋、蒜头以及其他佐料，放入冰箱里静置三天，等待所有味道渗入肉里，交融在一起。

◎ 刚出锅的醋肉酥脆可口，令人欲罢不能。（陈剑 摄）

The freshly fried vinegared pork is incredibly crispy and delicious. (Photo by Chen Jian)

用来炸醋肉的地瓜粉也极为讲究，很多考究的人会到种植地瓜的地方去挑选，以求得上好的地瓜粉。如此讲究，为的是让醋肉炸出来后色泽和口感俱佳。

醋肉趁热吃，口感酥脆，酸酸甜甜，既能当下酒的小菜，也能当日常零食。醋肉加小酒的搭配，让人觉得生活美滋滋的，和近几年受追捧的啤酒炸鸡比起来，丝毫不逊色。

醋肉淡淡的醋香、外酥里嫩的口感不但令泉州本地人欲罢不能，也吸引了很多慕名而来的外地游客。这种闽南经典的美食，因为炸得软硬适中，所以老少皆宜。在泉州的街头，很容易就可以买到这种小吃，泉州人也几乎家家户户都会做。闽南人家的祭祀案头上，我们也常能见到醋肉的影子。

醋肉，被称为闽南最具魔性的美食之一，无论是搭配面线糊还是卤面，抑或是酸辣汤，都可称得上是绝佳伴侣。

Vinegared Pork: Crispy Outside and Tender Inside; Rewarding Taste Buds

In the food map of Quanzhou, there is a kind of authentic food called vinegared pork, which always leaves eaters pleasant and endless aftertaste.

In Chinese food culture, time is often also an important "ingredient", and many delicacies require time to brew. This is confirmed in the production of vinegared pork. It is not at all easy to make it well. The step of marinating alone requires three days of waiting for those who are striving for perfection.

To make the best vinegared pork, streaky pork instead of pure lean meat is selected, so that fat and lean meat can mix well. Cut the large streaky pork into small pieces of moderate size, add vinegar, garlic, and other condiments, and put them in the refrigerator for three days, waiting for all the flavors to penetrate into the meat and blend together.

◎ 醋肉既可蘸酱吃，也可搭配着面线糊吃。（老丁 摄）
Vinegared pork can be eaten either with a dipping sauce or with mee sua paste. (Photo by Lao Ding)

The sweet potato powder used for frying vinegared pork is also very particular. Many demanding people will go to the place where sweet potatoes are grown to choose the best sweet potato powder, so that the color and taste are good after the pork is fried.

Eaten while it is hot, the vinegared pork is crispy, sour, and sweet. It can be used as a side dish for small liquor or as a daily snack. The combination of the pork and small liquor makes people feel that life is beautiful, and it is not inferior to the Korean fried chicken that have been sought after in recent years.

The light vinegar aroma of the small liquor and the tender texture on the outside not only make the locals in Quanzhou can not stop eating it, but also attract many tourists from other places. This classic cuisine of Southern Fujian is suitable for all ages because it is fried moderately hard and soft. You can easily buy this kind of snacks on the streets of Quanzhou, and almost every household in Quanzhou can make it. We can often see vinegared pork on the sacrificial desks of people in Southern Fujian.

Vinegared pork is known as one of the most magical delicacies in Southern Fujian. Whether it is paired with mee sua paste, braised noodles, or hot and sour soup, it can be regarded as an excellent companion.

鲜美海味：大海的馈赠

　　能够让人来去千里、甘之如饴的核心驱动力里，美景和美食当仁不让地名列前茅。

　　日本、澳大利亚及东南亚各国是海鲜狂热粉丝们心中的理想度假地，而从性价比来说，古城泉州，亦是不错的选择。如果说世界上最能吃海鲜的是日本人，那么中国最能吃海鲜的应该是福建人。据统计，福建的人均海产品产量和消费量稳居全国第一。

　　泉州的美食里有一个显著特征，那就是"鲜"。"鲜"之一字，来源于鱼和羊。所有的食物中，最能体现泉州"向海而吃"的特征的，当属海鲜。泉州菜系之风流典雅，离不开大海柔波里蕴藏的无穷鲜味和渔民们迎风破浪的辛勤劳作。泉州拥有421千米的海岸线，辽阔的海域里藏着丰富的美食资源和众多可供选择的食材，让泉州的"鲜"也有了最大程度的体现。

◎ 讨海去。（陈英杰 摄）
Make a living from the sea. (Photo by Chen Yingjie)

Delicious Seafood: a Gift from the Sea

In term of the core attractions that can make people come to a place pleasantly from thousands of miles away, the scenery and the food are rightfully at the top of the list.

Japan, Australia, and Southeast Asian countries are ideal holiday destinations for seafood enthusiasts. In terms of the price–performance ratio, the ancient city of Quanzhou is also a good choice. If the Japanese are the best eaters of seafood in the world, then the Fujianese are the best eaters of seafood in China. According to statistics, Fujian's per capita production and consumption of seafood steadily rank first in the country.

Among the food of Quanzhou, there is a distinctive feature, which is "fresh". In Chinese, the original meaning of the word "fresh" is related with fish and sheep. Among all the foods, seafood best reflects the heavy dependence of Quanzhou food on the sea. The elegance of Quanzhou cuisine is inseparable from the endless flavors contained in the gentle waves of the sea and the hard work of the fishermen against the wind and waves. With a coastline of 421 kilometers for the vast sea area, it is rich in gastronomic resources and has many ingredients to choose from, getting Quanzhou's "freshness" to the greatest degree.

◎ 丰富的渔获是大海的馈赠。（吴刚强 摄）
The rich catches are a gift from the sea. (Photo by Wu Gangqiang)

沙滩、阳光、琳琅满目的海鲜……这一切，散落在泉州的不同角落，只要你用心去寻，便可寻得到。说走就走去到海边赏海景、吃海鲜，是泉州人得天独厚的优势。在泉州，漂浮在海上的渔家饭店，都是船的样子。新鲜的鱼、虾、蟹有最简单的煮法和食法，无需多余的调料，便鲜美清甜。蟳埔、崇武、东石、金井、石狮、泉港等地，成了食客们追捧的圣地。他们不惜开车数十公里，只为品尝那一口原汁原味的鲜嫩。吹着海风，品着海鲜，身边知己良朋相伴，人生得意莫过于此。

　　若是无法亲临海边也不打紧，盛夏泉州的很多小店里，人声鼎沸，海味伴着猜拳和摇骰子，活色生香。餐桌上几瓶啤酒、一盘小红章鱼、一盘炒螺、几份炭烧生蚝，外加烧烤的秋刀鱼，应有尽有的海鲜粉墨登场。

◎ 泉州人的餐桌上总有几样海鲜。（向阳 摄）
Quanzhou people always have a few kinds of seafood for their meals. (Photo by Xiang Yang)

◎ 鲜美的海鲜产品不需高超的烹饪技法就能令人食指大动。（向阳 摄）
Tasty seafood do not require sophisticated cooking techniques to be appetizing. (Photo by Xiang Yang)

Beaches, sunshine, a dazzling array of seafood... all of these are scattered in different corners of Quanzhou. As long as you look for them with your heart, you can find them. Just walking to the beach to enjoy the sea view and eat seafood is the unique privilege of Quanzhou people. In Quanzhou, the fisherman's restaurants floating on the sea look like boats. Fresh fish, prawns, and crabs are cooked and eaten in the simplest way. No extra seasoning added, the seafood dishes are delicious and sweet. Xunpu, Chongwu, Dongshi, Jinjing, Shishi, Quangang and other places have become holy places sought after by diners. They do not hesitate to drive dozens of kilometers, just to taste the original taste of freshness. Blowing the sea breeze, tasting seafood, accompanying good friends, there is nothing better in life than these.

It doesn't matter if you can't go to the beach in person. During the midsummer in Quanzhou, the crowd is boisterous in many small shops. The seafood is accompanied by finger-guessing games and dice shaking. On tables, a few bottles of beer, a plate of small red octopus, a plate of fried snails, a few char-grilled oysters, plus barbecued saury, all the seafood is here.

土笋冻：滋味浓厚甘美的闽南传统小吃

在泉州的街头，有些土笋冻店门面不大，却总能看到人头攒动。你都不知道，有多少人是慕名而来；你也很难想象，小小的一家店平常一天的营业额竟是上万元，如果遇到节假日，收入更是成倍增加。至于墙上挂的各大电视台的采访照片，更是让人不禁感叹，到底是怎样的魔力让人对这样一碗小小的土笋冻垂涎三尺。

土笋冻发源于泉州，是一种色香味俱佳的闽南传统风味小吃，它是由一种像蚯蚓一样的海洋生物——土笋加工而成的冻品。要做出一碗晶莹透明、鲜嫩脆滑的土笋冻除了要花五个小时以上的工夫，上好的原材料更是必不可少，其中又以泉州安海和东石两地的土笋为最佳。做土笋冻的行家里手们，会很认真地和你说："土笋冻用的是土笋，而不是大家误以为的沙虫。"好的土笋要到海边浅滩处仔细寻找，然后用锄头挖出来。把挖回的新鲜土笋处理干净，倒入锅中，熬煮出胶质，尔后连汤倒出分装在小瓷碗里，待其自然冷却凝结。

土笋冻具有清凉降火、清热润肺的作用。又因其丰富的胶质，所以美容效果也特别好。在美容功效上，土笋冻和燕窝相仿。如今，市面上各种假燕窝不少，而土笋冻除了质量差别之外，很少有假。也因此，土笋冻可称得上广大爱美女性的福音。

虽然土笋冻味道如此诱人，第一次看到土笋冻的外地人却可能会被里面形似虫子的土笋吓到，没勇气品尝这美味。如何顺利克服这种恐惧，并顺利地吃上一口爽滑的土笋冻呢？这里有个诀窍：吃第一口的时候，先把眼睛闭上，那么第二口就不需要闭眼睛了，因为你一定会爱上土笋冻的味道。

◎ 土笋冻如同果冻一般，爽滑可口，佐以醋、酱油、蒜蓉，令人吃完还想再吃。（陈英杰 摄）
The sea worm jelly is as smooth and tasty as jelly. Accompanied by vinegar, soy sauce and garlic, it will make you want to eat repeatedly afterwards. (Photo by Chen Yingjie)

Sea Worm Jelly: a Traditional Southern Fujian Snack with a Rich and Sweet Taste

On the streets of Quanzhou, in some small-scale sea worm jelly shops, you can always see crowds of people. You can't find out how many people come here because of its name. It's hard to imagine that a small shop has a daily turnover of ten thousands *yuan*. In holidays, the revenue will double. As for the interview photos of major TV stations on the wall, people can't help but wonder, what kind of magic is it that makes people salivate for such a small bowl of sea worm jelly.

The sea worm jelly originates in Quanzhou. It is a traditional Southern Fujian snack with good color and flavor. It is a frozen product processed from a kind of sea creatures like earthworms—sea worms. It takes more than five hours to make a bowl of crystal-clear, fresh and crispy sea worm jelly. Good raw materials are also indispensable.

◎ 制作一碗土笋冻需要繁复的工序。（许兆恺 摄）
It takes a lot of work to make a bowl of sea worm jelly. (Photo by Xu Zhaokai)

Among them, the sea worms from Anhai and Dongshi in Quanzhou are the best. Experts who make sea worm jellies will say to you very seriously: "Sea worms but not sandworms that everyone mistakes are used for sea worm jelly." Good sea worms should be carefully searched in the shallows of the sea. Dig them out with a hoe. Dispose of the freshly dug up sea worms, pour them into a pot, boil the gum. Then pour out the soup and place them in small porcelain bowls, and let them cool and condense naturally.

Sea worm jellies have the effect of cooling and clearing internal heat and moistening the lungs. It also has a particularly good cosmetic effect because of its rich gelatinous content. In terms of beauty benefits, they are similar to bird's nest soup. Today, there are a lot of fake bird's nest soup on the market, while sea worm jellies are rarely fake except for the difference in quality. Therefore, they can be considered a blessing for the majority of beauty loving women.

Although the taste of sea worm jelly is so tempting, strangers who see it for the first time may be intimidated by the insect-like sea worms inside and may not have the courage to taste this delicious food. How can you overcome this fear and have a smooth bite of it? Here's a tip: when you take your first bite, close your eyes first. Then you don't need to close them for the second bite, because you may have fallen in love with the taste of them.

有一年元宵节，央视主持人李佳明到安海来录节目。他一口气吃了五六碗土笋冻，连连说好吃好吃。当时安海的老百姓并不知道李佳明这么有名，他们以为是平常那些慕名而来的外地记者或者是当地电视台的记者。到后来知道他是央视的主持人，他们也并不觉得惊讶，毕竟来安海寻找土笋冻之谜的人实在太多了。

安海出产的土笋冻没有生产工厂，即使再著名的品牌，也只是手工作坊。制作土笋冻的老师傅们遵循代代相传的纯手工做法。在他们眼中，只有这种"古早味"的方法做出的才能叫做土笋冻。而老饕们对此也挑剔得很！

安海虽然美食众多，但是土笋冻的地位依然是最特别、最有代表性的。安海凭借一碗土笋冻，走上央视的《走遍中国》栏目；论及土笋冻的历史时，那些老行家们很确定地说，安海土笋冻一定是最早的。如果要品尝到好吃又正宗的土笋冻，最好能亲临安海。

安海土笋冻的"大咖"肖园说他家土笋冻是从他曾祖父就开始了，到他儿子这代已经传承了五代。肖园的曾祖父最开始是挑着担子在街上卖，有时候也到邻近乡镇去卖，一代一代的手工技艺传下来。就连名声，也是从他曾祖父那时候就开始就打下的。

就像安海人说起安海的地标性建筑，他们会说五里桥；说起安海的香火圣地，他们会说龙山寺；若说起安海的美食，他们会推荐土笋冻。土笋冻的味道，就是安海的味道。

◎ 炎炎夏日，吃一块晶莹剔透的土笋冻让人暑意全消。（老丁 摄）
In hot summer, eating a piece of sea worm jelly will make you feel cool. (Photo by Lao Ding)

One year during the Lantern Festival, CCTV host Li Jiaming came to Anhai to record a show. He ate five or six bowls of sea worm jellies in one go, repeatedly saying that it was delicious. At that time, the people in Anhai didn't know that Li Jiaming was so famous. They thought he was a reporter from a local TV station or a nonlocal reporter who came here admiringly. They were not surprised even when they later learned that Li was a host of CCTV. After all, too many people came to Anhai to look for the mystery of the sea worm jelly.

◎ 土笋冻和五香卷是闽南宴会时常见的菜品。（陈英杰 摄）
Sea worm jelly and Ngoh Hiang Lobak (spiced meat rolls) are common banquet dishes in Southern Fujian. (Photo by Chen Yingjie)

There are no production plants for the sea worm jelly in Anhai. Even the famous brands are only from manual workshops. The masters who make the jelly follow the method of pure handwork passed down from one generation to another. In their eyes, only what made in this kind of "old-fashioned" method can be called sea worm jelly. Besides, the gluttons are also very picky about the method!

Although there are many delicacies in Anhai, the status of the sea worm jelly is still the most special and representative. With a bowl of sea worm jelly, Anhai embarked on CCTV's *Across China* column. When talking about the history of sea worm jelly, those old hands said with certainty that the sea worm jellies in Anhai must be the earliest. If you want to taste the delicious and authentic sea worm jellies, Anhai is the place you must come in person.

Xiao Yuan, the big shot of Anhai sea worm jelly, said that his family's business of sea worm jelly started from his great-grandfather and has been passed down for five generations to his son. Xiao Yuan's great-grandfather first carried sea worm jellies on a shoulder pole and sold them on the streets or neighboring towns. The craftsmanship was passed down from generation to generation. Even the brand's reputation has been established since his great-grandfather's time.

When Anhai people talk about Anhai's landmark building, they will mention Wuli Bridge. Speaking of Anhai's holy land of religion, they will talk about Longshan Temple. When it comes to Anhai's food, they will recommend sea worm jelly, the taste of which is the taste of Anhai.

石花膏：突破味觉甜美极限的消暑圣物

在泉州人心中，炎炎夏日何以消暑？石花膏虽不是唯一答案，但绝对是正确答案之一。

没有吃过石花膏，就不算度过了泉州的夏天。石花膏出现于清光绪年间，当时的泉州人发现了石花草。石花全藻皆可药用，能治痰结、瘰疬、肠炎、痔疮、支气管炎等症。石花草制成的石花膏因其清凉解暑、爽嫩有弹性而深受泉州人的喜爱。石花膏被誉为夏季解暑、降火之妙品。夏季酷暑燥热，泉州人坚信，饮用三碗石花膏，便可快速降火。

石花膏由石花草炼制而成。石花草是一种长在低潮带礁石上的食用海藻，每年初春，借由勤劳的渔家之手采集而来，历经多遍仔细地清洗、晾晒，方能下锅熬制石花膏。每一份石花膏，都要经过四五个小时的熬煮、过滤，再经由十二个小时的自然凝固。熬制好的胶液倒入盆中放凉，再放进冰箱冷却凝固成形，即可用石花刨刮出均匀的细条，这些细条便成了四果汤里的主料。正宗的石花膏，颜色偏黄，其味道独特，不同于用果冻粉煮出的味道。

纪录片《舌尖上的中国》第三季播出后，石花膏成了很多人来泉州旅游的又一理由。片中，店主丁秉正传承家业，把石花膏做得街知巷闻。秉正堂石花膏始于清光绪末年，由丁秉正的外婆黄韭菜开始经营。当年的黄阿婆为了生计，拜一个叫做石花阿婆的人为师，学习制作石花膏的手艺。出师后的黄阿婆挑着石花膏担子沿街叫卖。她卖的石花膏口感爽滑、冰凉消暑，深受食客追捧。

◎ 很难想象爽滑的石花膏是来自于这海边不起眼的石花草。（啊琴姐 摄）
It is hard to imagine that the smooth agar-made jelly is refined from these inconspicuous
agars growing in the sea. (Photo by Aqinjie)

Agar-made Jelly: a Sacred Dispeller of Summer Heat That Breaks the Limit of Sweet Taste

In the hearts of Quanzhou people, how do they cool off the hot summer? Although agar-made jelly is not the only answer, it is definitely one of the correct answers.

If you haven't eaten agar-made jelly, you can't say you spend a summer in Quanzhou. Agar-made jelly appeared during 1875 and 1908 of the Qing Dynasty, when agar was discovered in Quanzhou. The whole plant of agar can be used medicinally, and it can cure phlegm, gall tumor, enteritis, hemorrhoids, bronchitis, among other diseases. The agar-made jelly was deeply loved by the local people of Quanzhou because of its function of cooling and heat relieving, softness, and elasticity. Agar-made jelly is known as a wonderful product for relieving internal heat in summer. The summer is very hot in Quanzhou, but the local people firmly believe that drinking three bowls of agar-made jelly can quickly reduce the internal heat.

Agar-made jelly is refined from agars, a kind of edible seaweed that grows on reefs in the low tide zone. They are collected by the hard-working fishermen in early spring every year. They must be carefully washed and dried many times before they can be boiled to make the jelly. Each piece of the jelly needs to be boiled and filtered for four to five hours, and then solidified for twelve hours by itself. Pour the boiled glue into a basin and let it cool, and then put it in the refrigerator to cool and solidify. Then you can scrape out uniform thin strips with shredders. These thin strips become the main ingredient in the Ling Chee Kang. The authentic agar-made jelly is yellowish in color and has a unique taste, which is different from the taste of jelly powder.

After the third season of the documentary *A Bite of China* was broadcast, agar-made jelly became another reason for many people to travel to Quanzhou. In the film, the store owner Ding Bingzheng inherits the family business and makes his agar-made jellies well-known in the city. Bingzheng Shop's agar-made jelly was started by Ding Bingzheng's grandmother Huang Jiucai in 1908. In order to make a living, Granny Huang learnt the art of making the jelly from a woman called Agar-made Jelly Granny. After graduating from the master, Granny Huang carried a shoulder pole of agar-made jelly and sold them along the streets. The jellies she sold was smooth and cool, and were highly sought after by customers.

◎ 四果汤除了主料石花膏外还有十几二十种配料可以选择。（七桃生活 摄）

In addition to the main ingredient agar-made jelly, there are dozens of ingredients to choose from for making Ling Chee Kang. (Photo by Qitao Shenghuo)

◎ 秉正堂石花膏是许多老泉州人儿时的记忆。（七桃生活 摄）
Bingzheng Shop's agar-made jelly represents many old Quanzhou people's childhood memories. (Photo by Qitao Shenghuo)

手艺传到丁秉正父母这代，工艺上更是青出于蓝而胜于蓝，石花膏的风味更加迷人，名头也更响亮。丁秉正从小耳濡目染，探索出了一套既不破坏传统又与时俱进的制作技艺。用六晒六泡的方法做出来的秉正堂石花膏，外观清澈、口感脆嫩、清凉润肺、解暑去燥。从冰凉的井水到冰箱和冰块，从白砂糖到蜂蜜，从走街串巷到天后宫旁……秉正石花膏传承了几代泉州人的舌尖记忆。

石花膏可单吃，加入蜂蜜、冰水后喝起来就有亲近大海的口感；也可以搭配各式各样的配料混合成著名的四果汤，任选的四样小果可以是莲子、红豆沙、绿豆沙、香芋、仙草蜜、珍珠小丸子以及各种鲜果粒。

之所以叫"四果"，而不是"五果""六果"，乃是遵循了"过犹不及"的饮食均衡原理。一次选四样，其余几果，留待下次品尝。

盛夏，来一碗石花膏做成的四果汤，是直抵灵魂的冰凉——味甜爽口，清凉解毒。在许多泉州人的记忆里，美好的夏天通常是由一碗四果汤开启的。

When the craftsmanship passed down to Ding Bingzheng's parents, "the student surpasses the teacher". The flavor of agar-made jelly is more charming and the brand is more famous. Ding Bingzheng has been fascinated since he was a child, and has explored a set of production techniques that does not destroy tradition and keeps pace with the times. The agar-made jelly in Bingzheng Shop is made by the method of drying the ingredients in the sun and soaking them in water for six times separately. By doing so, the appearance becomes clear and the taste is crunchy. The jelly can cool and moisten the people's lungs and relieve the summer heat. From the cold well water to the refrigerator and ice cubes, from white sugar to honey, from a street vendor to a shop next door to Tianhou Temple...Bingzheng Shop's agar-made jelly has inherited the tongue-tip memories of generations of Quanzhou people.

Agar-made jelly can be eaten itself. After adding honey and ice water, it will have a taste close to the sea. It can also be mixed with various ingredients to form the famous Ling Chee Kang. The optional four ingredients can be lotus seeds, red bean paste, mung bean paste, sweet taro, grass honey, pearl balls and various fresh fruit pieces.

The reason why it is called "Four Fruits" instead of "Five Fruits" or "Six Fruits" is to follow the principle of balanced diet, namely "too much is as bad as too little". We can choose four ingredients at a time, and save the rest for next tastings.

In high summer, a bowl of Ling Chee Kang made of agars is cold to the soul, sweet and refreshing, cool and detoxifying. In the memories of many Quanzhou people, a good summer is usually started by a bowl of Ling Chee Kang.

◎ 一碗冰爽的四果汤陪伴泉州人度过一个个炎热的夏天。（七桃生活 摄）
A bowl of icy Ling Chee Kang accompanies Quanzhou people through hot summers. (Photo by Qitao Shenghuo)

◎ 如今行销于全世界的安溪铁观音载誉满满。2005年，安溪铁观音被国家工商总局认定为"中国驰名商标"，这是茶界第一枚中国驰名商标；2009年入选"中国世博十大名茶"；2015年被评为"百年世博中国名茶金奖"首位；2020年，安溪铁观音入选"中欧地理标志"首批保护清单……安溪铁观音荣誉之多数不胜数，茶产业规模亦是全国之最。（吴朝安 摄）

Nowadays, Anxi Tieguanyin, which is being sold all over the world, has gained tremendous honors. In 2005, it was recognized as "China's Well-known Trademark" by the former State Administration for Industry and Commerce of PRC, which was the first Chinese well-known trademark in the tea industry. In 2009, it was selected as one of the "Top Ten Famous Teas of China's World Expo". In 2015, it was ranked the first place in the "Gold Award of Chinese Famous Tea in the Century Expo". In 2020, Anxi Tieguanyin was enlisted in the first protection batch of Sino-European Geographical Indications... Anxi Tieguanyin has numerous honors, and the scale of its tea industry is also the largest in the country. (Photo by Wu Chao'an)

铁观音：一壶功夫茶，三两家常事

中国人喝茶的历史大概可以追溯到神农尝百草的年代，那一片神奇的东方树叶落到沸水之中产生的奇妙融合和变化，应该就是"茶"的起源了。而后，饮茶逐渐成了古人重要的生活场景，并发展出完整且复杂的茶文化。品茶，品的或许不只是茶，更是数千年来一路传承、绵延不绝的中华文化与精神。

唐代诗人韩偓有诗云："古崖觅芝叟，乡俗乐茶歌。"中国文人雅士的生活品位，记载于诗歌，呈现于丝绸和陶瓷，记录于茶文化。从陆羽的《茶经》开始，茶就成了一种品位，一种格调。

闽南的茶文化，承续中原茶文化精髓，并与地方文化相结合，发展出有别于其他地方的独特茶文化。而说起闽南的茶文化，铁观音是绕不开的。相传，清乾隆六年（1741年），安溪人王士让赴京拜谒礼部侍郎方苞，以茶相赠。方苞品后，觉得此茶甚好，便敬献乾隆。乾隆品后，召王士让问及茶的来处，王士让禀明茶的来龙去脉。乾隆细观茶叶形似观音脸，重如铁，便赐名"铁观音"。

铁观音，盛产于"中国茶都"——泉州安溪。安溪的产茶业历史悠久，源远流长。据《安溪县志》记载，安溪产茶始于唐代，宋代开始广泛种植，明清开始进入鼎盛时期。安溪四面环山，气候温暖湿润，雾露充足。土壤、温度、湿度、降水都非常适宜茶树的生长。宋代名士黄夷简茶联有云："宿雨一番疏甲嫩，春山几焙茗旗香。"寥寥数字，一幅遍地茶树雨后抽新芽的情景便跃然纸上。安溪盛产乌龙茶，其中铁观音为名贵品种之冠，有"绿叶红镶边，七泡有余香"的美称。

Tieguanyin Oolong Tea: Small Talks over a Pot of Kung Fu Tea

The history of Chinese tea drinking can probably be traced back to the time when Shennong tasted hundreds of plants. The miraculous fusion and change caused by that magical oriental leaf falling into boiling water should be the origin of "tea". Then, tea drinking gradually became an important life scene for the ancients, and a complete and complex tea culture was developed. What is tasted in tea tasting may not only be the tea, but also the Chinese culture and spirit that has been passed down all the way for thousands of years.

The poet Han Wo of the Tang Dynasty had a poem: "Old men are seeking glossy ganoderma on the ancient cliff. The local people like to sing tea songs." The life tastes of Chinese literati are recorded in poems, presented in silk and ceramics, and recorded in tea culture. Starting from Lu Yu's book *The Classic of Tea*, tea has become a kind of taste and style.

The tea culture of Southern Fujian inherits the essence of the tea culture of the Central Plains. Combining with the local culture, a unique local tea culture has been developed and is different from the tea culture of other places. Speaking of the tea culture of Southern Fujian, *Tieguanyin* is inseparable. According to legend, in 1741 of the Qing Dynasty, Wang Shirang, a native of Anxi, went to Beijing to pay a formal visit to Fang Bao, the Deputy Minister of Board of Rites and Ceremonies, and presented him with tea. After tasting the tea, Fang Bao felt that it was very good, so he dedicated it to Emperor Qianlong. After tasting the tea, Emperor Qianlong summoned Wang and asked where the tea came from. Wang Shirang reported the whole story of the tea to the emperor. Qianlong gave the tea the name "*Tieguanyin*" as he thought the tea leaves looked like the face of Kuan Yin and were as heavy as iron.

Tieguanyin is abundantly produced in Anxi, Quanzhou, the "Chinese Tea Capital". Anxi's tea industry can go back a long way. According to the *Anxi County Chronicles*, tea production in Anxi began in the Tang Dynasty, widely planted in the Song Dynasty, and entered its heyday in the Ming and Qing Dynasties. Surrounded by mountains, Anxi's climate is warm and humid, with plenty of fog and dew. Its soil, temperature, humidity, and precipitation are very suitable for the growth of tea plants. In his tea couplet, Song Dynasty celebrity Huang Yi Jian said: "After overnight rain the tea plants are even tenderer. Upon several roasting, the aroma of tea leaves can be smelt." From the couplet we can conjure up the scene that new buds sprout from tea trees after the rain. Anxi is abound in Oolong tea, among which *Tieguanyin* is the most precious variety, with the reputation of "green leaves with red borders, lingering fragrance even after seven brews".

◎ 安溪古厝晒茶。（陈英杰 摄）
Sun-drying tea leaves on the roof of an old house in Anxi. (Photo by Chen Yingjie)

◎ 泉州，作为海上丝绸之路的起点，过往是为世界各地的人们输送瓷器、丝绸和茶叶。现在，则是用上等的铁观音招待八方来客，文明交融的使命，在波澜起伏的历史轮回里，依旧没有改变。（吴俊仁 摄）

Quanzhou, as the starting point of the Maritime Silk Road, used to deliver porcelain, silk and tea to people all over the world. Now, it uses the first-class *Tieguanyin* Oolong tea to treat guests from all directions. Its mission of blending civilizations remains unchanged in the ups and downs of history. (Photo by Wu Junren)

泉州人喜饮乌龙茶！他们不是大碗牛饮，而是一小杯一小杯地慢品，人们称之为"呷茶"。泉州人对茶叶、茶具、茶器、茶水的选择都十分讲究，甚至苛刻，对泡茶的细节也极为关注。

繁复的泡茶程序，可以让人一窥中国茶道的精神内涵！可以说，每一次泡茶，都是一种仪式感的升华。在泉州的茶文化里，泡茶程序可以隆重到用这些词来形容——孟臣淋霖，乌龙入宫，悬壶高冲，春风拂面，熏洗仙颜，若琛出浴，玉液回壶，关公巡城，韩信点兵，鲤鱼翻身，品香审韵……仪式感，是当今这个快餐时代极度缺失的，而在泉州人的每一泡茶中都可找回。

泉州的茶文化，从宋、元、明、清至近现代，一直兴盛不衰。对于泉州人来讲，泡茶是一种精神享受，是一种艺术，更是一种修身养性的手段。无论是清晨刚醒来，还是在精神疲乏，抑或压力大的时候，泉州人总会不自觉坐到茶桌前，那悠悠的茶香，可以滋养身心。

在泉州，去别人家里做客，落座之后，主人的第一件事就是拿出茶具，沏上一壶铁观音。不多时，茶香便布满房间每个角落，而几杯茶盏之间，感情似乎又增进了几分。以茶话友，闲话家常，妙不可言。

泉州人饮茶，既有"何年青天坠长星"的浪漫情怀，亦有"星垂平野阔"的自由意境，茶话之间，天下之事，尽在杯中。在各种聚会上，总是少不了"茶"这个重要角色，以茶纾解心中郁闷之气，用茶追求与山水天地相融合，凡此种种皆离不开茶。

People in Quanzhou love Oolong tea! Instead of drinking from a large bowl, they sip slowly, with one small cup at a time. People call it sipping tea. Quanzhou people are very particular, even harsh, about the choice of tea, tea sets, tea utensils, and water for tea, and they are also very concerned about the details of tea making.

The complicated tea making procedures can give people a glimpse of the spiritual connotation of Chinese tea ceremony! It can be said that every time you make tea, it is a sublimation of a sense of ritual.

◎ 一壶功夫茶，三两好友，妙不可言。（成冬冬 摄）
It's fantastic for a few good friends to have a small talk over a pot of Kung Fu tea. (Photo by Cheng Dongdong)

In the tea culture of Quanzhou, the tea-making process can be described with these words: Mengchen Linlin (water the teapot with boiled water), Wulong Rugong (put the fermented tea leaves into the teapot with a teaspoon), Xuanhu Gaochong (pour the boiled water into the pot from high), Chunfeng Fumian (stroke the tea gently and delicately with the lid), Xunxi Xianyan (pour out the water after washing the surface dust if there are any), Ruochen Chuyu (warm the cups with the tea), Yuye Huihu (pour the tea into fair mug), Guangong Xuncheng (serve equal portions of the tea into the cups), Han Xin Dianbing (distribute the final drops evenly and humbly) , Liyu Fanshen (turn over the cups), Pinxiang Shenyun (smell the fragrance and taste the tea)...The sense of ritual is extremely missing in this fast-food era, and it can be found in every tea made by Quanzhou people.

The tea culture in Quanzhou has been flourishing from the Song, Yuan, Ming, Qing Dynasties to modern time. For Quangzhou people, making tea is a spiritual enjoyment, an art, and a means of self-cultivation. Whether they just wake up in the morning, or when mentally tired or stressed, Quanzhou people will always sit at the tea table unconsciously. The lingering tea fragrance can nourish their bodies and minds.

In Quanzhou, when you go to someone's home as a guest, the first thing the host does is to take out the tea set and make some *Tieguanyin* Oolong tea after you are seated. The fragrance of tea filled every corner of the room soon after. Between a few cups of tea, the relationship seems to have improved. Small talks about friends and families over the tea are so wonderful!

The people of Quanzhou drink tea, not only with the romantic feeling of "in what year did the comet shoot across the sky", but also the free artistic conception of "stars hanging down over the plains". In all kinds of gatherings, the important role of tea is always indispensable. To relieve the depression in the heart, and to pursue the integration with the natural landscape and the world, all of these are inseparable from tea.

03
旅行规划
Tours Recommended

经典游一日线路

线路一:

清源山（老君岩）──→灵山伊斯兰教圣墓──→南少林寺

线路二:

天后宫──→清净寺──→关岳庙──→泉州府文庙──→中山路──→西街──→开元寺

线路三:

五店市──→磁灶窑址（金交椅山窑址）──→草庵──→龙山寺──→安平桥

深度游主题线路

世遗之旅（三日）

开元寺——南外宗正司遗址——泉州府文庙——清净寺——泉州市舶司遗址——天后宫——德济门遗址——顺济桥遗址——真武庙——江口码头——灵山伊斯兰教圣墓——洛阳桥——九日山祈风石刻——磁灶窑址（金交椅山窑址）——草庵——安平桥——石湖码头——六胜塔——永宁古城——万寿塔——安溪青阳下草埔冶铁遗址——德化窑址（尾林−内坂窑址、屈斗宫窑址）

海丝寻迹之旅（二日）

南外宗正司遗址——泉州市舶司遗址——德济门——天后宫——清净寺——顺济桥遗址——泉州海外交通史博物馆——江口码头——真武庙——蟳埔村——洛阳桥——九日山——石湖码头——六胜塔——万寿塔——永宁古城——崇武古城

宗教文化之旅（三日）

真武庙——天后宫——关岳庙——清净寺——基督教泉南堂——元妙观——泉州府文庙——开元寺——温陵书院——承天寺——崇福寺——清源山（老君岩）——灵山伊斯兰教圣墓——南少林——草庵——龙山寺——南安雪峰寺——安溪清水岩寺

Classical Day-trip Tours

Option 1—1 Day

Qingyuan Mountain (Statue of Lao Tze)→Islamic Tombs in Lingshan Mountain→Southern Shaolin Temple

Option 2—1 Day

Tianhou Temple→Qingjing Mosque→Guanyue Temple→Confucius Temple and School in Quanzhou→Zhongshan Road→West Street→Kaiyuan Temple

Option 3—1 Day

Wudianshi Traditional Blocks→The Sites of Cizao Kilns (Kiln Sites at Jinjiaoyi Hill)→Cao'an Temple→Longshan Temple→Anping Bridge

泉
州

In-depth Theme Tours

Option 1—3 Days

World Heritage Journey

Kaiyuan Temple→Site of Southern Clan Office→Confucius Temple and School in Quanzhou→Qingjing Mosque→Site of Quanzhou Maritime Trade Office→Tianhou Temple→Site of Deji Gate→Site of Shunji Bridge→Zhenwu Temple→Jiangkou Docks→Islamic Tombs in Lingshan Mountain→Luoyang Bridge→Wind-praying Stone Inscriptions in Jiuri Mountain→The Sites of Cizao Kilns (Kiln Sites at Jinjiaoyi Hill)→Cao'an Temple→Anping Bridge→Shihu Dock→Liusheng Pagoda→Yongning Ancient Town→Wanshou Pagoda→Xiacaopu Iron Production Site of Qingyang Village in Anxi→Dehua Kiln Sites (Weilin-Neiban Kiln Site, Qudougong Kiln Site)

Option 2—2 Days

Maritime Silk Road Trail Journey

Site of Southern Clan Office→Site of Quanzhou Maritime Trade Office→Site of Deji Gate→Tianhou Temple→Qingjing Mosque→Site of Shunji Bridge→Quanzhou Maritime Museum→Jiangkou Docks→Zhenwu Temple→Xunpu Village→Luoyang Bridge→Jiuri Mountain→Shihu Dock→Liusheng Pagoda→Wanshou Pagoda→Yongning Ancient Town→Chongwu Ancient Town

Option 3—3 Days

Religion and Culture Journey

Zhenwu Temple→Tianhou Temple→Guanyue Temple→Qingjing Mosque→Christian Quannan Church→Yuanmiao Temple→Confucius Temple and School in Quanzhou→Kaiyuan Temple→Wenling Academy→Chengtian Temple→Chongfu Temple→Qingyuan Mountain (Statue of Lao Tze)→Islamic Tombs in Lingshan Mountain→Southern Shaolin Temple→Cao'an Temple→Longshan Temple→Xuefeng Temple in Nan'an→Anxi Qingshuiyan Temple